FIGHTER COMMAND
1939-1945

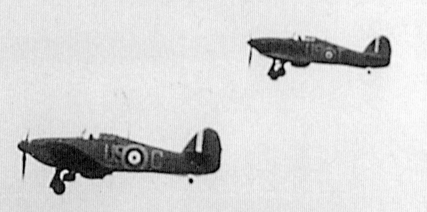

FIGHTER COMMAND 1939-1945

David Oliver

Acknowledgements

Of the many people who assisted me in writing this book with personal anecdotes or photographs, I would like to extend particular thanks to the following individuals and organisations:

John Davis and John Annals of the 604 Squadron Association; Fred Beacon and Paddy Calvert of the 607 Squadron Association; Ian Smith of the 615 Squadron Association; James A. Gray of the Eagle Squadron Association; Flt Sgt David Curry of the RAF Digby Operations Room Museum; Norman Bate of the Arnoldian Register; Eileen Robinson of the Caterpillar Club; Cyril W. Plimmer of the Boulton Paul Association; The Polish Institute and Sikorsky Museum.

I would also like to thank Ken Adam; Margaret Balfour; Eric Barwell; Roland Beamont; John S. Bennett; Marcel Boisot; Stella Burgess; Johnny Checketts; Royal Cooper; John Cunningham; Lettice Curtis; Kuni Deanesly; James F. Edwards; Ken Ellis; John C. Freeborn; Sadie Gibson Lewis; Mike F. Goodchap; Wilfred A. Goold; Dennis J. Hill; Tony Holmes; Richard Hough; Will Hoy; John Jordan; Dick Leggett; Tony Liskutin; Ken Mackenzie; Derek Morris; Paul Patten; Frances King (née Philip); Francois Prins; Bruce Robertson; Eric Shipp; Stan Shonfield; Doug Tidy; Diana Barnato Walker; P. E. Webster; Edward P. Wells; D. E. Wilson.

Picture credits

Ken Adam pp211, 212; Eric Barwell p159; John S. Bennett p224; Marcel Boisot p74; Max Collett pp63, 80; Royal Cooper p173; Ken Ellis Collection pp18, 25, 50, 51, 55, 109, 110, 130; Len Jordan p78; Dick Leggett pp47, 48, 162, 171, 173; Ian Le Sueur p229; Tony Liskutin pp70, 71

Ken Mackenzie pp132, 228; David Oliver pp10,12, 13, 18, 22, 24, 26, 35, 41, 53, 68, 86, 91, 93, 113, 114, 123, 124, 130, 135, 138, 143, 152, 181, 182, 187; Paul Patten pp112, 121, 160; C. W. Plimmer p16; Popperfoto pp23, 40, 105; Francois Prins Collection pp14, 15, 16, 17, 18, 27, 31, 32, 33, 34, 36, 38, 49, 52, 54, 57, 58, 59, 60, 61, 66, 67, 68, 79, 88, 97, 99, 102, 103, 104, 106, 107, 111, 115, 117, 120, 121, 122, 125, 126, 135, 136, 141, 150, 174, 176, 178, 181, 182, 183, 184, 189, 190, 191, 194, 195, 199, 200, 202, 204, 205, 209, 210, 211, 217; Bruce Robertson pp19, 21, 25, 28, 30, 45, 54, 55, 56, 58, 62, 70, 72, 73, 76, 79, 84, 85, 88, 89, 92, 93, 98, 112, 129, 130, 133, 134, 137, 142, 154, 158, 161, 163, 164, 165, 166, 167, 168, 170, 172, 175, 176, 178, 180, 183, 186, 188, 190, 191, 192, 193, 196, 198, 201, 204, 205, 208, 209, 214, 215, 216, 217, 220, 221, 222, 225, 226; Eric Shipp pp43, 195, 198, 206, 207; Stan Shonfield p203; D. E. Wilson p172

No 604 Squadron Archives pp23, 24, 28, 62, 119, 120, 148, 149, 156, 157, 161, 165; RAF Digby pp64, 82, 88, 90, 115, 144, 145, 155

Quotations are taken from the following sources:

CITA *Challenge in the Air* by Tony Liskutin (William Kimber)
DT 'Battle of Britain supplement' (*The Daily Telegraph*, 1990)
FP *FlyPast* magazine (Key Publishing)
OOTB *Out of the Blue* by Laddie Lucas (Grafton Books)
Pan *The Dangerous Skies* by A. E. Clouston (Pan Books)
  Against the Sun by Edward Lanchbery (Pan Books)
RAFN *RAF News*
RD *Yesterday's Britain* (Reader's Digest Association)
249AW *249 Sqn at War* by Brian Cull (Grub Street Books)

This edition produced for The Book People Ltd,
Hall Wood Avenue,
Haydock, St Helens, WA11 9UL

HarperCollins*Publishers*
77-85 Fulham Palace Road
Hammersmith
London W6 8JB

First published in Great Britain by HarperCollins*Publishers* 2000

1 3 5 7 9 10 9 6 4 2

Copyright © David Oliver

The author asserts the moral right to be identified as the author of this work

ISBN 0 00 762908 7

British Library Cataloguing in Publication Data:
A catalogue record for this book is available from the British Library.

Contents

Foreword

For a few months in 1940 the future of this Nation, and probably the future of the whole of the Western civilised world, lay in the hands of Royal Air Force Fighter Command. This first great air battle, the Battle of Britain, remains a powerful image in the public mind, and rightly so. But the contribution of Fighter Command during the Second World War extended through the whole conflict, from the early days of the Battle of France to D-Day and beyond. This book documents the considerable achievements of Fighter Command throughout this period. With its excellent illustrations and photographs, it provides the reader with a wealth of information made more vital by the first hand accounts of those who served in the Command during those momentous years.

Air Chief Marshal Sir Peter Squire KCB DFC AFC FRAeS RAF
Chief of the Air Staff

Preface

As we enter a new century, the Second World War fades further into history. However, for that very reason it is time to take a new look at the events, battles and, above all, the people who took part in the six-year conflict, and re-evaluate their place in history.

Air warfare was less than 30 years old when war broke out, and the Royal Air Force was the newest of Britain's fighting services. It was more by luck than judgement that Fighter Command had been established only three short years before war was declared in Europe, and few could have predicted the enormous contribution it would be called on to make in the Allied victory.

It was a remarkable combination of personalities and equipment that formed the basis for its success in wartime. Sir Hugh Dowding, Winston Churchill, Sir Henry Royce, R. J. Mitchell and Sydney Camm came together in history to give Fighter Command the tools to win its most important victory – the Battle of Britain.

While the Hurricane, Spitfire and, later, the Typhoon and Mosquito all played a vital part in Fighter Command's successes, more important was the quality of the young men who flew and maintained these aircraft, later joined by young women working behind the scenes to support them in their fight to liberate occupied continental Europe.

Theirs is a story of inspiration, determination, and personal bravery and sacrifice. Yet many Fighter Command pilots considered the real heroes to be the foot soldiers who fought their way on to the beaches of Dunkirk, and fought their way out from the beachheads of Normandy towards Germany four years later.

David Oliver
Arkley
May 2000

Chapter 1
Home defence

At the end of the First World War the newly independent Royal Air Force had a struggle to survive. The newly re-elected Prime Minister, Lloyd George, announced that the days of the fledgling RAF as a separate department were numbered. This move was immediately opposed by Winston Churchill, Lloyd George's Secretary of State for Air, who threw his weight behind the RAF's first Commander-in-Chief, Air Marshal Sir Hugh Trenchard, and his campaign to retain the service's independence. Their campaign met with success when Parliament voted to accept in principle Trenchard's proposals for the future organisation of an independent RAF at the end of 1919. It was a far-reaching decision. However, the RAF budget for 1920 was limited to £15 million with provision for 19 overseas squadrons but only six home squadrons plus two training wings.

In 1925 the Air Defence of Great Britain (ADGB) was placed under the control of Air Marshal Sir John Salmon, a First World War pilot who had risen to GOC of the RAF in the Field by 1918, and included under his command was the newly created Auxiliary Air Force (AAF), the first squadrons of which were 602 (City of Glasgow) and 600 (City of London), another important step in the build-up to the future conflict. Trenchard's aim was to make the part-time Auxiliary Air Force a sought-after elite force by restricting membership to only the very best volunteers. Squadrons were formed as units based on cities or counties – 504 (County of Nottingham); 603 (City of Edinburgh) – and soon gained the reputation of being the 'Best Clubs in Town'. The AAF also became an integral part of Great Britain's air defence and regularly took part in exercises with regular RAF squadrons. Its aircraft were part of the 700 that took part in the 'greatest air manoeuvres in history' defending South East England from 'foreign' invaders in August 1928.

When Sir Hugh Trenchard retired as Chief of the Air Staff in 1930, he was replaced by Sir John Salmon, who had successfully reorganised the ADGB into a modern fighting force despite the severe economic constraints. The ADGB command HQ had moved to RAF Uxbridge, while the home defence squadrons became No 1 Air Defence Group.

Unfortunately, with economic decline threatening most of Europe, the RAF again became an obvious target for cuts in government spending. In February 1932 the Rt Hon Arthur Henderson MP, leader of the Labour Party, opened the League of Nations Disarmament Conference in Geneva, and, following five years of slow and cautious expansion, the Air Estimates announced two months later showed a 10 per cent reduction over the previous year, once again bringing the long-term future of the RAF into doubt.

However, a boost to the cash-strapped RAF's reputation as a professional pioneering service came in the early 1930s when its flying boats captured the world headlines with a series of record long-distance cruises between England and the Far East. The 'Flying Boat Union' was now a powerful faction within the RAF and was able to place contracts for new types while the bomber and fighter force had to rely on what were in essence updated versions of First World War designs.

However, in 1933 Germany, now led by Adolf Hitler, walked out of the League's Disarmament Conference; suddenly pacifism was out of fashion and there were immediate calls by certain Members of Parliament, including Winston Churchill, the forces and industrialists for Britain to re-arm without delay. At the time Britain's air defences rested on 13 RAF squadrons, the majority of which were equipped with outdated Bristol Bulldog biplanes.

The 1934 Air Estimates gave little indication of any extensive re-armament, although the Prime Minister, Stanley Baldwin, assured the house that 'if the Disarmament Conference failed, steps would be taken to bring about an Air-Disarmament Convention; if that failed, the British Government would proceed to bring the strength of our Air Force up to the strength of the strongest air force within striking distance of this country.' Reassuring words!

During the summer of 1934 the political situation in Europe deteriorated further. Baldwin's Disarmament Conference did fail and Germany resigned from the League of Nations. However, Britain's aircraft industry began to grasp the reality of the situation even if the politicians did not, and geared itself up for a period of rapid military

Right *From 1930 to the formation of Fighter Command in 1936, the Bristol Bulldog was the RAF's most widely used fighter, equipping nine ADGB squadrons. Here a tight formation of 19 Sqn Bulldogs, led by F/Lt Harry Broadhurst, performs at the 1934 RAF Display.*

Below *The prototype of the Rolls-Royce Merlin-powered Supermarine Spitfire monoplane fighter, seen here parked outside the Woolston works at Southampton, made its maiden flight on 5 March 1936.*

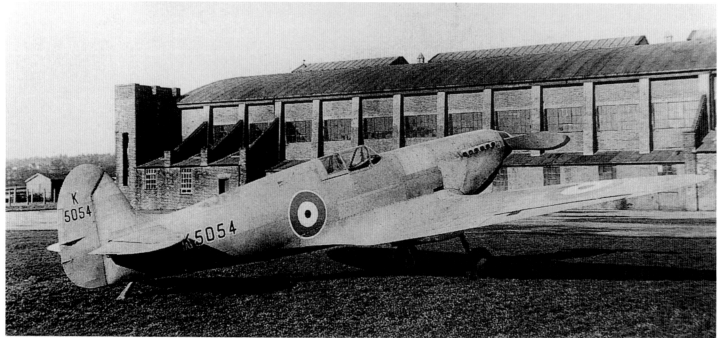

expansion. In July the House of Commons was prompted to pass a motion to increase the strength of the RAF by 41 squadrons, and even the Air Ministry began to move forward, albeit slowly, by issuing specifications for new monoplane fighter aircraft, one of which was F7/30, which led indirectly to the birth of the Hawker Hurricane and Supermarine Spitfire powered by the Merlin engine. This had been developed by Rolls-Royce as a private venture from the 'R'-type engine that powered the Schneider Trophy-winning Supermarine S.6 float planes in 1931.

By March 1935 the existence of Germany's *Luftwaffe* was officially revealed to the world, together with the astounding fact that it possessed almost 2,000 aircraft of all types manned by some 20,000 officers and men. Two months later the British Government announced proposals for further expansion of the RAF, whereby the strength of the Air Force based at home would reach 1,500 first-line aircraft by March 1937. This figure compared with the then current total of only 850 first-line aircraft, many of which were approaching obsolescence. However, even these proposals looked inadequate when later in the year growing political turmoil in Europe added to Great Britain's vulnerability. Germany had re-introduced conscription, a civil war raged in Austria, and in October Italy invaded Abyssinia (Ethiopia). The following March Hitler's forces moved into the disputed Rhineland in violation of the Treaty of Versailles that had brought the First World War to an end.

In response to these threatening developments, the Air Estimates for 1936-7 were almost twice as much as the previous year and made provisions for the establishment of no fewer that 123 squadrons for the Home Defence Force. In the RAF Display held at Hendon on 27 June 1936, the Merlin-engined Hurricane and Spitfire made their first public appearance, although neither would be in service for almost another two years.

Fighter Command

In order to cope with the gathering speed and scope of RAF expansion, only three weeks after the Hendon display the ADGB was replaced by five separate Commands – Training, Coastal, Bomber, Maintenance and Fighter – the last-named under the command of Air Marshal Sir Hugh Caswell Tremenheere Dowding.

Like Salmon, Dowding had learned to fly before the outbreak of the First World War and was a group commander at its end. A career officer with a single-minded determination to see the RAF given equal opportunities with its more senior service rivals, Dowding's set views and uncompromising stand on RAF issues denied him the rapid promotion some of his contemporaries enjoyed during the interwar years. He was, however, appointed to the Air Council in 1931 with the rank of Air Marshal as a Member of Supply and Research, and used that position to further his support of the latest advances of the day such as monoplane fighter aircraft, which led to the Hurricane and Spitfire, and developing a system of fighter control using the latest radio/telephone and radio direction-finding technology.

Fighter Command's Headquarters was established at Bentley Priory in Stanmore, North London, and the Command was divided into two Fighter Groups, No 11, with Headquarters at RAF Uxbridge and covering South East England and the defence of London, and No 12, with Headquarters at RAF Watnall in Nottinghamshire and covering the Midlands; the Groups were commanded by Air Vice Marshals Sir Philip Joubert de la Ferte and Trafford Leigh-Mallory respectively.

Only a month after Fighter Command was born, when the new King, Edward VIII, reviewed the Royal Air Force at RAF Mildenhall in July 1936, its 13 squadrons for home defence were equipped with Bulldog, Fury, Demon and Gauntlet front-line fighters – all biplanes.

In the meantime, the international situation showed no sign of improving. Germany had formed an Axis with Italy, and civil war had broken out in Spain, involving pilots and aircraft from Germany's fledgling *Luftwaffe*. In 1937 Winston Churchill, now a backbencher, was again in the forefront of the re-armament faction in Parliament. He had already made his position clear in a recent speech on the subject, stating that 'the only real security upon which sound military principles will rely is that you should be master of your own air', and in the House he deplored the London County Council's decision to ban local cadet corps and schoolchildren from attending the RAF Display dress rehearsal.

In August some 400 RAF aircraft were engaged in a mock attack on London, which was 'effectively defended' by RAF interceptors and anti-aircraft guns. By now the interim phase of the RAF's expansion programme, scheduled to be implemented between December 1935 and December 1937, had been covered by the introduction of Hawker Fury and Hart derivatives, and Gladiators – still all biplanes – as well as diverse transport, training and communications types. The only modern monoplanes then in RAF

Above *One of the first duties of King Edward VIII was to tour RAF stations in a Rapide of the newly formed Royal Flight in July 1936, the month RAF Fighter Command was formed. The aircraft is seen here at RAF Martlesham Heath.*

Left *Fighter Command's latest fighter in 1937 was the Gloster Gladiator, here seen in 73 Sqn's colourful pre-war scheme, which equipped five home defence squadrons at the time of the Munich Crisis.*

service were Coastal Command's Anson and Bomber Command's Blenheim.

The Blenheim was faster than any of Fighter Command's fighters, and was another example of the RAF being 'sponsored' by a wealthy patriot, this time the newspaper magnate Lord Rothermere, who agreed to underwrite the cost of a high-performance all-metal eight-seat airliner designed by the Bristol Aeroplane Company. The performance of the twin-engined Bristol 142, christened 'Britain First', which made its maiden flight in 1935, was so impressive that the RAF asked to test it and Lord Rothermere presented it to the nation.

The Type 142 was originally developed into the Blenheim light bomber, the first of which flew on 25 July 1936. As war loomed in Europe, the Air Ministry ordered some 200 aircraft to be converted to long-range day fighters by fitting four .303in Browning machine-guns in a ventral gun pack.

By January 1938 Fighter Command possessed or was in the process of forming 26 Regular and Auxiliary fighter squadrons, only one of which had taken delivery of the RAF's first monoplane fighter – the Hawker Hurricane. Days after the RAF's annual air defence exercises had taken place in August, which involved bombers from 'Eastland', an imaginary territory over the North Sea, all RAF leave was cancelled and Fighter Command was bought to an operational state of readiness. The Munich Crisis had begun.

In June 1936 Dowding's appointment had been considered a sideways step by the Air Ministry, but the post gave him control of all of Britain's air defence assets – fighter aircraft, anti-aircraft guns and barrage balloons. He was already preparing for the Battle of Britain, and the 1938 Munich Crisis enabled him to acquire new support equipment for the RAF such as Sector Operation Rooms and paved runways at main fighter bases. He also oversaw the establishment of the Observer Corps, established in September 1938 as a direct result of the Munich Crisis; this was a volunteer organisation of sky-watchers manned by ex-servicemen located in South East England who were to make visual reports of unidentified aircraft. Fighter Command was also responsible for the administration of No 22 Army Co-operation Group.

By this time radio direction-finding equipment, which would become known as radar, had become an important aspect of Britain's air defence structure. Following successful Radio Direction Finding (RDF) experiments in 1935, the decision had been taken to build a chain of radar stations covering the South and East Coasts of England and Scotland, the first of which was opened at Dover in 1937. In operation by the start of the Battle of Britain were 21 Chain Home (CH) stations, with a range of 120 miles and able to detect aircraft at heights of between 5,000 and 20,000 feet, and 30 Chain Home Low (CHL) stations, which were able to detect aircraft flying below 5,000 feet at a maximum range of 50 miles.

Along with other Auxiliary Air Force squadrons, No 604 Sqn's Hawker Demons had their colourful silver overall and red/orange markings replaced by a dull camouflage during the Munich Crisis.

These radar aerials were mounted on 350-foot-high towers – those on the South Coast could be seen from France – and were vital to the defence of Britain; they therefore became priority targets for the *Luftwaffe*. Mobile Radar Units (MLU), with a maximum range of 90 miles, were also brought into operation during the Battle to supplement fixed sites or those put temporarily out of action by air attacks.

Many of the Observer Corps volunteers were ex-servicemen and women, and they manned observation posts throughout the country, although by the outbreak of war the Corps was commanded by full-time officers. On the eve of the Battle of Britain some 30,000 observers manned more than 1,000 posts reporting to 32 centres. Aircraft recognition was all-important. While radar stations gave accurate information about the range of enemy aircraft, pinpointing their altitude was more difficult and

verification often fell to the observers using simple but effective measuring devices. They were also used to track enemy formations that had passed over the radar stations, which could only look one way. On cloudy days the observers had to rely on sound alone to identify an aircraft's altitude and bearing.

Other advanced technology was under development as Fighter Command came into being. In 1933 S/Ldr Chandler recommended that High Frequency/Direction-Finders (HF/DF), or 'huff-duff', be set up in each sector of what was then the ADGB. By late 1935 four stations were operating at Biggin Hill, Northolt, Hornchurch and North Weald. Homing and position-fixing using two or more HF/DF stations was tried, although co-ordination of HF/DF, the Observer Corps and radios in aircraft was necessary to achieve this.

When Fighter Command was established it was decided to fit HF/DF at all sector airfields, seven in No 11 Group and five in No 12 Group. It was necessary to take the radar or Observer Corps information in filtered form and convert it into 'vectors' on which pilots should fly to intercept enemy aircraft.

Below *Hurricanes of 'Treble One' Squadron appeared for a short period in February 1938 wearing the numbers '111' painted on the camouflaged aircraft. These were later replaced by the letters 'TM'.*

Right *The second RAF squadron to be re-equipped with the Merlin-engined Hurricane was No 3, based at RAF Kenley; this took place in March 1938, when others were being issued with new Gladiator biplanes.*

Below *Still on the pre-war secret list was the two-seat Boulton Paul Defiant. Designed as a bomber-destroyer, the prototype, seen here under construction, made its first flight in July 1939 without its rear turret.*

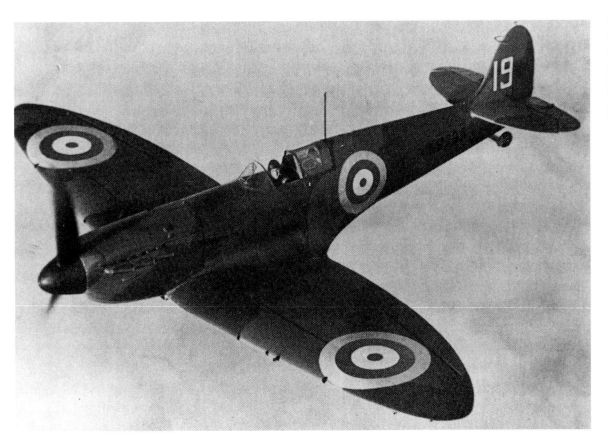

The first RAF squadron to receive the Supermarine Spitfire I was No 19 based at Duxford. They were delivered in September 1938 with number '19' on the tail, unlike '111' on the Hurricane's rear fuselage.

The DF stations picked up the aircraft Morse signal – the Wireless Operator in the leading aircraft held down his key for the DF operator to take a bearing on the goniometer. This was plotted and telephoned to the ops room where the tests were first carried out.

Inaccuracy of the DF information, and in the conversion of track and ground speed into airspeed, together with the fighter pilots using dead reckoning to navigate, meant a very approximate result. Eventually it was W/C E. O. Grenfell who met with success by the principle of equal angles. By drawing a line from approaching bombers to the fighters and making it the base of an isosceles triangle, with the fighter angle always equal to the bomber angle, the two formations met at the apex of the triangle. Thus was born the sector control and vectoring procedure later used in the Battle of Britain.

The importance of the sector controller was paramount, and three HF/DF stations for each fighter sector were proposed. Automatic periodic DF transmissions from aircraft were achieved by 'Pip-Squeak', named after cartoon characters of the day, a system that automatically switched on the HF transmitter in the aircraft for 14 seconds every minute. A clock in the control room, with a hand rotating once a minute, showed by the use of four coloured sections which aircraft should be

transmitting. Thus each of four aircraft had its position plotted once a minute and navigation was not necessary. If an aircraft crew forgot to switch on, the controller would say, 'Is your cockerel crowing?', 'cockerel' being the codeword for 'Pip-Squeak'.

The DF system and radar were the keys to all the interceptions made, and meant that it was unnecessary to fly standing patrols, which were impossible anyway. The heart of the system was the Fighter Command Operations Room at Bentley Priory. Here was the filter centre where all radar plots showing perceived position, strength, height and direction were received from CH (Chain Home) and inland CHL (Chain Home Low) stations, which were added to track low-flying aircraft.

Operational control was to be exercised through Operations Rooms located at Command, Group and Sector Stations. The first of these regional Groups was No 11, and work on its underground operations complex was completed in 1939. The purpose of these complexes was to act as a nerve centre through which information was fed, evaluated, and acted upon. By a system of visual displays, up-to-the-minute information would be available on the resources of the Group, and, from a variety of other sources, the strength, position and course of approaching enemy aircraft.

Hurricane I L1609 of 56 Sqn based at RAF North Weald, the third RAF squadron to re-equip with the type in April 1938, seen the summer of 1939.

Wearing its pre-war code letters 'PN', this two-bladed Spitfire I was delivered to 41 Sqn at RAF Catterick in the spring of 1939 and took part in Fighter Command's last pre-war air defence manoeuvres.

This 29 Sqn Bristol Blenheim IF, the RAF's first night-fighter, seen here taking part in a pre-war exercise at RAF Debden, would remain on the secret list until the Battle of Britain.

Above *The new family of monoplane fighters entering RAF service, the first with enclosed cockpits and retractable undercarriages, led to many accidents; this 3 Sqn Hurricane, L1936, has suffered a heavy landing.*

Left *This 25 Sqn Gladiator II, seen in Munich Crisis camouflage and code letters, was replaced by a Bristol Blenheim IF when the squadron converted to night-fighting at the end of 1938.*

1939: Bullet-proof

'Our task was to modify the Merlin IIs of 74 Sqn's Spitfire Is to Merlin IIIs by changing the airscrew shaft to accommodate the standard airscrew hub, or "spider", and fitting the constant speed unit and 24-volt starting system. Simultaneously we were engaged in installing armour plate to the fire-proof bulkhead, and lowering the main fuel tank to accommodate an enveloping ricochet shield.

We were also fitting a rather clumsy casting, incorporating bullet-proof glass, to the existing windscreen perspex with as little damage as possible – a very difficult, fiddly task that I was actually working on when Mr Chamberlain's voice was relayed over the Station tannoy at 1100 hours on 3 September 1939, telling Great Britain that we were at war with Germany. The announcement was immediately followed by the dramatic wailing of the air raid sirens, which proved to be a false alarm.'

P. E. Webster – Fighter Command AC1 Fitter Two

The manning of these Operations Rooms required a large number of personnel, which comprised a Senior or Group Controller and his assistants, who were seated in the raised centre cabin overlooking the large plotting table, which was effectively a map of South East England. They were flanked by Naval, Anti-Aircraft Command and Observer Corps personnel with supervisory personnel in front of them at a lower level. The plotting table itself was surrounded by WAAF plotters moving small indicator markers, which showed details of enemy formations, over the map with long magnetic rakes.

None of these innovations were operational at the start of the Munich Crisis, when Auxiliary Air Force squadrons were deployed to their war stations and their aircraft's silver overall paint schemes and colourful squadron markings were replaced by unfamiliar drab camouflage. The RAF's first operational Hurricane Squadron, No 111 based at Northolt, had only just been declared operational.

In an effort to prevent events from escalating into another major war in Europe, British Prime Minister Neville Chamberlain had asked for a head-to-head meeting with German Chancellor Adolf Hitler, and flew to Germany to attend the Munich Conference on 29 September 1938 as the RAF took delivery of its first Spitfires. Chamberlain returned the following day having signed the Munich Agreement, which effectively allowed Hitler to seize the Czechoslovak frontier region of Sudetenland, Germany having already annexed Austria in March. The Agreement, which was condemned by Churchill as appeasement, nevertheless temporarily held Europe back from the brink of all-out war, while the crisis gave added impetus to the RAF and AAF expansion programmes.

It did not, however, curb Hitler's appetite for enlarging his 'empire'. In March 1939 Bohemia-Moravia and Memel were annexed and German troops entered the Czech capital, Prague. On 28 March Madrid fell to General Franco's forces, supported by Heinkel He 111 bombers and Messerschmitt Bf 109 fighters of the German Condor Legion. Three days later the British Government abandoned its appeasement policy and announced that it would guarantee the sovereignty of Poland against any attack from Germany. There was now no turning back. War was all but inevitable.

Deliveries of the new RAF fighter types were increased to a steady flow with the first Auxiliary Air Force Squadron, No 602 (City of Glasgow), replacing its Gauntlet biplanes with Spitfires in May 1938. Large-scale air defence exercises in which 1,300 RAF aircraft and 53,000 personnel participated were held over several days in August 1939, and at the end of the month Royal Air Force and RAF reservists were mobilised. On 1 September Operation *Weiss* began when Hitler's forces invaded Poland, and two days later Britain, Australia and New Zealand declared war on Germany. The second World War had begun.

To war

When war broke out, 58-year-old Dowding was putting the finishing touches to Britain's air defence network, a central part of which was the Spitfire force that was still in the early stages of its creation.

The *Luftwaffe*, meanwhile, claimed to have more than 4,000 aircraft of all types in service, while the RAF had 3,555 aircraft of all types on strength and 20,033 aircrew. Britain's main fighter defences still comprised more than 100 biplanes, although 347 Hurricanes equipped a total of 16 squadrons. Of the 270 Spitfire Mk 1s delivered to the RAF at the time, 187 had been issued to nine operational squadrons while two others were in the process of re-equipping.

The pilots of 'B' Flight of 56 Sqn are seen here at North Weald on 3 September 1939, the day war was declared. Three days later P/Off Montague Hulton-Harrop, front row left, was killed in the 'Battle of Barking Creek'.

Four squadrons were still equipped with Gladiator biplanes, and one with Gauntlets.

It was only three days into the war when RAF Spitfires and Hurricanes fired their guns in anger – but with tragic results. On 6 September a flight of unidentified aircraft was reported to have crossed the Essex coast heading for London. As a precautionary measure the North Weald Sector Controller 'scrambled' a flight of six 56 Sqn Hurricanes from North Weald airfield. However, the Squadron CO decided to order all of his serviceable aircraft, 14 in all, into the air. Responding to reports from a jittery Observer Corps of more aircraft in the air, six more Hurricanes from No 151 Sqn were scrambled. When this force of 20 aircraft failed to find any 'bandits', they turned inland heading east and were fired on by 'trigger-happy' anti-aircraft guns. This in turn led to 24 Spitfires from Nos 54, 65 and 74 Sqns at Hornchurch being scrambled. Guided towards the 'enemy' aircraft by the anti-aircraft fire, the Spitfires shot down two of 56 Sqn's Hurricanes, the pilot of one being killed. By now air raid sirens were sounding throughout East London and Essex, and yet more Spitfires, this time from 19 and 66 Sqns at Duxford, were scrambled to join the confusion.

1939: Home comforts

'As an ex-Halton aircraft apprentice, my training was accelerated when war was declared. I was posted as a newly qualified Fitter (Armourer) in late October 1939 to No 74 Squadron at RAF Hornchurch. When I arrived at the station, barrack room space was in short supply. There were three squadrons at Hornchurch – 74, 65 and 600 – the first two with Spitfires and 600 with fighter Blenheims.

Us armourers were packed in one room of 74 Squadron's block. There were about 16 beds, and in the spaces between the beds latecomers such as me slept on bedboards – two low trestles about 6 inches high with three 1-foot-wide boards resting on them – actually quite comfortable!'

Derek Morris – Fighter Command Fitter (Armourer)

At the last minute the commanding officer of 151 Sqn realised that the sky was full of RAF fighters attacking each other and, using his R/T, managed to warn those in the air and on the ground to call off the action. Unfortunately the 'ack-ack' batteries at Sheerness and Chelmsford did not get the message in time and fired on the Spitfires returning to Hornchurch, damaging at least one in the process. This unfortunate 'accident of war' became known as the 'Battle of Barking Creek'.

Lessons learned from this incident included the recommendation that coded Identification, Friend or Foe (IFF) signal equipment should be fitted to Fighter Command aircraft to avoid the practice of all unidentified aircraft being treated as hostile, or 'X' on the plotting table, thus overloading the system. However, this gave group and sector controllers untold trouble and, by the time the Battle of Britain commenced, a 'tote' board (named after the 'Totalisator' board at horse-racing tracks) had been erected on the rear walls of control rooms to record all

A pilot of 602 (City of Glasgow) Sqn, the very first AAF unit to be formed, adjusts his helmet before climbing aboard his Spitfire at Grangemouth in October 1939.

details of enemy raids, and the fighters intercepting them, leaving the table map with just the raid numbers and squadron symbols. Each 5-minute section of the control room clock was coloured red, yellow or blue and the colours of counters indicating the raids were changed to indicate their age to match the clock.

Thankfully, the next occasion on which RAF Spitfires went into combat was altogether more successful. On 16 October *Luftwaffe* Ju 88 bombers of KG 30 based at Westerland attacked Royal Navy facilities in the Firth of Forth, and were intercepted by Spitfires of No 602 (City of Glasgow) Sqn – the very first AAF unit to be formed and the first to re-equip with the type – and No 603 (City of Edinburgh) Sqn from RAF Turnhouse. Two Ju 88s were shot down during the encounter, while 603 Sqn shot down an He 111 of KG 26 in a separate raid, Fighter Command's first aerial victories. The following day Gladiator Is of No 607 (County of Durham) Sqn shot down a *Luftwaffe* Do 18 flying-boat off the Yorkshire coast.

Two weeks later Spitfires of No 72 Sqn joined Hurricanes of 46 Sqn in destroying seven He 115B float planes, which had been hunting British merchant ships in the North Sea. The two Scottish AAF Spitfire squadrons were also responsible for bringing down the first *Luftwaffe* aircraft on the British mainland when they shot down another KG 26 He 111 in Lothian on 29 November. Several Hurricane squadrons were deployed to the North of England to carry out 'Kipper' patrols to protect Britain's fishing fleet in the North Sea. It was during this period that F/Lt Peter Townsend and Sgt 'Darkie' Hallowes of 43 Sqn shared the destruction of the first German aircraft to fall on

English soil, another KG 26 He 111, on 3 February 1940.

Fighter Command was involved in a number of skirmishes with the *Luftwaffe* over the North Sea well into the New Year, but it was not until 6 February 1940 that the first Fighter Command aircraft, another 43 Sqn Hurricane, was shot down by a German aircraft. It crashed into the North Sea following air combat with an He 111, but its New Zealander pilot, F/Off M. K. Carswell, was rescued unharmed. He would repeat the experience over Dunkirk and during the Battle of Britain. However, it would be another three months before British-based fighters would tangle with *Luftwaffe* fighters in earnest.

Above *The KG 26 He 111 shot down by Spitfire Is of 602 (City of Glasgow) and 603 (City of Edinburgh) Sqns on 29 November 1939, the first German aircraft to be brought down on the British mainland.*

Below *The RAF's first AAF night-fighter unit was 604 (County of Middlesex) Sqn, which re-equipped with Blenheim IFs on the eve of the outbreak of war; one of the new aircraft is seen at North Weald in the winter of 1939.*

Right Its Honorary Air Commodore, Sir Samuel Hoare, and Air Vice-Marshal Welsh visit 604 Sqn at Northolt in April 1940; notice the then classified gun pack below the fuselage.

Below At RAF Digby 611 Sqn Spitfire Is are seen flying in the pre-war line-astern formation over other similar aircraft in February 1940. The Squadron would remain part of No 12 Group throughout the Battle of Britain.

Above *P/Off Leon Collingbridge with his 66 Sqn Spitfire I, still in its pre-war code letters, at RAF Duxford in early 1940. The second Spitfire unit, 66 Sqn was another No 12 Group squadron.*

Left *Another example of the new technology catching out an unwary pilot. However, despite the damage this 66 Sqn Spitfire I, K9823, was repaired and served in various units until the end of 1943.*

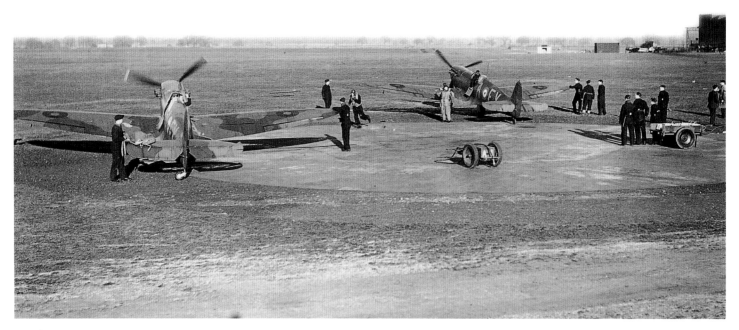

Above A practice 'scramble' by No 611 (West Lancashire) Sqn personnel at RAF Digby during the 'Phoney War' period in February 1940. It would have to wait until Dunkirk for the real thing.

Below An RAF Spitfire pilot in shiny shoes struggles to fasten his parachute straps over his thick fleece-lined pre-war flying suit during a practice scramble during the 'Phoney War' period of early 1940.

Norway

Meanwhile, on mainland Europe Germany's invasion and defeat of Poland, which was achieved in only 27 days, was followed by a lull in the fighting, a period known as the 'Phoney War', which lasted until 9 April 1940, when neutral Denmark and Norway were invaded by Germany under an operation codenamed *Weserubung*. Although RAF bombers supported by Fleet Air Arm Sea Gladiators and Skuas from the carrier HMS *Glorious* attempted to repulse the German advance in Norway, it was too little, too late.

In February W/C Dore DSO had been touring Scandinavian countries, including Finland, to establish bases for RAF operations in the event of a German invasion in the region. In fact, Blenheim IFs of No 604 Sqn based at Northolt had secretly been painted with the blue and white swastikas of the Finnish Air Force on 11 March, the day before Finland's 'Winter War' with Russia ended. This event and the speed of the German advance into Scandinavia precluded any deployment of the Fighter Command Blenheims. The day before the German invasion began, P/Off Whitney Straight, an Anglo-American 601 Sqn Hurricane pilot with excellent diplomatic contacts, flew into Norway to make preparations for some sort of RAF operations.

It was No 263 Sqn, equipped with obsolete Gladiators of the type operated by the Royal Norwegian Air Force and neighbouring Finland and neutral Sweden, that was ordered aboard the carrier HMS *Glorious*, which had been hurriedly recalled from the Mediterranean. Fleet Air Arm pilots flew 18 of No 263 Sqn's biplanes on to the carrier, and it set sail for Norwegian waters on 24 April. All successfully took off and were guided by a Fleet Air Arm Skua to two frozen lakes in central Norway.

In spite of the overwhelming odds, sub-zero weather conditions and almost total lack of fuel, spares and groundcrews, the Gladiators accounted for at least six enemy aircraft before they were all destroyed on the ground by 28 April. Meanwhile,

A 263 Sqn Gladiator II attempting to hide from the Luftwaffe under a flimsy camouflage of branches at its temporary airfield in Norway, the frozen Lake Leskajog, in April 1940.

Above *In preparation for deployment to Finland in April 1940, 604 Sqn Blenheims based at Northolt were painted in Finnish Air Force markings. The deployment was cancelled days later.*

Below *The remains of F/Lt Mills's 263 Sqn Gladiator II in Norway on 21 May after he had shot down an He 111 on 25 April; he was later seriously wounded.*

another 18 Gladiators, which had been dispatched aboard HMS *Glorious* to join them, arrived at Bardufoss on 22 May.

By 26 May *Glorious* had returned yet again, this time with 18 Hurricanes of No 46 Sqn. After ten days of heroic action, however, the evacuation of British forces commenced and the surviving RAF fighters, ten Gladiators and ten Hurricanes, landed safely on board *Glorious*. Only two of the biplanes had been lost in air combat, while 263 Sqn pilots had shot down 36 enemy aircraft and the Hurricane pilots claimed 11 German aircraft for the loss of two.

On the afternoon of 8 June HMS *Glorious* and her destroyer escort were sunk by the German battlecruisers *Scharnhorst* and *Gneisenau*. A total of 59 RAF personnel perished that day; only two Hurricane pilots, S/Ldr K. B. Cross, No 46 Squadron's CO, and F/Lt 'Pat' Jameson, survived.

Battle of France

Since the Munich Crisis the British Government had planned for the formation of an Expeditionary Force that would move into France on the outbreak of hostilities to support Allied forces. Part of this force was an Air Component, which, under the command of Air Vice-Marshal C. H. B. Blount, was deployed to France on 15 September 1939.

The Air Component of the BEF comprised four squadrons of Lysander Army Co-operation aircraft, four of Bomber Command Blenheims and four Fighter Command Hurricane squadrons. They scored their first victory when a No 1 Sqn Hurricane shot down a *Luftwaffe* Do 17 near Toul on 30 October. The force was reorganised in January 1940 with the formation of the British Air Forces in France (BAFF) Command under Air Marshal Sir Arthur Barratt. Nos 1 and 73 Sqns were transferred to No 67 Wing of the Advanced Air Striking Force (AASF), and Nos 85 and 87 Sqn to No 60 Wing of the Air Component with two Gladiator Squadrons, Nos 607 and 615.

Although air combat on the Western Front was sporadic during the early months of the year, action on 2 March gave British fighters a taste of what was to come. That day four Hurricanes, two each from 1 and 73 Sqns, were forced down by *Luftwaffe* aircraft. One of No 1 Sqn pilots was killed in the action, while F/Off E. J. Kain would bale out of his 73 Sqn Hurricane after combat with a Bf 109 only three weeks later. Before the Battle of France was over, New Zealander 'Cobber' Kain would become Fighter Command's first 'ace' – scoring five victories.

On 10 May Operation *Gelb*, the German offensive against France and the Low Countries – the Netherlands and Belgium – commenced and the RAF found itself fighting on a second front. On the same day Neville Chamberlain resigned as British Prime Minister in favour of Winston Churchill and his coalition government, which included Sir Archibald Sinclair as Secretary of State for Air, and Lord Beaverbrook as head of the newly created Ministry of Aircraft Production. The following day No 74 Sqn Spitfires flew cover over a British destroyer crossing the English Channel bearing Queen Wilhelmina of the Netherlands, Princess Juliana, Prince Bernhard and their families. Holland had capitulated.

During the next week the two Gladiator squadrons claimed to have destroyed more than 50 German aircraft before they were withdrawn to re-equip with Hurricanes. During 11 hectic days that followed the invasion No 607 alone claimed a total of 23 enemy aircraft destroyed, but its successes were not obtained without loss, and among those killed was its CO, S/Ldr L. E. Smith.

Their place was taken by three more Hurricane squadrons, Nos 3, 79 and 504, but in spite of repeated pleas from the French Government and demands from high places at home, Sir Hugh Dowding refused to commit any Fighter Command Spitfires to the Battle of France. On 16 May Churchill flew to Le Bourget, ironically escorted by RAF Spitfires of No 92 Sqn, to inform the French Government in person that Britain could spare no more fighters for the defence of France.

However, Spitfires did see action over France. On 23 May Spitfires of Nos 74 and 92 Sqns, operating from Hornchurch, met the Messerschmitt Bf 109 in combat for the first time, resulting in the loss of six Spitfires, one of which was captured intact after a forced landing at Calais, although the squadrons claimed to have destroyed six Bf 109s in the encounter.

One Spitfire of No 212 Sqn, a detachment of the RAF's Special Survey Flight, had in fact been based in France since November 1939. This was a specially modified photo reconnaissance aircraft, which provided valuable intelligence for the BEF as the war situation in France deteriorated and German units closed up to the coastline. The unit continued its covert operations until the fall of France.

It was left to the Hurricane units in France, which were now joined by detachments from 56, 601, 253, 111, 229, 213, 242 and 245 Sqns from No 11 Group, to bear the brunt of air battles in France. The three weeks of hectic fighting produced more than 40 RAF 'aces', but 180 of their Hurricanes were lost and more than 60 pilots killed.

1939: Chickened out

'I could claim an early intervention by Lady Luck when a posting to the aircraft carrier HMS Glorious was cancelled by my squadron commander at the beginning of September 1939. Glorious was sunk off Norway less than a year later with the loss of 1,474 officers and men of the Royal Navy and 41 of the RAF. Only 39 of her compliment were rescued. Instead, I went to France with the two Hurricane squadrons from RAF Debden in Essex, Nos 85 and 87, as part of the British Expeditionary Force (BEF) Air Component. I was Warrant Officer, Engineer for 87, and my old pal, Dan Newton, held a similar spot in 85.

We arrived at Boos, a small French airfield 4 or 5 miles from Rouen, on 3 September. Within three weeks orders were issued to move to Merville, but before moving the two squadron commanders, S/Ldrs David Atcherley (later AVM D. F. Atcherley) of 85 Squadron and W. Coote of 87, flew Dan and I over there to "case the joint". We were wined and dined sumptuously at a hotel named the Seraphim, which was renamed the "Paraffin" when the squadrons arrived.

After farewell salutes and handshakes, we left in our two Magisters for the run back to Boos, travelling at nought feet and scaring chickens, cattle and peasants as we went.

Approaching Rouen, David Atcherley pointed to the transporter bridge over the River Seine, obviously intending to fly under it! The transporter looked like a large-scale pan, suspended from a beam perched on the top of two towers, one on each riverbank.

When we got within 300 or 400 yards of the bridge, I noticed that the transporter was moving slowly, but inexorably, from left to right. My pilot had spotted this too and yanked viciously back on the stick, clearing the right-hand tower by only a few feet. No 85 Squadron's Magister got through with little to spare.

We landed together, and as I stepped out of the "Maggie" Dan yelled across, "So 87 Squadron chickened out!"

I thought that 87 had been particularly lucky.'

W. J. 'Spanner' Hendley – Fighter Command Engineer Officer (OOTB)

Above *King George VI visited Lille/Seclin on 6 December 1939 to inspect Hurricanes of Nos 85 (with hexagon markings on the tail) and 87 Sqns, and 615 Sqn Gladiators.*

Left *When No 11 Group first sent 17 Sqn Hurricanes from Martlesham Heath to carry out daylight patrols over France on 10 May, the Squadron lost five aircraft and two pilots. At the end of the Battle of France it was the top No 11 Group scorer, with 16 victories.*

Right *RAF AOCs during the Battle of France were Air Marshals Barratt, left, and Playfair, who commanded the British Air Forces in France (BAFF) and the Advanced Air Striking Force (AASF) respectively.*

HOME DEFENCE

Opposite top F/Offs Newell 'Fanny' Orton and Edgar James 'Cobber' Kain, both of 73 Sqn, became Fighter Command's first 'aces' during the Battle of France with scores of 15 and 16 destroyed respectively.

Opposite bottom The primitive 73 Sqn duty 'office' in France during the winter of 1939, with the Cranwellian 'Dickie' Martin seated second from the right.

Left S/Ldr 'Bull' Halahan, Commanding Officer of No 1 Sqn, and flight commander F/Lt 'Johnnie' Walker led the Squadron in France from October 1939 to 20 May 1940, and became the leading scorers in the Battle of France, with 63 destroyed.

Below Posted to France with 73 Sqn, F/Off R. F. Martin crash-landed in Belgium in November after an oxygen problem and was interned. He later escaped to claim 4½ destroyed in the Battle of France.

Below *Groundcrew servicing a No 501 Sqn Hurricane in the open at Anglure on a hot day in late May 1940. The squadron was the last to leave France on 21 June.*

HOME DEFENCE

Dunkirk

Following the surrender of the Belgian Army on 25 May and the fall of Calais and Boulogne two days later, the British War Cabinet issued the order to activate Operation *Dynamo* – the seaborne evacuation of the entire British Expeditionary Force from the continent from the only North Sea port still in Allied hands, Dunkirk. British fighter cover for the operation, which began on 26 May, was to be provided by 16 Fighter Command squadrons drawn from the 32 units from all over Great Britain.

The nine-day evacuation of 338,226 men from the beaches of Dunkirk was carried out under heavy air attacks by *Luftwaffe* bombers, which were attacked by British Hurricanes and Spitfires. These air defence fighters were built for speed and agility, and consequently had small fuel tanks and limited range; the Spitfires in particular could fight for only a few minutes over the beaches of Dunkirk before breaking off to return to their bases in South East England to refuel. Their pilots also had less air combat experience than the Hurricane pilots and suffered heavy losses in the first days of fighting.

At the same time, Fighter Command was carrying out night patrols over Dunkirk with Blenheim IFs of No 604 Sqn operating out of Manston. Ironically, the Squadron was in the process of replacing its twin-engined fighters with Gladiators, but although it flew its first operation with the obsolete biplanes, they were withdrawn by the end of May.

RAF Fighter Command flew 2,739 sorties during Operation *Dynamo*, losing over 100 aircraft – 49 of them Spitfires – and nearly 100 aircrew were killed. Top scoring pilots over Dunkirk were two of the RAF's first Spitfire 'aces', Bob Tuck and 'Al' Deere, who claimed ten kills each, and the Canadian Hurricane pilot 'Willie' McKnight, with a similar score.

Dunkirk also saw Fighter Command's two-seat Defiant in action for the first time with No 264 Sqn. Originally developed as an anti-bomber fighter and first flying in August 1937, the Defiant was similar in size to the Hurricane, powered by the same Merlin III engine, but differed radically in its armament. Its firepower came from a manned power-operated .303in Browning machine-gun turret fitted behind the pilot's cockpit. It had no forward-firing guns. Defiants were used with great success when they shot down more than 40 enemy aircraft for the loss of 11 pilots and gunners.

One of Fighter Command's pioneer photo-reconnaissance pilots was the French-Canadian S/Ldr Le Mesurier, OC 1416 Flt, who flew Blenheims in France and later Spitfires with 140 Sqn. He was killed over France in 1941.

Defiant crews of 264 Sqn, which claimed 31 destroyed over Dunkirk on 29 May. Back row, left to right: F/Off Hickman, F/Lt 'Lanky' Cooke, CO S/Ldr Philip Hunter, P/Off Michael Young, P/Off Gerald Hackwood, F/Lt Eric Barwell, P/Off Thomas and P/Off 'Bull' Whitley. Front row, left to right: Sgt E. R. Thorne, Sgt Kay, Sgt Lauder and Sgt Stokes.

1940: A lift home

'During the Dunkirk period I was in No 264 Squadron, the first to be equipped with the Defiant two-seat fighter based at Duxford.

Every day we flew down to Manston airfield to operate over the French coast. On 29 May 1940 we had what was to be our most successful day as the squadron was credited with the destruction of 37 enemy aircraft, three of which fell to me and my gunner, for the loss of one air gunner. All of our aircraft returned safely.

Then, on 31 May, we went over again and on that occasion we met a very large number of enemy aircraft over Dunkirk. As far as I was concerned I saw one of our Defiants breaking up in mid-air. I though it had been hit by "ack-ack", but in fact it had been hit by another aircraft. We did not spot any parachutes coming from it and assumed that the pilot, P/Off Young, and his gunner had been killed.

On that patrol I accounted for one Me 109. On the

next patrol that day we were again in the thick of it and I attacked some He 111 bombers, one of which I shot down, seeing parachutes appear before it hit the water almost over Dunkirk harbour. Almost immediately I had the cockpit full of glycol, which meant that I had been hit in the engine. I obviously could not remain airborne for very long and immediately headed for home, and from 10,000 feet slowly lost altitude. Going across the Channel I kept the line of small boats stretching from Dunkirk to Dover in sight the whole way. When my engine finally slowed down and eventually packed up I decided to ditch.

I saw two Royal Navy destroyers going in opposite directions so I decided to ditch the aircraft between them, hoping that one of them would be able to pick us up. I stood up in the cockpit to undo all the straps of my harness and parachute and concentrated on landing on water. It was difficult to judge my height above the water as it was a very smooth sea. The aircraft broke up after hitting the water and I found myself pulled down but eventually swam up towards the surface. When I looked around for my gunner,

P/Off Williams, I eventually spotted his parachute pack floating some way off. I turned it over to find him unconscious with a bit of a gash on his head.

I started to swim towards the nearest destroyer, which was some distance away, and after some difficulty in keeping my gunner's head – and my own – above water, was relieved to see the ship slowly turning towards us. A sailor dived off the bow and took control of my gunner while I was hauled aboard. The first person I saw on board was P/Off Young, who we thought had been killed earlier that day. The amusing thing was that when Williams came to on the destroyer, he saw Young silhouetted against what he though were red flames. In fact it was the setting sun, but in his woozy state he was convinced that he had joined Young in the flames of hell!

Anyway, we were landed safely at Dover in due course having accounted for five enemy aircraft in two days of action over Dunkirk.'

Eric Gordon Barwell – Fighter Command pilot

No 92 Sqn's Spitfires flew their first patrols over Dunkirk on 23 May to claim six destroyed on the day, but the squadron lost its CO, S/Ldr Roger Bushell, who was later shot in 1944 for his part in the 'Great Escape' from Stalag Luft III.

1940: A learning curve

'We had only converted from the Blenheim to Spitfires a few weeks earlier and 29 May was my first patrol with No 64 Sqn. Our 12 Spitfires, in four close-vic formations, were flying straight and level across the Channel heading for the Dunkirk area at 15,000 feet when I noticed small black clouds appearing in the sky around us.

The next thing I knew was that my aircraft was suddenly lifted up by an unseen hand as I smelled cordite for the first time. I had nearly been hit by German "ack-ack"! A few minutes later the leading aircraft disappeared in a small cloud of thick acrid black smoke.

That day we lost three aircraft and their pilots, including our CO, S/Ldr E. G. Rogers. We also learned a valuable lesson in air combat. From then on we weaved all over the sky to give the "ack-ack" gunners a more difficult target, but it would be some time before Fighter Command realised that flying in close pre-war vic formations meant that the pilots spent more time looking at each other to avoid mid-air collisions than searching the sky above and behind for enemy aircraft.'

Paul Patten – Fighter Command pilot

With the evacuation of the BEF, France's ability to withstand the German onslaught was effectively ended. On 12 June, two days after Italy declared war on Great Britain and France, Churchill flew to Tours in a last vain effort to convince the French Prime Minister not to give up. It was only the low fuel state of his escorting Spitfires that made him leave with his mission unaccomplished.

Paris was declared an open city on 13 June and the victorious Germans marched in the next day. The remnants of 1, 17, 73, 242 and 501 Hurricane Squadrons fought on in France until 15 June, when they finally withdrew and made their various ways back to England. Of the 261 Hurricanes sent to France, only 66 returned. In the six weeks following the German invasion of France, the RAF had lost a total of 386 Hurricanes, 67 Spitfires, 11 Blenheims, 10 Defiants and a Gladiator.

Several of Fighter Command's first 'aces', including 'Cobber' Kain and Leslie Clisby, each with 16 victories, were killed in France, while many others, such as 'Killy' Kilmartin, 'Max' Aitken and 'Ginger' Lacey, would soon become household names.

On 21 June France signed an armistice with Germany. The Battle of France was over and Britain now faced its own battle for survival.

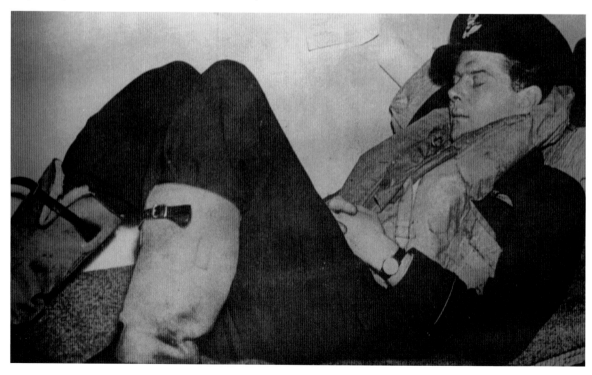

Former British skier 'Billy' Clyde left Mexico to join 601 (County of London) Sqn at the outbreak of war and became a Dunkirk and Battle of Britain 'ace'.

Chapter 2

Flying training

Many of Fighter Command's battles were won by the quality of its pilots as much as the quality of the aircraft they flew. At the outbreak of war, pilots for Fighter Command's new state-of-the-art interceptors were drawn from a variety of backgrounds: Royal Air Force Regulars, Auxiliary Air Force 'weekend playboys', RAF Volunteer Reservists – spare-time flyers – and student volunteers in University Air Squadrons. It was said at the time that 'Auxiliaries are gentlemen trying to be officers, Regulars are officers trying to be gentlemen, and VRs are neither trying to be both.'

However, this did not take into account the abilities of pilots with differing backgrounds. Regular entry was via either the RAF College, Cranwell, or a Short Service commission. The academic standard for entry to Cranwell was extremely high and was restricted to a privileged few who included such future 'aces' as Douglas Bader, Peter Townsend, George Barclay and Dicky Lee. On the outbreak of war it was announced that during the period of hostilities no further permanent commissions in the RAF would be granted, and the RAF College became Cranwell Flying Training School (FTS).

Up to that time all successful applicants were given their basic and advanced training on biplane types before being commissioned as officers and posted to Fighter or Army Co-operation squadrons. In the late 1930s these were equipped with Hawker Fury IIs and Hinds, or Gloster Gauntlets – all fabric-and-wire biplanes.

However, the Auxiliary pilots were well educated, intelligent and good pilots who adapted well to metal monoplanes when they came into service. All commissioned officers, they tended to be up to five years older than their Regular counterparts. Most were men of independent means and their lifestyles were reflected in the names given to Auxiliary squadron members, such as the 'Millionaires Mob', the 'Legionnaires' or the 'Brains Trust'. These units were manned by friends and colleagues from the city or county to which all the AAF squadrons were affiliated – 'The County of Kent', 'The City of Edinburgh', 'South Yorkshire', etc.

The Royal Air Force Volunteer Reserve had been created in 1936, although entry did not commence until April 1937. Conceived by the Director of Training at the Air Ministry, Air Commodore A. W. Tedder, the RAFVR was to become a 'Citizen Air Force', which, with the Auxiliaries, would form a second line of defence behind the Regulars. RAFVR pilots were enthusiasts who sacrificed much of their spare time in order to maintain the high standards demanded of them. They received weekend flying training and £25 per annum retainer from the government, and on gaining their wings became Sergeant Pilots or Pilot Officers, depending on their 'social class'. Some 300 VR pilots were serving with Fighter Command at the outbreak of war.

A separate RAF Training Command, under the command of Air Marshal Sir Charles Burnett, was not established until May 1936, a time when the RAF was in the throes of a rapid expansion programme. The Air Ministry's Fighter Production Scheme 'F' called for 500 Hurricanes and 300 Spitfires to be in service by 1939. When Training Command was formed, four new flying training schools were opened in addition to the existing five, but a shortage of qualified flying instructors was aggravated by the new front-line equipment coming on line.

By the mid-1930s most RAF pilots, irrespective of their method of entry, were being given their basic training on the DH Tiger Moth. This two-seat biplane primary trainer had entered service with RAF Elementary and Reserve Flying Schools in 1932, replacing First World War-vintage Avro 504s, and was destined to remain in service for more than 20 years. After some 50 hours on the Tiger Moth, trainee fighter pilots graduated to the two-seat Hart trainer, another biplane introduced in the same year as the Tiger Moth. However, the Hart's top speed was only 165mph and hardly prepared the student pilot for the new generation of 350mph monoplane fighters about to enter service.

To address this problem new monoplane training types were also ordered. These were the Miles Magister elementary trainer, or 'Maggie', and the Miles Master advanced trainer, which had a retractable undercarriage, an enclosed cockpit and a top speed of 225mph! However, few of these new

1941: The best Hurricane pilots ever

'A month after arriving in Britain in October 1941, I was posted to a Hurricane OTU at RAF Crosby-on-Eden near Carlisle with two other Australians from my course, Ron Charmain and Bruce Watson, both Melbournites.

It was very cold and our billets were Nissan huts – so cold! We were quickly into it – a couple of flights in a Miles Magister to get our hands back into flying, and to see where we lived in the countryside. We were given a verbal and visual rundown on a Hurricane cockpit – there were no dual-control Hurricanes. After some few hours memorising all the controls and instruments, an instructor strolled out, leaned on the cockpit and asked questions about where certain controls were, etc – all very casual.

Then it was, "OK – off you go!" So I grabbed my parachute and climbed into the Hurricane allocated to me. This was it. I was to fly a top-line fighter plane.

The first hurdle to get over was starting the engine. I remembered petrol on, trim OK, brakes on, a few pumps of the "Wobble" pump, press the starter button and the engine fired. This was not always the case, as one tended to over-prime and the engine wouldn't start.

The next hurdle was to taxi out to the strip. With such a long nose you had to swing the aircraft from side to side to see where you are going. I was finally at the end of the strip and did my cockpit drill – "TMPFF" ("Trim nose down, Mixture rich, Pitch fine, Fuel on, Flaps up"). I got a green light from the control tower – this was it! I opened the throttle and away we went. The power, compared with what I had been used to, was incredible.

I was at 3,000 feet before I realised that I hadn't retracted my wheels. I then flew around for 30 minutes or so. It was fantastic! Then I pulled off a reasonable landing. I had made it!

From here on we flew incessant exercises – formation flying, air-to-air combat and gun firing. I finished the course and we considered ourselves the best Hurricane pilots ever.'

Wilfred A. Goold – Australian Fighter Command pilot

A student pilot climbs into the rear cockpit of a North American Harvard I advanced trainer to get his first experience of an enclosed-cockpit, retractable-undercarriage fighter trainer.

One of the last Spitfire Is to be built, AR212 served with No 57 OTU at Hawarden in 1941 before being written off in a mid-air collision while serving with 27 OTU a year later.

Having survived the Battle of Britain with No 11 Group's 145 Sqn, this veteran Bristol Blenheim IF went on to serve with 54 OTU, Fighter Command's first night-fighter Operational Training Unit.

trainers were in service when war broke out, and in an attempt to make up the shortfall, 400 North American Harvard I advanced trainers, one of the first American types to be ordered by the RAF, were ordered, the first of which were delivered to RAF Flying Training Schools in early 1939. This popular and robust trainer would remain in RAF service throughout the war years. It was considered at the time that it would take at least a year to train an operational fighter pilot, accumulating the minimum of 250 hours of flying training that was required.

One problem was converting RAF instructors to these new types before *ab initio* students could get their hands on them. Consequently, many pilots took part in the Battles of France and Britain having been taught to fly on obsolete biplane trainers, with little or no radio/telephone (R/T), weapons or tactics training.

Both Regulars and Auxiliaries continued to practice set piece air battle scenarios based on 1914-18 fighting techniques up to the outbreak of the Second World War. At the end of 1939 the RAF was receiving 200 pilots a month from flying training of all types, many of whom had never flown a monoplane or used a radio, and had been taught by instructors with no operational experience. Operational training concentrated on tight-formation flying and practising 'Fighting Area Attacks', in which a line of fighters queued up to take it in turns to fire at a target aircraft. There were also few opportunities for firing guns at a moving target.

The concept of separate operational training units was not adopted by the RAF until the eve of war. Prior to this all advanced training – night flying, gunnery and formation flying – was carried out by front-line squadrons. Fighter Command Operational Training Units (OTUs) were officially established on 1 September 1939, but it was almost two years before they were fully functional. In the meantime, Fighter Command Group Pools, known initially as Advanced Flying Training Centres (AFTCs) were established, and these were supplemented by having advanced trainers such as the Master I attached to operational Hurricane and Spitfire units, and Oxford T.Is with Blenheim squadrons.

The first OTUs were not opened until March 1940 when 5 and 6 OTUs at Aston Down and Sutton Bridge respectively were formed, equipped with Hurricanes, while the first Spitfire OTU, No 7 at Hawarden, was not established until the eve of the Battle of Britain. Initially each unit was equipped with up to 50 battle-worn aircraft, which were regularly written off following misuse by pupils, especially those who had trained on biplanes and had no experience of retractable undercarriages and

constant-speed airscrews. A series of fines were levied for various misdemeanours – 5 shillings (25p) for bending the prop by hitting the brakes too hard, taxiing with flaps down or boiling the glycol coolant, and £5 for a belly landing! The fines were shared out among the groundcrews.

As RAF losses mounted during the Battle of Britain, replacing pilots became a greater priority than replacing Spitfires. Having lost a high percentage of squadron commanders, an Air Staff ruling decreed that fighter pilots over 30 years old should be withdrawn from front-line units – the average age during the Battle of Britain was 23. This would mean that many experienced AAF pilots and older Regulars such as 'Max' Aitken, 'Sailor' Malan and Douglas Bader would be given desk jobs. However, in the event many of these 'veteran' officers were posted to squadrons withdrawn from the Battle to re-equip and train replacement pilots.

Some of these replacements had even less flying experience than their commanders would have wished. In an effort to speed up the training process, the vital six-month OTU course was reduced to only four weeks! Pilots were now being posted with only 10 hours on Spitfires or Hurricanes and virtually no knowledge of the latest German tactics that they would have to encounter during combat. Many would be lost on their first sorties.

When the Battle of Britain began in July 1940, the pilots who manned Fighter Command's combat-ready squadrons were a mix of 'veterans', who had fought in the Battle of France, and 'new boys', who had recently completed their operational training. It was not until the Battle was over that Fighter Command formed No 81 Group in December 1940, under the command of Air Commodore F. J. Vincent DFC, to control all operational training. Existing units were renumbered as Nos 55, 56 and 57 OTUs, while at the same time the first night-fighter OTU, No 54, was formed at Church Fenton with Defiants. No 81 Group was about to expand rapidly during 1941 to cope with a huge influx of overseas-trained pilots who were about to gain their RAF 'wings'.

These pilots were the product of one of the RAF's most important training schemes, negotiated soon after the outbreak of war but too late to contribute to the Battles of France and Britain. An agreement was reached in Ottawa on 17 December 1939 to establish the Empire Air Training Scheme (EATS), under which the majority of British and Commonwealth aircrew would be trained for the duration of the war.

Later known as the British Commonwealth Air Training Plan (BCATP), the scheme covered elementary, basic or intermediate and advanced flying

P/Off Eric Shipp recording a
Link Trainer exercise at
Tangmere in November
1942. Invented by the
Americans, this was the first
flight simulator, and was
made available to Fighter
Command in 1941.

A member of the groundcrew
refuels a well-worn Spitfire I
belonging to No 61 OTU at
Rednal, with P/Off Eric
Shipp in the cockpit ready for
a solo exercise in July 1942.

training, and the first Canadian flying schools, operated by the Royal Canadian Air Force, opened at Camp Borden, Ontario, in April 1940. BCATP Elementary Flying Training Schools (EFTSs) were equipped with the American Boeing Stearman PT-17/PT-27 Kaydet, Fairchild PT-19/26, Canadian Fleet Finch and DH Tiger Moth. Intermediate FTSs used North American Yales originally ordered for the French Air Force, while all advanced training was carried out on the Harvard.

At its peak in 1943 there were almost 200 BCATP schools in eight Commonwealth countries stretching from New Zealand to the Bahamas. Most participating countries sent their pilots to Canada for advanced training, with New Zealand sending more than 500 per year. Rhodesia operated 25 BCATP schools, while neighbouring South Africa established a separate organisation, the Joint Air Training Scheme (JATS), which had 36 schools training aircrew for the Allied Desert Air Force. There were no fewer than 93 Canadian FTSs using nearly 7,000 aircraft for pilot training, some of which were supplied under the Lend-Lease agreement with the United States, while others, such as the Tiger Moth, PT-26 Cornell and Harvard, were built under licence in Canada. By the time the Scheme was terminated in March 1945, some 50,000 pilots had been trained in Canada, with 856 students being lost in training accidents.

At the height of the Battle of Britain the British Under-Secretary of State for Air, Capt Harold Balfour MC, flew to the United States by Empire flying boat to ask US President Roosevelt for flying training facilities. He reached an agreement in August 1940 for the establishment of six British Flying Training Schools (BFTSs) to be established in the United States for elementary to advanced flying training. To be administered by RAF personnel and staffed by US Army Air Force (USAAF) pilot instructors, the schools, in Florida, Oklahoma, Texas and California, opened in September 1941.

A separate American scheme came about following a visit to Britain by Major General Henry H. 'Hap' Arnold, the Commander-in-Chief of the USAAF, in early 1941. He offered the British Government access to civilian-run contract flight training schools in the southern United States. A 30-week course would consist of 8-10 hours primary, 10 hours basic and 10 hours advanced flying training on Southeast Air Corps Training Center (SEACTC) types. These were the same training aircraft as those used by the BFTSs, namely the PT-17 primary trainer, the BT-13 basic trainer, and the AT-6, AT-9 and AT-10 advanced trainers. The six Arnold Scheme Primary FTSs were Carlstrom at Arcadia and Lakeland, Florida, and

1943: Betrothed

'The "marriage ceremony" between pilot and navigator had to be concluded within the first few days of our arrival at No 51 OTU, Cranfield. This pantomime took the form of a shotgun wedding event, although it was such an important step in our young lives. We were allowed one evening in the Sergeants' Mess and the next evening in the Officers' Mess. For better or worse, the betrothal was final.

By chance, both I and my navigator-to-be – E. J. "Midi" Midlane – had bribed a corporal in the personnel section of Station Headquarters to show us the respective documents of our careers to date. It seems that this "old-time" corporal used to make a financial success of this ruse! Although Midi was rather ancient, being 27 years old, he was head and shoulders above any of the other pupil navigators with regard to both academic and practical performance. Similarly, I was one of the most experienced pilots on the course, hence within the first half-hour in the Sergeants' Mess we had found each other and our partnership blossomed over the next 18 months.'

Richard W. 'Dick' Leggett – Fighter Command night fighter pilot

Camden, North Carolina; Darr Aero Tech at Albany, Georgia; Souther at Americus and Georgia; and Van de Graff at Tuscaloosa, Alabama. Basic training took place at Cochran Field, Macon, Georgia, and at Gunter Field, Montgomery, Alabama. The advanced course took place at Turner, Napier and Craig Fields in Georgia, and Moody Field, Valdosta.

As America was still a neutral country, the first 500 British Arnold Scheme 'cadets' had to be discharged from the RAF and RAFVR and travel to the United States via Canada in civilian grey suits. Not all were welcomed on their arrival. They were known as 'Lower-classmen', while American students were 'Upper-classmen'. Whereas Commonwealth student pilots suffered from the extreme cold at Canadian BCATP schools, BFTS and Arnold Scheme students found the humid heat and southern US accents difficult to deal with. However, the most difficult

The staff of an OTU watch from their black and yellow mobile control van as a student pilot executes the text-book curved approach to a Spitfire landing.

aspect of the US training system was the threat of instant 'wash-out'. This could occur within minutes of a trainee's first dual flight, and led to over 40 per cent of Arnold Scheme cadets being eliminated and some 25 per cent of BFTS students. Nevertheless, more than 13,000 RAF pilots graduated in the United States, including some 7,000 from the BFTSs, and 4,370 during the Arnold Scheme. During the schemes' 20-month lifespan 81 lost their lives in accidents.

When the *Luftwaffe* began its night Blitz on London and other major British cities, the RAF was forced to respond. Although most fighter pilots had some experience of night flying, usually with OTUs or their operational squadrons, the Hurricane and

1942: Those with promise

'At the controls of a Hurricane during operational training, the joy of flying hit me. Then those who showed promise were sent to fly the new Typhoon fighter, with such a powerful – and experimental – engine that it would have to be throttled back when chasing an Me 109. It was a very macho aeroplane to fly and you could express all your aggression.'

Richard Hough – Fighter Command pilot

Spitfire were designed as day fighters and few of their pilots were formally trained to fly, let alone fight, at night. Following night flying trials carried out in 1939, test pilot reports revealed that exhaust flare restricted forward view, cockpit lighting was poor, internal reflections unacceptable, battery life marginal for the landing lamp, and the undercarriage lights too bright at night. Night take-offs required the lengthening of flarepaths to 800 yards – double the normal take-off distance – and while the Hurricane's wide undercarriage track gave pilots added confidence when making night landings, the Spitfire's long nose and narrow undercarriage track made landing after dark potentially hazardous.

One of the few pilots to achieve success at night while flying the Spitfire was the South African former merchant seaman, Adolph Gysbert 'Sailor' Malan, who shot down two He 111 bombers in 30 minutes on a clear moonlit night in June 1940. A few days earlier Douglas Bader, on the other hand, carrying out a fruitless search in his lone Spitfire for a 'bogey' on a cloudy night over the River Humber, described the experience as like 'being blindfolded and chasing a rabbit in the woods'. On his return to base at Kirton-in-Lindsey, he wrote off his Spitfire after misjudging the flarepath in the pouring rain.

In the event no Spitfire squadrons were committed to night fighting, although several Hurricane squadrons, including Peter Townsend's 85 Sqn, would become night fighter units by the end of 1940. The RAF's first successful night fighter was the Defiant, which had been withdrawn from daylight operations early in the Battle of Britain due to unacceptable losses. It did, however, have the advantage of being a two-seater, thus enabling an instructor to sit in the rear cockpit, and the type was chosen to equip the first night-fighter OTU, No 4, which was opened at Church Fenton in October 1940.

In the year following the establishment of No 81 Group, another six Operational Training Units were opened, including two more night-fighting OTUs, while several new types coming into service included the Beaufighter, and the Mosquito, Typhoon and Mustang in 1942.

With Fighter Command taking the offensive over occupied Europe, more emphasis was placed on tactical and ground attack training, which previously had only been addressed in very general terms at OTUs and operational squadrons. Air gunnery was an acquired art, and how 'sprog' pilots learned it was largely down to how good their flight and squadron commanders were at passing on their experience. In

George Henry Gibson Lewis's certificate of Graduation from Riddle-McKay College. Lewis went on to serve only briefly with Fighter Command, then moved to the ATA at the end of the war.

1941: Above average

'The telegram instructed me to report immediately to No 9 Service Flying Training School (SFTS) at RAF Hullavington in Wiltshire. As I approached the airfield I was astonished to see lots of Hart and Audax biplane aircraft buzzing around the sky. However, it was a relief to find out that my course would be on Miles Master Mk 1 aircraft fitted with the Rolls-Royce Kestrel engine.

Compared with the Tiger Moth this really was a step in the right direction. This fast monoplane with its retractable undercarriage and high landing speed was just right for a budding fighter pilot. It became even better when, due to a shortage of Master aircraft, we were delighted to be authorised to do our aerobatic and formation flying in the Hurricane Mk 1 with its Merlin engine. Now it seemed inevitable that then unqualified pilots should be permitted to dash around in a front-line aircraft.

However, we were now convinced that the next posting would be to either a Spitfire or Hurricane OTU. On the completion of the course my instructor gave me a chit and directed me to the station clothing store where I signed for my pilot's badge ("wings") and sergeant's stripe – no ceremony! That evening a WAAF girlfriend sewed them on to my uniform before we celebrated.

On 31 May, soon after my 19th birthday, I collected my log-book from the CFI who said, "Good show, Leggett, you're going to be a flying instructor." Naturally I protested, as this painful remark left me numb, but the Wing Commander smiled and said, "Off you go and enjoy your leave as it is unlikely that you will be getting much more."

When commiserating with my friends it seemed that only three of us had been assessed as "above average", so we all had to go and be taught to be flying instructors. Out of 20 students on my instructor course, only one failed and he was given the option of going to an Operational Training Unit of his choice. He was a happy man and went to a Spitfire OTU! Some of us were furious at having passed as "Average Instructor".

After 18 months of compulsory instructing in the UK and Canada, it was not until the spring of 1943 that my operational training commenced.'

Richard W. 'Dick' Leggett – Fighter Command night fighter pilot

After being assessed 'above average' during training, P/Off Dick Leggett was sent to Canada as part of the BCAPT. He is seen here on the right with 'a girlfriend' and fellow instructor Ralf Reavill, later killed flying a Bomber Command Halifax.

The up side of being a frustrated fighter pilot was the social life as an RAF instructor in Canada. Here Dick Leggett dances with an American heiress at the Hotel Nicolette, Minneapolis, on New Year's Day, 1943.

an effort to rationalise gunnery and tactics training, a number of specialist units such as the Pilot Attack Gunnery School, whose first CO was G/C 'Sailor' Malan, and the Air Fighter Development Unit were established in 1942. The unsuccessful Dieppe raid was another learning curve for Fighter Command planners, and in the run-up to D-Day the Fighter

Leader School was established at Milfield and Tactical Exercise Units and Armament Practice Camps were formed under the control of No 9 Group.

By 1945 Fighter Command had more aircraft on strength with its training units that it had had with front-line squadrons in September 1939.

Chapter 3
Groundcrew

Like the pilots, RAF groundcrews had faced a leap in technology with the introduction of Fighter Command's new Hurricanes and Spitfires at the beginning of the war. In a short space of time, and with little specialist training, they had to come to terms with V12 Merlins, stressed skin, split flaps, hydraulics, pneumatics and electrics.

Again, as with their aircrew colleagues called to duty on 24 August 1939, the Aircraftsmen Mechanics came from diverse backgrounds ranging from ex-RFC (First World War) reservists, RAF apprentices ('brats') and direct entry Regulars. They had a few months to adjust to the new high-technology fighters that were about to defend Great Britain against almost certain invasion by seemingly invincible German forces spearheaded by the *Luftwaffe*.

RAF groundcrews, or 'erks' as they were known, had already been blooded in the Battles of Norway and France, where many lost their lives or were captured. Now they were again in the front line as the Battle of Britain gathered momentum. As they followed their squadrons into action, often moving at a few hours' notice, the groundcrews had to take whatever accommodation they could – in many cases tents or the outhouses of the local stately home vacated for the duration by its owner. At the height of the Battle squadrons were flying up to four or five sorties a day. When the fighters landed they were expected to be refuelled, re-armed and gun ports taped, have their engines checked, including topping up the oil and glycol coolant tanks, oxygen cylinders replaced and R/T tested, all within 10 minutes!

Early Spitfires had to have their eight Browning machine-guns washed in a petrol solution to prevent them from jamming at high altitudes while at the same time lubricated with oil to stop them rusting. Sometimes repairs and routine maintenance had to be carried out in the open during bad weather, when flying was cancelled, or at night in the blackout. During night raids, power and water mains were often put out of action, making the groundcrew's life even more difficult.

Armourers re-arm a No 601 Sqn Hurricane's eight .303 Brownings – the gun bays had only two panels with 32 turnbuttons – while an 'erk' refuels the fighter at Tangmere in July 1940.

1939: A visit to the cinema

'On 1 September 1939 I was detailed to join a salvage party to collect the wreckage of one of our squadron's Spitfires from where it had crashed into the corner of a school playground in Grays, Essex, killing the pilot, F/Sgt Gower. He had not baled out and was the sole casualty as the crash occurred during the school holidays. It was my first experience of a fatal aircraft accident.

The gardens of a row of houses backed on to the edge of the playground separated by the perimeter fence. The occupants plied us with tea, and snatches of the latest wireless news of the invasion of Poland with excited statements such as "Warsaw bombed – thousands killed!" During the morning flights of Wellingtons and Battle bombers passed overhead.

The wreckage lay in a heap giving off its distinctive peculiar smell. Other lasting impressions were of retrieving the pilot's crushed seat from the back of the supercharger casing of the partially embedded engine, which was enfolded by the bent metal DH propeller blades. The mainplane had split from the trailing edge, opening up on impact like a book, scattering the ammunition. The leading edge had carved a dihedral-shaped tapered groove or furrow deep into the tarmac surface of the playground.

We also thought of the boyish, fresh-faced, crop-haired enthusiastic chap who had been the pilot, with whom my friend Ted Thompson and I had arranged to visit the cinema on our next six-hour pass.'

P. E. Webster – Fighter Command ACI
Fitter Two

In contrast, at Duxford in June 1940, groundcrews refuel and re-arm 12 Group's Spitfire Is of 66 Sqn, the gun bays of which had 22 panels and 150 turnbuttons.

In August and September 11 Group's main fighter bases came under heavy attacks by the *Luftwaffe* during which groundcrew were expected to help man the airfield defence anti-aircraft guns. These raids often destroyed accommodation blocks and killed many aircraftsmen and women. When the raids were over airfield damage was repaired by the groundcrews, before moving to the base's satellite field where their squadron's Spitfires were operating. Few were able to take any leave during this period.

When at a state of readiness, a member of the groundcrew, the engine fitter, would warm up the fighter's engine at regular intervals, while the other member of the 'team', the airframe rigger, would be ready to help the pilot into his parachute and strap him into the seat in the event of a 'scramble'.

The Merlin engine fitted to the first RAF Hurricanes, Defiants and Spitfires had to be started by using an external battery mounted on a trolley accumulator, which had to be manhandled into place by the groundcrew; the Spitfire II's engine was fitted with an internal Koffman cartridge starter. The Bristol Mercury radial that powered the Gladiator and Blenheim 1F had to be cranked into life by an 'erk' with a starting handle. A backfire could result in a broken wrist.

Most pilots appreciated their groundcrews' part in their ability to operate effectively. A smooth-running engine, clean and well-oiled canopy and non-jamming guns would often not only increase a pilot's chances of shooting down the enemy, but may save his life. Many long-term relationships between groundcrew and aircrew were forged during the hectic months of the Battle of Britain.

A team of armourers open the Spitfire's numerous gun and ammunition bay access doors to replace the Browning's .303 ammunition boxes during a 30-minute re-arming turnround.

This relationship continued during the offensive stages of Fighter Command's strategy when even more pilots were lost over the continent. However, while conditions for 'erks' improved at permanent sector stations, new units were being formed weekly during 1942-44 and many of these were deployed to new airfields that were often still under construction when the groundcrews moved in. With few hangars, workshops or even accommodation, apart from tents, the groundcrews were hard put to maintain the ever-increasing number of sophisticated types that entered service prior to D-Day.

In the days following the start of Operation *Overlord*, the groundcrews of squadrons assigned to 2TAF were shipped off to 31 temporary airstrips being bulldozed out of empty French farmland around Caen, a few miles inland from the D-Day invasion

beaches. RAF groundcrew helped Sappers and Pioneers lay hundreds of tons of wire mesh over miles of hessian. Conditions were primitive and facilities non-existent. Groundcrews set up workshops in open cornfields and under fruit trees in orchards, and slept where and when they could while battles raged around the airfield perimeters.

The weather was either hot and dry, which whenever aircraft took off or landed caused clouds of dust that found its way into engines, hydraulics and gun mechanisms, or cold and wet, when the airfields were turned into quagmires. The ends of the wire mesh would bend upwards with constant use, becoming a bed of needles that punctured aircraft tyres, often with fatal results. Ground attack sorties were measured in minutes rather than hours, with 'cab-ranks' of Spitfires, Mustangs and Typhoons

A team of engine fitters pore over a Hurricane I's 1,029hp Rolls-Royce Merlin III engine at a No 11 Group airfield in southern England during the Battle of Britain.

attacking on demand targets that were easily in view of their groundcrews. The fighters had to be refuelled and re-armed twice an hour from dawn to dusk in the long summer days of July.

Three months after D-Day the Allies' race to Germany was on, and 2TAF fighters moved from France to Belgium and on to Holland, with their groundcrews trying to keep up. This continued until the last weeks of the war in Europe, when they moved into battered *Luftwaffe* airfields in Germany, which they often occupied for many months after VE-Day.

1940: Vanishing trick

'The squadron had a Fairey Battle for general training purposes and a Miles Magister for communications work at the time, which was a sod to start. The prop had to be hand swung and it was usually very reluctant to catch.

All of us who worked on the Spitfires in and around the squadron hangar helped with handling and starting. So every time the Magister was pushed out we all vanished from sight.'

Derek Morris – Fighter Command Fitter (Armourer)

No 504 (City of Nottingham) Sqn groundcrew work on a Hurricane's radio compartment watched by their pilot, F/Lt M. E. A. 'Scruffy' Royce, who shot down two enemy aircraft in September 1940.

Opposite above *A 601 Sqn Hurricane, which was credited with the destruction of three enemy aircraft in the previous month, gets the full attention of a team of engine fitters and airframe riggers at Exeter airfield in September 1940.*

Opposite below *No 3 Sqn armourers load a Hurricane IIC with 20mm ammunition for its four 20mm cannon under the watchful eye of its pilot.*

Above left *With its tail lashed to a trestle and main wheels firmly chocked, 72 Sqn groundcrew protect their ears during the harmonisation of a Spitfire's eight Brownings at Acklington.*

Left *An 'erk' paints the name of 65 Sqn on the nose of a Spitfire. Two other squadrons, Nos 92 and 123, were also known as 'East India' squadrons.*

1940: Last Gauntlet

'No 74 Squadron had been re-equipped with Spitfires in February 1939 and the Gloster Gauntlets that it replaced were all flown away – all except one. That was on a 180-hour inspection and was dismantled at the time so it was just written off and left – its wings off and stripped of its fabric. It was piled up in an annex of the hangar and allowed to collect dust.

It was nearly a year later in January 1940 when the CO looked at it on his weekly hangar inspection and ordered it to be put back together. All trades concerned worked on it for a few weeks in spare moments and it was assembled and flying again by February. We had no guns for it, but apart from that it was fine. It was used as a hack between Hornchurch and its satellite airfield at Rochford, and continued to fly throughout the Battle of Britain to become the last of its type to serve with Fighter Command.'

Derek Morris – Fighter Command Fitter (Armourer)

One of the groundcrew's less popular tasks was holding down the tail of a Spitfire while the pilot gave the Merlin full boost during an engine test.

Armourers re-arm the four closely grouped 20mm Hispano cannon mounted in the nose of a twin-engined Whirlwind long-range fighter. Below the guns is a cine-camera gun.

Above *Air Training Corps cadets assist a member of the regular groundcrew to start a 65 Sqn Spitfire V at Eastchurch in early 1942.*

Below *At North Weald in March 1942 a rigger straps in the pilot of 222 Sqn Spitfire VB BM202; it was named 'Flying Scotsman', having been presented to the RAF by the London & North Eastern Railway.*

The complexity of the Hawker Typhoon's 2,200hp Napier Sabre IIB can be seen as 56 Sqn groundcrew work on it.

The Typhoon's four 20mm Hispano cannon are re-armed by 257 Squadron's armourers at Warmwell in May 1943.

Armourers loading 16 60lb
3-inch rocket projectiles
(R/Ps) under the wings of a
247 Sqn Typhoon at Hurn in
late 1943.

Groundcrew winching up
250lb bombs to the
underwing hardpoints of a
Hawker Typhoon in the
spring of 1943.

The entire groundcrew section of No 56 Sqn poses with newly delivered Typhoon IB DL317 at Matlaske in August 1942.

1943: Typhoon work-up

'*After No 181 Squadron had replaced its Hawker Hurricanes with its latest stablemate, the Typhoon, at Duxford in late 1942, we moved down to Snailwell near Newmarket to work up before being declared operational. The thing I remember about this period was the stable lads exercising their racehorses early every morning as though there was no war going on. It was also a time when our CO, S/L Crowley-Milling, who had flown with Douglas Bader's 242 Squadron in the Battle of Britain, during which he shot down three enemy aircraft, would stand on the wing of a Typhoon with a stopwatch in his hand while we repeatedly exercised refuelling and re-arming the aircraft.*

We were declared operational in June 1943 and the squadron moved to Gravesend where the Typhoons began operating against enemy shipping armed with a pair of 250lb bombs as part of the "Channel Stop" campaign. The squadron also became the first to add the 60lb 3-inch rocket projectile to its armoury in October 1943. A month later we became part of the newly formed 2nd Tactical Air Force (2TAF) and were on the move again.

Gravesend was a pre-war fighter station with comfortable sleeping quarters, messes, permanent hangars and workshops. We were now given four blankets and transported out to a desolate airfield in Hampshire where we would spend the winter. Lasham was still under construction when we arrived and the only accommodation was tents. It was a shock to the system.'

Stan Shonfield – Australian Fighter Command Wireless Operator Mechanic (WOM)

Right Engine fitters Tom Grange and 'Taffy' Mills take time off from servicing the 1,425hp Bristol Hercules III radial engines of a 604 Sqn Beaufighter IF.

Below Groundcrew re-arm, refuel and inspect a 127 Sqn Spitfire LF XVI operating from a wet Woensdrecht airfield (B.57) in Belgium in late 1944.

1944: Over the top

'Our squadron went over to Normandy very early after D-Day. The groundcrews went by ship and, after landing at Omaha Beach and wearily climbing the towering cliffs, were instructed to "spread out your groundsheets", and in a few moments we were all firmly asleep!

Our Mosquitos were at Manpertus (A.15) in the American sector although it was not equipped for night fighters. No 604 Sqn was the first Allied night fighter unit to operate from French soil. We had no contact with the US airmen but we did, however, have the benefit of their weekly PX rations – cigarettes, chocolate, chewing-gum, etc.

After a month or so we moved over to Picauville (A.8) near Caen in the British sector and, I regret to say, diminished living standards. However, we put up with it – being British!'

D. E. Wilson – Fighter Command Groundcrew

Armourers loading 500lb bombs on a 485 (RNZAF) Sqn Spitfire LF IXB used for dive-bombing missions from Merville (B.53) in France late in 1944.

No 66 Sqn 'erks' refuel and re-arm one of their Spitfire Is at Duxford in early 1940.

A Canadian fitter works on the instrument panel in the cockpit of a No 401 (RCAF) Sqn Hurricane IIB at Digby in April 1941.

Chapter 4
Brothers in arms

Free Europeans: escape to fight

'I must confess that I had been a little doubtful of the effect that their experience in their own countries might have had upon Polish and Czech pilots. But my doubts were laid to rest. The squadrons swung into the fight with a dash and enthusiasm that is beyond praise. They were inspired by a burning hatred for the Germans, which made them very deadly opponents. The first Polish Squadron, No 303 in 11 Group, during the course of a month, shot down more German aircraft than any British unit in the same period.'

Air Chief Marshal Dowding,
AOC Fighter Command, 1941

When Germany invaded Poland, the latter's Air Force had only some 300 warplanes, less than half of which were fighters, to face a *Luftwaffe* with more than ten times that number.

However, Poland was a country under conscription and the number of recruits to the Air Force each year was therefore considerable. If its reserves of aircraft were poor and soon to be used up, its reserves of men were enormous; if it was not possible to save its aircraft from destruction by the *Luftwaffe*, it became evident as early as 14 September 1939 that it would be possible to save the men. Even before active resistance in Poland had ended, the escape of thousands of its airmen had been planned

Their escape routes would take them through every single country within Europe – except Germany – and beyond. They would go through Romania, where thousands of Polish soldiers and airmen first gathered after their defeat, through Greece and Yugoslavia, Turkey, France and Spain. Other Polish exiles would return to Europe from the United States and South America.

The first of these men of the Polish Air Force began to reach England in early December 1939, only three

months after the collapse of their country. In a sense they were lucky, as the rest of Continental Europe had not yet fallen to the German *Blitzkrieg*. France was still a free country with avenues of escape still open. Many Polish airmen had reached France by skiing across the Carpathians to Hungary and on to Yugoslavia, where they boarded steamers for Marseilles.

But by this time they found themselves in a France on the verge of defeat and disunity, so in June 1940 their escape began again. There was only one country left to them – Britain. The Poles were now joined by others escaping from the German onslaught, including Czechoslovaks. Many Czechoslovak airmen, anticipating correctly the German take-over of their air force following the Munich Agreement, escaped to Poland in 1938 and 1939, and some fought with the Polish Air Force. After the fall of Poland most reached France and joined the only military unit open to them – the French Foreign Legion – and it was not until France's entry into the war that they were incorporated into the French Air Force.

During the winter of 1939 there was still little air fighting and it was only in the spring of 1940, a few weeks before the collapse of France, that the Czechoslovak National Committee and the French Government agreed to Czech airmen officially joining operational units.

There was little time to organise, but in the event more than 100 Czechoslovak pilots were attached to various front-line French squadrons, including GC1/5 equipped with American Hawk 75As. During the next few weeks these airmen fought with distinction, and one of them claimed the destruction of 15 aircraft to become the second highest scorer in the Battle of France.

Ironically, some of these Polish escapees flew Koolhoven FK.58 fighters, a 'Dutch aircraft with French engines armed with Belgian machine-guns' assigned to the aerial protection of French towns, mainly in the South of France. For a few weeks they also flew with GC/1/145 equipped with Morane 406s in the defence of Paris, shooting down 12 German aircraft in the process.

1942: One down and one home

'On 4 May I was flying as Yellow 1 of a section of 303 (Polish) Sqn between St Omer and Calais on a bomber escort mission. The first attack by enemy aircraft was made on my squadron while turning left over the target area. As two Fw 190s dived on us and I turned towards them, the enemy aircraft broke away from my attack and dived down. I followed about 300 yards behind. As the enemy aircraft turned to starboard I gave the left-hand Fw 190 a short burst but saw no results.

I broke away and turned left towards my squadron. I was now at 10-11,000 feet when I heard someone calling over the R/T – "Attention – Fw" – and saw an Fw 190 attacking a Spitfire from 50 yards astern. I turned to starboard towards the enemy aircraft and at a range of 25-30 yards with no deflection I gave him a long burst of cannon and machine-gun fire. The Spitfire was now issuing black smoke and the Fw 190 was still firing at it. The Spitfire then went into a spin with smoke still pouring from it. A fraction of a second later I saw flames then black smoke coming from the Fw 190 and it too went into a spin. It was last seen at about 4,000 feet still spinning towards the earth. I had fired 17 rounds from each of the two 20mm cannon and 42 rounds from the four .303in machine-guns.

Near Calais I joined up with one of the Bostons whose starboard engine had stopped and escorted it as far as Sandwich. In the middle of the Channel I was joined by F/Sgt Popek and we then left for our base at RAF Northolt.'

Eugeniusz Horbaczewski – Polish Fighter Command pilot

Typical of many RAF squadrons in 1940 was 257 Sqn, which had pilots from many different nations including the Polish 'ace' P/Off K. Priak – seen wearing an Italian helmet – and Canadian 'ace' F/Lt H. P. Howard 'Cowboy' Blatchford, kneeling to his right. Standing between them is the CO, S/Ldr Bob Tuck, who claimed 17 destroyed and four probables during 1940.

Pilots of No 306 (Polish) Sqn led by S/Ldr Kazimierz Rutkowski with Spitfire IX UZ-T at Northolt. The squadron had lost four pilots over Dieppe a few weeks earlier.

1944: Two down

'On an armed patrol of 315 (Polish) Sqn Mustangs in the Caen, Lisieux, Argentian, Mamere and Sees area on 12 June, flying at 8,000 feet 8 miles south-east of Sees, I spotted four unidentified aircraft flying at zero feet in a westerly direction. I warned my leader, who gave the order to lose height, jettison our bombs and attack. I attacked one of the enemy aircraft, which I recognised as an Fw 190, and it undertook evasive action. I fired from an angle of 20-50 degrees and after a few bursts I noticed pieces breaking off from the

cockpit of the enemy aircraft as well as fire. The target shortly crashed in flames.

I attacked the next Fw 190 as it tried to avoid another Mustang attack by flying half loops. I fired several head-on bursts when he was on his back and noticed bits and pieces flying off the engine as well as fire. The Fw 190 was still on its back when it crashed into the ground in flames. I had fired 560 rounds from my 0.50in guns.'

Jakub Bargielowski – Polish Fighter Command pilot

Right *One of four Spitfire VBs presented to the nation by the residents of Hendon in 1941, 'Hendon Lamb', W3505, was lost on 12 April 1942 when serving with 303 (Polish) Sqn from Northolt.*

Below *One of No 316 (Warsawski) Sqn's Northolt-based clipped-wing Spitfire LF IXBs in late 1943 when the CO was S/Ldr P. Niemic.*

When France fell in June 1940 the Czech and Polish airmen, almost 5,500 of the latter, joined those from Norway, Denmark, Belgium, Holland and now France itself in attempting to reach Britain to carry on their fight against Germany. Most assembled in unoccupied Southern France and even North Africa to board merchant ships to Gibraltar, or sailed direct to England. Others arrived across the Channel in Belgian and Dutch merchant ships, fishing-boats or even rowing-boats. Many walked across the Pyrenees to Spain, then on to neutral Portugal.

Norwegian airmen flew a Northrop N-3PB seaplane to Scotland, while others escaped to Iceland to form 330 (Norwegian) Sqn of RAF Coastal Command. Some 20 Dutch Navy Fokker C.19W and T.8W float planes were flown to England in May 1940, forming the initial equipment of 320 (Dutch) Squadron, Coastal Command, at Pembroke Dock in Wales.

Before the end of 1940 the Norwegian Air-Force-in-exile had established a military flying training school known as 'Little Norway' at Island Airport, Toronto, Canada. By 1942 the school was equipped with more than 50 aircraft, including Hawk 75A-8 fighters, and would go on to train some 3,000 aircrew and groundcrew, plus 15 WAAFs, with at least three Norwegian and one Danish RAF 'aces' among them.

Finally, the first French pilots arrived in England on 26 June. Their position was the most difficult of all. Whereas the Poles, Czechoslovaks, Norwegians, Dutch and Belgians had reached England together with their governments in exile, the French had no such privileges. Their country was divided into the Occupied and the Unoccupied, and the Vichy Government treated any soldiers, sailors or airmen who escaped to Britain in order to continue fighting Germany as traitors and deserters, and therefore liable in their absence to be condemned to death. In spite of this, many hundreds of airmen left France by ship, while a handful managed to steal aircraft from Vichy airfields and fly them to Gibraltar.

On 12 July the Independent Czechoslovak Air Force was re-born in England with the formation of 310 (Czechoslovak) Sqn at Duxford as part of No 12 Group, RAF Fighter Command. It was soon followed by Nos 312 (Czechoslovak) and 302 and 303 (Polish) Sqns, declared operational in September 1940, at the height of the Battle of Britain. Of over 5,500 Polish airmen who arrived in England by mid-1940, 147 Polish pilots took part in the Battle of Britain, all flying the rugged Hurricane. No fewer than 15 of them became 'aces' (five or more victories) during the Battle, the top scorer being F/Off Witold Urbanowicz with 14 confirmed victories. These scores were, however, achieved at a high cost with 30 Polish pilots being killed in action.

1944: More luck than brains

'There was an operation on 1 September, a No 307 (Polish) Sqn night-intruder mission to the Luftwaffe's night-training establishment near Stettin on the Baltic. After a fruitless search during which my navigator was taken ill, we were north of Kiel when we ran slap over a German flak ship, which he would normally have picked up on the AI screen and which I could easily have avoided. I felt the Mosquito NF.XII being repeatedly hit amid the searchlight beams and coloured tracers. All hell had broken loose, but the Mosquito kept flying, although in a somewhat wobbly fashion.

It was on the run-in to Coltishall, the forward base near the Norfolk coast, that the damage became manifest. As I lowered the flaps on the approach, the aircraft banked over to the left and nearly turned over on its back. A quick retraction of the flaps saved us and I landed successfully without them at a very high speed.

After taxiing in and switching off, all was quiet except for some gentle hissing and gurgling in the pipes. The sick navigator was given immediate attention, then one of the groundcrew, shining a torch underneath the wing, shouted out, "Jesus bloody Christ! Come and look at this, sir."

The mess was unbelievable. A big shell had gone through the port wing, missing the main fuel tank by inches. The flap on that side had only a few ribs left. We finished counting the bullet holes in the aircraft at 300. But neither my navigator nor I had even a scratch – a clear case of "more luck than brains".

The aeroplane was a write-off, and another was sent to take us back to our base at Church Fenton. But I doubt whether anything but a Mosquito could have stood up to that kind of punishment and still got us back. That's why I love the Mosquito.'

Karol Ranoszek – Polish Fighter Command night fighter pilot (OOTB)

Right S/Ldr G. D. M.
Blackwood and F/Lt G. L.
Sinclair, CO and Flight
Commander of 310 (Czech)
Sqn, surrounded by their
Czechoslovak pilots who
destroyed 37½ German
aircraft during the
Battle of Britain.

Below Members of 'B'
Flight, 312 (Czech) Sqn,
with a Spitfire VB at RAF
Angle in March 1942. Left to
right: Josef Novotny, Vic
Kaslik, Vaclav Slouf, Jaroslav
Sodek and Tony Liskutin.

1943: Beyond visual contact

'I was returning from a dusk patrol with No 312 (Czech) Sqn in mid-Channel on 6 January 1943. The night was pitch-black, the cloud base at about 400 feet, with heavy rain. The visibility was poor even while I could still see the convoy. The return to base was more on instruments than visual contact, and I certainly felt elated to find RAF Churchstanton so easily in such conditions. The air traffic control did not expect me back that night and assumed I was going to land at Exeter. On arrival I found the flarepath half extinguished. In those circumstances it did look marginal but I decided to try one approach for landing before considering the diversion to our master airfield at Exeter.

Just before the airfield perimeter was a piece of slightly elevated ground, which I never even noticed in daylight. I was compelled to take notice of this insignificant obstruction now, in the dark!

In my final turn to line up with the runway I must have been a little too low and my left wing touched the ground at some 100-110mph. The impact was staggering. The control column flew out of my hand, and the Spitfire performed a multiple flick-roll on the ground and completely disintegrated over a distance of 500 yards. My clearly remembered thought during those few seconds was, "Well, goodbye, this is it!"

When things around me eventually stopped moving I found myself alive, strapped in my seat in the wet grass and with only the engine remaining near me. This all felt quite incredible. Contrary to all expectation, this crash did not kill me! In the dark there was not much to see, but I knew the size of the disaster. My thoughts were, "Oh Christ, what a mess!" Indeed there was not much left of my aircraft, Spitfire VC AR548, DU-V.'

**Miroslav Antonin 'Tony' Liskutin –
Czechoslovak Fighter Command pilot (CITA)**

After shooting down a Do 217 over Dieppe on 19 August 1942, F/Lt Tony Liskutin (third from right) surveys the damage to his 312 (Czech) Sqn's Spitfire VB EP559 inflicted by an Fw 190 on his second sortie of the day.

This clipped-wing Spitfire LF IXC was delivered to the first Czechoslovak squadron, No 310, in late 1944 and later served with the 'new' Czechoslovak Air Force.

1942: Lucky chair

'I was in a hurry to get to my favourite chair for the briefing at Hornchurch. However, "my" chair had already been taken by a 64 Sqn pilot. I was too embarrassed to tell the occupant that "my" chair was my lucky charm. I sat elsewhere and felt uneasy. As the intelligence officer unveiled the target map I heard a voice behind me: "Hell, it's Lille again."

Halfway across the Channel I remembered "my" chair and what its "loss" meant, but drove away my apprehension by convincing myself that the operation would go well. As CO of 122 Sqn, I concentrated on leading my squadron.

As the Bostons, which we were covering, bombed and turned for home, we were attacked by German fighters. In the mêlée my aircraft was hit. I had to dive away to escape my pursuers. When I levelled off right down on the deck, my Spitfire was on fire and smoke was filling the cockpit. Then the motor quit and I had no alternative but to land straight ahead.

Fate smiles. There was a flat field right in front and I landed the aircraft in it, wheels up. The moisture in the ground quelled the fire underneath. I ran quickly away, fortunately electing to head south. Soon I came across an old woman working in a field with a teenage boy.

"Are there any Germans about here?" I said.

"Over there," she replied, pointing to a large building in the direction from which I had come.

I moved fast. Our intelligence officers had always advised us to get as far away as possible from a crashed aircraft, and never to enter the nearest inhabited place. I ran as far as I could, then lay down in a ditch to rest. "Find something better than this," my brain dictated.

Avoiding another village and scouring the terrain, I came upon a stream. I sank down into the water on my back. Only my nose protruded through the surface so I wouldn't suffocate. This dodge probably saved my life, as the inevitable search party with sniffer dogs lost my trail.

Three months later I was back in England, arriving just before my 30th birthday and was soon back flying again.'

Frantisek Fajtl – Czechoslovak Fighter Command pilot (OOTB)

The RAF's top-scoring Battle of Britain pilot was Sgt Josef Frantisek, one of 87 Czech pilots to participate in the Battle; ironically, he scored all of his 17 victories flying with 303 (*Kosciuszko*) Sqn, which was also the highest scoring Fighter Command squadron for the month of September 1940.

Twenty-nine Belgian pilots also flew in the Battle, and were perhaps the most fortunate of the Allied pilots who did so, many of them having trained on BAF Hurricanes before the war. Their transition to RAF operating procedures was therefore rather easier than for the Poles and Czechoslovaks, who had trained on

aircraft from not only their own countries but of American, Russian and French origin. Also, very few spoke English, although most spoke good French, which caused some initial problems with training and R/T procedures. This was largely overcome by having British pilots attached to their squadrons, so least one of the 'gang' could speak to their Sector Controllers during training and combat sorties.

It was not until November 1941 that the first dedicated Free French and Belgian Squadrons, 340 and 345 respectively, were formed. It had been nearly 18 months since the first French pilots had reached

An RAF mess steward fills a Spitfire's long-range fuel tank with beer for the Norwegian pilot of 331 (Norwegian) Sqn to fly to Allied troops in Norway from Grimbergen in October 1944.

1944: My D-Day

'At the time of D-Day I was serving with No 340 (Free French) Squadron – part of 145 Wing, which comprised four Free French squadrons within the RAF – stationed at RAF Merston near Chichester.

At about 1700 hours on 5 June 1944 G/C "Sailor" Malan, a South African Battle of Britain "ace", called the Wing together for a briefing. His laconic "Boys, this is it!" was greeted with a roar.

You may well imagine the excitement. I was due to take off next morning at approximately 0430 hours. I took off in the dim light of dawn heading for the beachhead. At about 1,000 feet my Spitfire's Merlin stopped dead, and so did my heart. First reactions – drop the 90-gallon drop tank and tighten the safety straps. By sheer luck I found myself gliding over Bognor where the Norwegian Spitfires were operating. I could see below me a flare path and thought that I may be able to save my aircraft. After pumping the undercarriage down manually – I had no power – I somehow managed to land downwind with no flap at high speed.

Free French pilot Marcel Boisot with his leader, Charles de Gaulle. Boisot served with 340 (Ile-de-France) Sqn, one of the first 2TAF units operating over the Normandy beaches on D-Day.

To my horror, I could see in front of me the Norwegians lining up to take off – towards me! I was lucky enough to squeeze between two Spits, but my problem was far from over.

I was still travelling too fast to use my brakes and the end of the field was approaching dangerously fast. My only solution was to crash into the perimeter ditch, which wrecked my poor "Kamasutra", the name I had given my Spitfire. Apart from what would became spectacular bruises, I was unhurt. I was then flown back to Merston, only a few miles away, extremely disappointed to miss the operation for which I had joined the RAF. However, a silly idea suddenly crossed my mind. What would prevent me from taking off in another Spitfire to rejoin my squadron over the beachhead, as I knew exactly which area we were supposed to protect? In fact, was it not my duty to do so?

So I did, and half an hour later, quite proud of myself, I joined the squadron as it patrolled its sector. This lasted only a short while, however, as I was called on the radio to report to the CO immediately after "pancake" (landing). This I did, and our exchange went like this:

"Sailor" Malan: "Was it you, Boisot, who was seen taking off alone this morning around 05.00 hours?"

Me: "I guess it was me, sir."

"May I ask where you were flying to?"

"To the beachhead, sir, as you briefed us yesterday evening."

"Do you realise that you were picked up on radar and taken for an enemy plane, and we had two squadrons of Spitfires sent into the air with the mission to shoot you down?"

"Thank heaven they did not find me."

"This is the biggest operation of all time and a fool like you comes along and buggers it up. You should be court martialled!"

"I understand, sir, and apologise, but you may not know that I had an engine failure on take-off and it is a miracle that I am still alive.

Moreover, I escaped from Morocco in order to join the RAF precisely for today's mission and it is not my fault if the British engine packed up. Now if after 150 missions the RAF is not satisfied with my conduct, I shall steal a Spitfire and fly back to France!"

"Sailor" Malan looked at me intently and mouthed two words: "F___ off."

Later, at the end of the day as the whole Wing was discussing that memorable day in the mess, and perhaps shooting a few lines, I went to the CO and said, "Sir, may I offer you a drink?"

This was my D-Day.'

Marcel Boisot – Free French Fighter Command pilot

England, but due to their large divided country, and the complex political position, they arrived over a longer period and were slower to be integrated into the RAF. Only 14 Free French pilots flew with RAF squadrons during the Battle of Britain, but as more and more of them responded to the Gaullist call and gathered together in Britain from all parts of Metropolitan France and the French Empire, their first squadron was formed under the emblem of the Croix de Lorraine at Turnhouse in Scotland.

Many of that squadron's groundcrews were men from the French Navy who had arrived in Britain from as far away as North Africa, South America, Indo-China and the Pacific island of Tahiti. Capitaine Philippe de Scitivaux was a former naval pilot who claimed one German aircraft before being shot down and wounded in May 1940. After reaching England via Gibraltar, he joined 245 Squadron at the end of the Battle of Britain and two years later became the first French Commanding Officer of 340 (*Ile-de-France*) Sqn before being shot down over France and taken prisoner in April 1942.

Other Free French squadrons were formed during the next two years, while many other Free French pilots, including their leading 'ace', Pierre Clostermann, who claimed 19 victories, flew with other RAF units.

Spitfires of 340 (*Ile-de-France*) Squadron were among the first RAF Fighter Command fighters to tangle with *Luftwaffe* Fw 190s over Dieppe in the early hours of 19 August 1942, the day of Operation *Jubilee*, the Anglo-Canadian raid on Dieppe. This was the first time many of the French pilots had fought over their native soil for more than two years and they were looking forward to the battle. However, after a day of fierce fighting during which the raid was repulsed with heavy casualties and the RAF lost 88 fighters, the Polish 303 (*Kosciuszko*) Sqn shot down the highest number of enemy aircraft with its sister unit, 317 (*Wilenski*) Sqn, having the next best score. One of Poland's most successful pilots of this period

was Eugeniusz Horbaczewski, who joined 303 Sqn in late 1940, shot down an Fw 190 over Dieppe, and was selected for the Special Polish Flying Team with the Desert Air Force in 1943. Returning to England a year later, he took command of 315 (Polish) Sqn flying Mustang IIIs, and was shot down and killed on 18 August 1944 after downing three Fw 190s in 15 minutes, giving him a total of 16 victories.

In the build-up to D-Day in 1944 there were no fewer than ten Polish, seven Free French, three Czechoslovak and Norwegian, two Belgian and one Dutch fighter squadrons assigned to the Air Defence of Great Britain (ADGB) and the 2nd Tactical Air Force (2TAF), which was formed within Fighter Command on 1 June 1943. Two Belgian pilots of note who were in action during the period were Remy van Lierde and Lucien Leboutte.

'Mony' van Lierde was shot down and wounded when the Germans invaded Belgium in 1940. He escaped from a German military hospital and made his way overland to Spain where he was imprisoned for almost a year. He eventually reached England in June 1941 and soon began to make up for lost time. By the end of the war he had flown 437 missions, shot down six enemy aircraft and destroyed 34 V-1 flying bombs, as well as countless vehicles and trains.

Lucien Leboutte was the pre-war leader of the Belgian Air Force's finest aerobatic team. When Germany overran his country, he too was captured and managed to escape. After crossing the Pyrenees on foot and spending five months in Spanish prisons, he reached England a few months after his compatriot, and at the age of 43 succeeded in joining an operational RAF night-fighter squadron with the rank of Pilot Officer. After the war Lt General Leboutte became the Chief of the General Staff of the Belgian Air Force.

By the end of 1944 the French and Belgian squadrons were operating from bases in their own countries, although it would take many more months of heavy fighting before the other Free European

Above Pilots of the second Belgian squadron in the RAF, No 349, led by the Belgian 'ace' S/Ldr Count Yvan Georges Arsene Felician Du Monceau de Bergendael, who claimed eight destroyed and three probables in 1941.

Right A seasonal scene of No 349 (Belgian) Sqn Spitfire LF IXEs at Friston in February 1944 prior to a Ramrod operation.

1943: Lucky break

'My first Ramrod mission with No 609 Sqn in December, to escort USAAF B-26 bombers over France, ended in disaster. First the bombers were late at the rendezvous and we had the circle over Manston for 10 minutes at 20,000 feet waiting for them. My Typhoon was the only one not fitted with 160-gallon drop tanks and it was soon clear, as we picked up the B-26s over the Channel, that I would not have enough fuel for the whole mission.

When I informed the CO, S/Ldr Thornton-Brown, of my predicament, he called me an idiot and instructed me to return to base immediately. I had just enough fuel to reach Manston safely but soon heard that the rest of the squadron, which was flying at medium level, had been attacked by 8th Air Force P-47s acting as high-level escort. The US fighters had mistaken the Typhoons for Fw 190s and shot down two. One of the pilots was Pat Thornton-Brown, who was killed in the action.

The next day one of our pilots, the American F/Off "Arty" Ross, was sent off to visit USAAF fighter units in his Typhoon.'

Ken 'Heinie' Adam – German-born Fighter Command pilot

units could return home, and in the cases of the gallant Poles and Czechs, to an uncertain future.

A few RAF pilots who were not anxious to return to their homelands included Count Manfred Beckett Czermin, the son of an Austrian diplomat who was born in Berlin and who joined the RAF in 1935 as a bomber pilot. On the outbreak of war he retrained as a fighter pilot and fought throughout the Battle of Britain, scoring 13½ victories flying Hurricanes with 85 and 17 Sqns. He later joined the Special Operations Executive (SOE) and was dropped behind enemy lines to train resistance groups.

The most unlikely Fighter Command pilots were two German Jewish brothers who were born in Berlin. Klaus, later Ken, Adam's family moved to Scotland in 1934 and he promptly applied to join the RAF. He was rejected. Trained as an architect, he was designing air raid shelters for the Government at the outbreak of war and therefore avoided internment. His younger brother Dennis was interned on the Isle of Man. It was not until he joined the OTC (AMPC), a para-military defence organisation, that he was accepted for RAF pilot training in 1941.

After a first taste of flying on Tiger Moths with the Perth EFTS, Ken was sent to the USA in 1942 for primary, basic and advanced flying training with the Arnold Scheme. After graduating with 'above average' classification, Sgt K. H. Adam was commissioned, but on his arrival back in Britain aboard the *Queen Elizabeth*, this was rescinded. Following a stint at 59 OTU at Carlisle, F/Sgt Ken Adam was posted to 609 Sqn in October 1943, flying the Typhoon. After the squadron converted to rockets in early 1944, 'Heinie'

Adam attacked enemy communications and radar installations before moving to Normandy after D-Day. With the squadron in Holland, he ended his tour in November 1944 with his belated commission, and his brother serving with him; as a serving officer, Ken had been able to request his brother's release from internment to join the RAF.

Dennis Adam subsequently learned to fly under the EATS in Rhodesia and joined 609 Sqn at the beginning of 1945. The brothers were based at Plantlunne in Germany when the war in Europe ended on 8 May. A month later Ken was in charge of 10,000 German prisoners at Wunstorf, although still a serving member of 609 Sqn.

After the war Ken Adam went on to become a famous movie art director, working on several of the James Bond films among many others; he won an Oscar for his art direction on the 1994 film *The Madness of King George*.

The Commonwealth

'…if the British Commonwealth and its Empire lasts for a thousand years, men will still say, "This was their finest hour."'

Winston Churchill,
British Prime Minister, June 1940

Almost half of the pilots that served with the RAF during the Second World War, many of them with Fighter Command, came from the British Commonwealth.

One of Fighter Command's most brilliant commanders was the New Zealander Keith Park, who was appointed AOC No 11 Group early in 1940. A First World War 'ace' with 20 victories, Air Vice-Marshal Park flew his personal Hurricane on frequently unannounced visits to operational units throughout Operation *Dynamo* and the Battle of Britain, and inspired his pilots by being one of them.

Even before war broke out in Europe, many aspiring fighter pilots were making their own way to England from the far-flung corners of the British Empire to join the RAF. Among these early arrivals who would become Battle of France and Britain 'aces' was the former South African merchant seaman, Adolph Gysbert 'Sailor' Malan, the Canadian John Maxwell 'Max' Aitken and New Zealanders Alan Christopher 'Al' Deere, Edgar James 'Cobber' Kain and Colin Falkland Gray.

One of the most resilient of the RAF's Commonwealth contingent was the New Zealander Pat Jameson. As a Flight Commander with 46

Squadron equipped with Hurricanes, F/Lt P. J. Jameson was sent to Norway in April 1940 aboard the carrier HMS *Glorious*. As recorded in an earlier chapter, after a hectic month of fighting against overwhelming odds, the squadron was ordered to evacuate on 7 June. Ten surviving Hurricanes all landed safely on *Glorious*, the first modern fighters to do so. The following day the aged carrier was sunk by the German cruisers *Scharnhorst* and *Gneisenau*, taking the Hurricanes and all their pilots with her, except 46 Sqn's CO and F/Lt Jameson.

Promoted to Squadron Leader, Jameson was back in the thick of it only a few months later leading 266 Sqn in the Battle of Britain. His war-long career included appointments as Wittering Wing Leader, 12 Group Wing Leader at Dieppe, North Weald Wing Leader, when his personnel callsign was *Mahjong*, Maori for 'chieftain', and as a Group Captain planning the 2nd Tactical Air Force's strategy for D-Day, together with being credited with nine kills.

Fellow New Zealanders Kain and Gray initially

An impressive line-up of Commonwealth 'aces' poses in front of a 485 (RNZAF) Spitfire IXB at Biggin Hill in July 1943; included is the squadron's New Zealander CO, S/Ldr Johnny Checketts, fifth from right, and his dogs, with Station Commander G/C 'Sailor' Malan to his left and next to him Wing leader W/C Al Deere.

failed their RAF medicals after travelling to England at their own expense, but this did not stop them from becoming two of Fighter Command's most successful pilots. 'Cobber' became the RAF's first 'ace' of the war when, flying Hurricanes with 1 Sqn during the Battle of France, he shot down 17 German aircraft only to be killed in a flying accident the day before he was due to be withdrawn from the battlefield. Colin Gray became the highest scoring and most decorated New Zealand pilot of the war with 28 confirmed victories.

Another 'failure' was the Canadian George 'Screwball' Beurling, who was turned down by the RCAF because of his academic standards despite having a private pilot's licence and 250 flying hours in his log-book. He eventually made his way to Scotland as a deck hand, and went on to score 31 victories flying with the RAF.

In contrast, Ernest Archibald McNab joined the RCAF in 1926 and was the oldest Battle of Britain 'ace' and the first commander of Fighter Command's No 1 (RCAF) Sqn. Canadian-born John William Maxwell Aitken was the son of the wartime Minister of Aircraft Production, Lord Beaverbrook. The Honourable 'Max' Aitken had joined 601 (County of London) Sqn, known as the 'Millionaire Mob', in 1935 and fought with it in the Battles of France and Britain before taking command of a new night fighter unit, No 68 Sqn, in February 1941. He finished the war with 14 confirmed victories.

During the Battle of Britain the first CO of the Polish 303 Sqn was a Canadian, S/Ldr J. A. Kent. Born in Winnipeg, Johnny Kent held a private pilot's licence at 17, the youngest to do so in Canada at the time, and joined the RAF in 1935. Due to his excellent flying ability he was posted to Farnborough as a test pilot, then to Photographic Development at Heston. He subsequently joined 303 (Polish) Sqn in August 1940 as a Flight Commander before being given command of 92 Sqn two months later. He subsequently became Kenley Wing Leader, ending the war with a score of 12 destroyed and three probables. On the other hand, the predominately Canadian-manned 242 Sqn, led by Douglas Bader in 1940, had no fewer than five Canadian 'aces' on its strength, including William L. 'Willie' McKnight, J. B. Latta, George Bell and Hugh Tamblyn. All four had been killed in action by mid-1941.

Almost 250 Commonwealth pilots took part in the Battle of Britain, 101 from New Zealand, 94 from Canada, 22 from South Africa, 22 from Australia – almost 30 per cent of whom were killed – two Southern Rhodesians and a solitary Jamaican.

In December 1939 the Empire Air Training Scheme (EATS), later known as the British

Above *The South African 'Sailor' Malan (second from right) joined 74 Sqn in 1936 and became its Commanding Officer in August 1940, by which time he was credited with the destruction of 14 German aircraft.*

Left *New Zealander Al Deere flew with No 54 Sqn throughout 1940, during which time he crashed-landed three Spitfires, baled out of another two, and claimed the destruction of 14 aircraft.*

Right New Zealander F/Off
Max Collett with his 485
(RNZAF) Sqn Spitfire IXB
assigned to 2TAF at Merville
(B.53) in October 1944.

Below Max Collett taxies
his Spitfire LF IXE MH432,
named 'Waipawa Special',
carrying 250lb bombs at
Merville, the French airfield
from which AASF Gladiators
operated five years earlier.

1940: I had never seen him

'During Dunkirk No 54 Squadron was patrolling in the Gravelines area when we came across a couple of dozen Me 110s escorted by a dozen or so Bf 109s. During the ensuing mêlée I had a squirt at a '109, and was wondering what to do next when I heard a tremendous clattering interspersed with a couple of lusty crumps. It took a moment or two to realise that the noise was caused by bullets striking the aircraft all along the fuselage and that the crumps were obviously cannon shells. The first of these exploded at the rear of my Spitfire, severing the elevator and the rudder trimmer wires, knocking out the hydraulic system and, as I discovered later, the air bottle. The second cannon shell missed my head by a cat's whisker, exploded in the port aileron, neatly removing the pitot head and, with it, my airspeed indication and throwing the aircraft into a spiral dive.

This was a most fortunate chance as it was probably better and quicker than any escape manoeuvre I could have devised. Indeed, I saw no more of my attacker – not that I had seen him in the first place!

My second piece of luck was that neither the cannon shells nor the 50 or so bullets that we subsequently counted seemed to have done any vital damage, to the coolant system for example, or to me for that matter, and everything held together for the 30-minute flight back across the Channel to base at Hornchurch.

The loss of air pressure meant that I could not fire my guns, which were air-operated in the Spitfire, but frankly I was not very interested in hanging around to try them out anyway. It also meant that I had no flaps or brake, which made landing tricky especially as I had no airspeed indicator. The loss of hydraulic fluid meant the undercarriage would not come down in the normal way. However, the emergency CO_2 bottle worked like a charm.

Subsequent investigation showed that the main elevator controls were almost severed and were only hanging on by a few strands.'

Colin Falkland Gray – New Zealand Fighter Command pilot (OOTB)

Commonwealth Air Training Plan, had been agreed, which led to the establishment of almost 200 flying training schools in eight Commonwealth countries ranging from New Zealand to the Bahamas.

As freshly qualified pilots were shipped to England at the end of 1940, the Air Ministry decided to form 'Commonwealth' squadrons. The first was in fact No 1 (RCAF) Sqn, which had been formed in July 1940 and fought throughout the Battle of Britain. It was re-numbered 401 (RCAF) Sqn to avoid confusion with No 1 (Fighter) Sqn RAF, and in April 1941 it was joined by several other RCAF, RNZAF and RAAF units, and several New Zealand and Australian units were re-formed in the UK after being withdrawn from the Far East following the fall of Singapore.

With Fighter Command turning to the offensive after the Battle of Britain, the Commonwealth squadrons were thrown in at the deep end undertaking hazardous fighter sweeps, bomber escorts and ground attack sorties over occupied Europe. When the Anglo-Canadian amphibious landings at Dieppe began in the early hours of 19 August 1942, almost half the RAF fighter aircraft supporting Operation *Jubilee* were Hurricanes,

Spitfires and Typhoons of Fighter Command's Commonwealth and Free European squadrons.

Although Bomber Command held centre stage during the Allied 'round the clock' strategic bombing offensive that began in 1943, Fighter Command continued to harry the enemy in France and the Low Countries, culminating in a series of daring intruder raids. In February 1944 Mosquito FB.VIs of 464 (RAAF) and 487 (RNZAF) Sqns carried out a low-level attack on Amiens prison, which held members of the Resistance, during which nearly 300 prisoners escaped.

By 6 June 1944 – D-Day – a total of 32 Canadian, Australian and New Zealand squadrons were assigned to the ADGB and 2TAF. The first deployment of Allied fighter aircraft to temporary airstrips in Normandy occurred on 9 June when Spitfires of No 144 (RCAF) Wing began operations at Ste Croix-sur-Mer (B.3). Only days later ADGB fighters were involved in a life-and-death struggle with Hitler's unmanned flying bomb menace, the V-1. Four squadrons bore the brunt of shooting down the 'doodlebugs', one of which was 486 (RNZAF) Sqn equipped with Tempest Vs, which accounted for

1940: Unacceptable behaviour

'On 11 November No 41 Squadron was scrambled and ordered to gain maximum height on a vector towards North Foreland. Unfortunately my Spitfire was slow to start so my squadron had to leave without me. Within a minute or so my engine fired and as I was keen to join the squadron and already knew the vector to follow, I set off at full boost hoping to catch them up.

But the sky is a very big place and by Southend there was still no sign of them. Shortly after this and still climbing, I had to enter cloud. At about 10,000 feet I broke cloud to find myself surrounded – or so it seemed to me – by a very loose and open formation of biplanes flying just above the cloud sill. I could not recognise them, but I assumed them to be a friendly training flight that seemed to have lost its way and strayed into a highly operational area.

Almost at once two or three of them opened fire on me at what seemed extreme range. I found this behaviour to be unacceptable, irritating and even slightly dangerous. I turned on the nearest biplane and gave him a good burst of 3 or 4 seconds. He immediately disappeared into the cloud sill and was not seen again. I repeated this performance with three other planes, by which time I had exhausted my ammunition – Spitfires at the time had only about 15 seconds fire time. By then I decided to give up any hope of rejoining the squadron and returned to Hornchurch.

There the intelligence officer, who saw my gunports blasted open, was all agog to know what had happened to the rest of the squadron. When I told him I had never made contact with them, but that I had been attacked by a formation of biplanes, he was as astonished as I had been. After a quick look at the identification chart in the dispersal hut I was able to positively identify the aircraft as Italian Fiat CR.42 fighters. I claimed only one damaged, as I had seen some parts fly off one of the targets before he disappeared in the cloud. I now believe that all four CR.42s must have fallen into the sea somewhere between Southend and the North Foreland. As far as I know the Italian Air Force never came to England again.'

Edward Preston 'Hawkeye' Wells – New Zealand Fighter Command pilot

New Zealander W/C Bob Yule, Detling Wing leader in 1943, claimed four destroyed and a further four shared destroyed during five years of operational flying with Fighter Command beginning in 1939.

1942: Tail-end Charlie

'As a "sprog" Pilot Officer I was flying a Spitfire V with No 485 (RNZAF) Sqn on a sortie with Havoc bombers to Le Havre. Our squadron was acting as close escort on the port side. We were in that stupid old formation of three sections of four aircraft in line astern, with No 4 weaving.

I was tail-end Charlie in "Blue" section, keeping a good look out behind, when I saw two aircraft, which were not weaving, coming towards us. I thought they had become detached from the squadron and were going to join us.

They were certainly going to join us – but they were 109s and they started firing at me. I turned into the attack and squealed for help. I was scared, and groped for the handle to lower the seat and get down behind the armour plating. I pulled the knob and

there was a terrific bang. I looked astern and the Huns had broken off the attack and were diving away.

The action I had taken to lower my seat was not designed for this. I had in my panic mistakenly fired the recognition colour from the signal gun on the starboard side of the fuselage.

I hastened to rejoin the squadron. I don't know how I came to pull that "tit" because it was on the opposite side from the seat handle. Did the signal flare scare the Huns off, or was it just chance that I did not get shot down? I don't know, but the bang I heard was the noise of the recognition signal being activated. I found this out later, but was too self-conscious to tell my companions about it.'

John Milne 'Johnny' Checketts – New Zealand Fighter Command pilot (OOTB)

---

the destruction of no fewer than 221 flying bombs; two of its New Zealand pilots, F/Off R. J. Cammock and F/Lt O. D. Eagleson, claimed more than 20 each. The Australian night fighter unit, No 456 (RAAF) Sqn based at Ford, accounted for 24 V-1s with its Mosquito NF.II aircraft, while 418 (RCAF) Sqn's Mosquitos downed more than 50, the squadron's top pilot, S/Ldr Russ Bannock, claiming 19 V-1s plus nine enemy aircraft destroyed in a 10-month campaign.

The privilege of undertaking the RAF's first operational sortie in a jet aircraft fell to Canadian F/Off 'Mac' McKenzie of 616 Sqn when on 27 July he took off from RAF Manston on a 'Diver' (V-1) patrol in a Gloster Meteor F.1. 'Mac' successfully 'wing-tipped' a V-1 into a terminal dive of destruction near Maidstone on 16 August, while fellow Canadian F/Off Jack Ritchone accounted for another the following day.

Back on the Continent, over Holland on 6 October, a Spitfire of 401 (RCAF) Sqn became the first RAF fighter to shoot down an Me 262, the *Luftwaffe's* first operational jet fighter. The Squadron was part of 126 (RCAF) Wing, which had been the first Allied fighter unit to be deployed to Holland a few weeks earlier. On Christmas Day F/Lt John J. Boyle of 411 (RCAF) Sqn downed another Me 262 in his Spitfire IX to add to one he had damaged two days earlier.

Two months earlier, Mosquitos of 464 (RAAF) and

487 (RNZAF) Sqns took part in another successful pinpoint low-level attack when they destroyed the Gestapo HQ at Aarhus, Denmark; they followed this with a similar raid on the Gestapo's Copenhagen HQ on 21 March 1945.

When 616 Sqn, now equipped with Meteor F.IIIs, moved to German soil for the first time in April 1945, W/C W. E. 'Smokey' Schrader, a New Zealander who had destroyed nine enemy aircraft in Tempest Vs while leading 486 (RNZAF) Sqn, took over command, with fellow antipodean W/C Tony Gaze, an Australian Spitfire 'ace' with 12½ victories, as one of his Flight Commanders.

Two Canadian Spitfire 'aces', who both scored a total of 14 victories each, ended their wars in very different ways. After a high-scoring year with 412 (RCAF) Sqn, S/Ldr Don Laubman was posted to command 402 (RCAF) Sqn, but only two weeks before the end of the war, on 14 April 1945, he was shot down and captured. S/Ldr Bill Klersy of 401 (RCAF) Sqn, on the other hand, finished the war unscathed after nearly two years of operations, only to be killed in a training accident two weeks after VE-Day.

Many of Fighter Command's Commonwealth squadrons remained in action beyond 4 May 1945, the last day of air operations in North West Europe, carrying out daylight sweeps over Germany in support of the Allied occupation forces.

A Spitfire II of No 452 Sqn, the first Royal Australian Air Force unit in Fighter Command,
at Kirton-in-Lindsey where the squadron was formed on 8 April 1941.

Left *Australian 609 Sqn pilot F/Lt Johnnie Curchin, seen here in his presentation Spitfire II 'Enfield Spitfire', shot down eight enemy aircraft before he went missing over the Channel in June 1941.*

Below *Pilots of the newly re-formed 453 (RAAF) Sqn commanded by S/Ldr F. Morello with one of their Spitfire VBs at Drem in June 1942. The squadron had previously been involved in the defence of Singapore.*

Pilots of 453 (RAAF) Sqn are briefed by their CO, S/Ldr D. G. Andrews, from an impromptu stage of jerrycans at Ford airfield a few days before D-Day.

1942: On the beat

'I had now been with No 607 Squadron for some months and was given weekend leave, so of course we headed for London. Most of the Australian and New Zealand aircrews stayed at either the Strand Palace or Regent Palace hotels. You were bound to find someone you knew there.

We used to frequent the "Codgers" pub where Eve was the barmaid. It was near Fleet Street and was the favourite watering hole for journalists who adopted Australian aircrews. Eve kept a visitor's book that had everyone in it.

The weather was cold and one weekend we had leave in London. There was a real "pea-souper" fog – so thick that you could really see it swirling. Of course, in the blackout it was almost impossible to try and get around at night. After drinks at the "Codgers", we wanted to go to the Astoria Dance Hall in Tottenham Court Road. We went outside and ran into a Police Constable. When we told him of our plan, he said, "Come with me." We walked from beat to beat. At the end of a beat he would blow his whistle and out of the fog another PC would appear. After a few of these greetings, away we went and eventually arrived at the Astoria Dance Hall. There were hundreds of people and continuous bands. It was London at its best in the post-Blitz period.'

Wilfred A. Goold – Australian Fighter Command pilot

1944: Fumes in the tanks

'We were assigned to a Beach Patrol flying a 125 Squadron Mosquito NF.XVII covering the area Le Havre, Rouen and Paris. Shortly after we began our patrol we were vectored by Durrington Radar Control to investigate a "bogey" in our vicinity. Almost immediately my Scots navigator, Patrick O'Malley, made radar contact about a mile away at "Angels Three" (3,000 feet) and we attempted to close in and identify the aircraft. We closed in to about 500 yards when the target began to take violent evasive action and headed into an easterly direction. We had a great deal of difficulty keeping it on radar.

We followed it for about half an hour. Every time we tried to get near enough for a visual sighting, the pilot started rolling the machine around. It was a very dark, overcast night, making it very difficult to see anything. Eventually I got a fleeting glance of a shape that I thought to be an Me 410, one of the latest German night fighters. I was unable to keep it visual, as he peeled off into a steep diving turn to the right and Pat lost him on the radar. We were unable to pick him up again due to the low altitude causing ground returns on the radar.

By this time we were out of touch with ground radar and running low on fuel, so we headed home. We climbed to 4,000 feet and contacted control. We were immediately told that "our tail was dirty", meaning that we were being followed at fairly close range, probably by the same night fighter we had been chasing ourselves.

We did not have enough fuel to fool around so I began to really throw the Mossie around. With the throttles wide open we headed for the treetops, as low as we estimated we could safely get. We shook off our tail and arrived back at Middle Wallop after 3 hours 30 minutes in the air with little more than fumes left in our tanks.

We had encountered a lot of flak on that patrol but were not hit and the only damage was to our egos. We had missed our chance for a kill and we learned that just after we left the area it was hit hard by enemy bombers.'

Royal 'Roy' Cooper – Canadian Fighter Command night fighter pilot

Right *Pilots of 242 Sqn at Coltishall in September 1940. Left to right: P/Off Denis Crowley-Milling, Canadian F/Offs Hugh Tamblyn and Stan Turner, Sgt John Savill, P/Off N. Campbell, P/Off 'Willie' McKnight (the squadron's leading Battle of Britain 'ace'), its British CO, S/Ldr Douglas Bader, F/Off Eric Ball, and P/Offs M. Homer and M. K. Brown.*

Right *A pre-war test pilot, Canadian F/Lt Johnny Kent shot down four enemy aircraft while serving as a Flight Commander with the first Polish Squadron, No 303, during the Battle of Britain.*

Far right *Group Captain Ernie McNab was the first Canadian CO of No 1 (RCAF) Sqn during the Battle of Britain, when he claimed five destroyed. He commanded RAF Digby from 1942 to 1945.*

Above *An Allison-engined North American Mustang I reconnaissance fighter of 400 (RCAF) Sqn, which was shot down over St Valery in France on 17 April 1943 on a Popular sortie.*

Below *Spitfire XVIs of 421 (RCAF) Sqn, with its Red Indian's head painted on the cowlings, parked on a snow-covered Evere (B.56) airfield in January 1945 as an RAF Hudson takes off.*

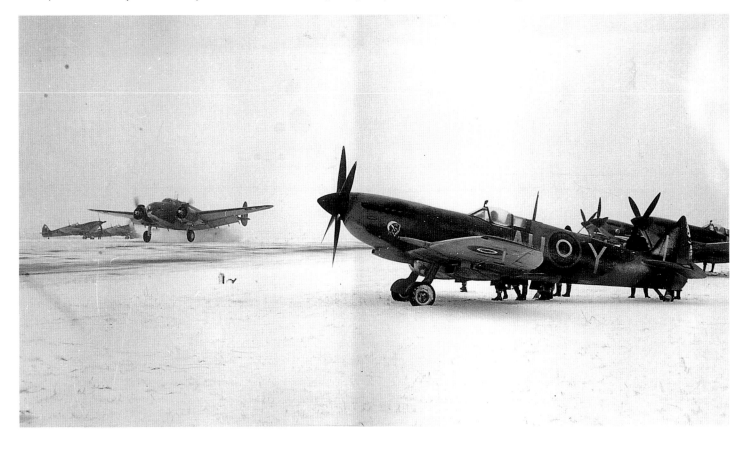

Canadian Digby Wing leader W/C Lloyd Chadburn, on the right, with six of his 402 (RCAF) pilots who shot down nine enemy aircraft during a Ramrod *over Holland on 3 November 1943, two of which fell to Chadburn.*

HM Queen Elizabeth meets a Canadian Wing Leader at Digby in 1943 accompanied by Commander No 12 Group and senior WAAF officers.

The 'Eagles'

'We shall not forget those gallant American soldiers, sailors and airmen who fought with us, some in our own ranks, countless others from our own shores. To those who did not return the best memorial is the fellowship of our two countries, which by their valour they created and by their sacrifice they have preserved.'

Winston Churchill,
former British Prime Minister, 1945

Inspired by the legendary deeds of the famed *Escadrille Lafayette*, the First World War squadron manned by American Volunteers, there was no shortage of volunteers from the neutral United States eager to join the European conflict.

A few Americans had already joined the pre-war RAF, including P/Off Willard Whitney Straight, the famous grand prix racing driver and air racing pilot, who became one of the 601 Sqn 'Millionaire

Mobsters' in April 1939 flying Blenheims, and F/Off Cyril D. 'Pussy' Palmer from Cleveland, Ohio, who became the first American pilot to claim a victory flying a No 1 Sqn Hurricane in France.

At the outbreak of war there was no organisation to deal with 'foreign' volunteers, and the first Americans to join the RAF during the Second World War came from varied and diverse backgrounds. For example, after seeing the film *China Clipper*, which starred Humphrey Bogart and PanAm 'Clipper' flying boats, William Meade Lindsley Fiske, son of a well-to-do banker, decided to take up flying. The next day he started private flying lessons in a Fleet biplane with a South African friend, Patrick 'Paddy' Green, who later became an RAF night-fighting 'ace' with a score of 11 destroyed. 'Billy' Fiske made his way to England soon after the outbreak of war and, with over 200 hours of flying light aircraft in the USA, was granted a King's Commission and sent to an RAF OTU. On 15 July 1940 P/Off Fiske was posted to 601 Sqn at Tangmere to serve alongside his fellow American, Whitney Straight.

After missing out on the Battle of France, Eugene Quimby 'Red' Tobin was one of the few American pilots to fight in the Battle of Britain, but lost his life flying with 71 'Eagle' Sqn in 1941.

Above *The damaged 71 'Eagle' Sqn Spitfire II at Hawkinge after its pilot, P/Off Bill Dunn, Fighter Command's first American 'ace', had tangled with Bf 109s on 27 August 1941, shooting two of them down.*

Right *P/Off Wendell Pendleton looks at the 'Eagle Squadron' badge painted on the cowling of his 71 Sqn Spitfire II based at North Weald in 1941.*

Eagle 'aces': S/Ldr Chesley 'Pete' Peterson, CO of 71 Sqn (left), claimed six destroyed with the squadron during 1941/2, while F/Off Gus Daymond shot down seven enemy aircraft, also with 71 Sqn.

After serving with 71 'Eagle' Sqn, S/Ldr James C. Nelson, from Denver, Colorado, commanded 124 Sqn at North Weald in 1943, which was equipped with high-altitude Spitfire HF VIIs.

Three other experienced American civil pilots had made their way to France hoping to fight the Germans with the *Armée de l'Air*, but had to escape to England when France fell. Eugene Quimby 'Red' Tobin, son of a Los Angeles real estate salesman, who worked as a messenger at MGM's Hollywood studios, had volunteered to fly for the Finnish Air Force to fight the Russians in the spring of 1940, but left for France when the 'Winter War' ended. There he was joined by A. B. 'Andy' Mamedorff, the son of Russian immigrant parents from Miami and a pre-war barnstorming pilot, and a Brooklyn-born professional parachutist, V. C. 'Shorty' Keough.

After joining the RAF as 'Canadians', the trio were sent on a four-week Spitfire conversion course before all being posted to 609 Sqn at Middle Wallop on 8 August. 'Billy' Fiske opened the Americans' scoreboard in the Battle of Britain by downing a Ju 88 on 13 August, but three days later he was wounded and, while attempting a belly landing at Tangmere, his aircraft burst into flames and he died as the result of severe burns the following day. A bronze tablet was later erected to his memory in St Paul's Cathedral, London, reading 'An American citizen who died that England might live'.

A total of seven American pilots took part in the Battle of Britain, three of whom, P/Offs Fiske, Tobin and Keough, were each credited with the destruction of at least one enemy aircraft. Another was P/Off Arthur Donahue, who was posted to Singapore at the end of 1940.

On 8 August 1940 Britain's Secretary of State for Air, Sir Archibald Sinclair, announced that an 'Eagle' squadron would be formed within Fighter Command to be manned by American pilots. In Montreal, Canada, an 'office' was opened to officially recruit American aircrew, and amongst the many who joined the RAF by this route were James A. Goodson and Donald S. Gentile.

On the outbreak of war in Europe, Goodson, then a student in Paris, immediately travelled to England to apply to join the RAF, but at the time was advised to enlist via the RCAF. On 2 September he boarded the British liner *Athenia*, which was sailing to New York. On the morning of 4 September she was sunk by a German U-boat 200 miles west of Ireland with the loss of 112 lives. Goodson was one of the survivors picked up by a Norwegian tanker and landed in southern Ireland. He later continued his voyage aboard a Canadian tanker and joined the RCAF in early 1940. Donald Gentile, a pre-war private pilot, volunteered to join the RAF through the Montreal recruiting office. Both pilots were later to serve together in the third 'Eagle' squadron.

Some of the first Americans to cross the 49th parallel to fight the German menace in Europe included Donald James Blakeslee and Charles E. McDonald. After flight training, Sgt 'Mac' McDonald was posted to 403 (RCAF) Sqn at Hornchurch in August 1941. Shot down over France and badly burned a month later, he was captured and sent to

1942: Jumped by Fw 190s

'No 133 (Eagle) Squadron was based at Lympne on 19 August 1942 when we were ordered to patrol the Dieppe area as part of Operation Jubilee. I was flying Spitfire "Yellow 3" in the third sortie, my second of the day. I had claimed a "damaged" Fw 190 on the first patrol.

I saw "Yellow 1" attack an Fw 190 that was flying at 12,000 feet in a south-westerly direction. The enemy aircraft broke away in a dive and I broke down after him and closed to 200 yards. I fired two bursts with cannon and machine-gun but did not observe any effects of my fire. The enemy aircraft was taking strong evasive action by jinking and turning, diving and climbing. I followed him down to about 3,000 feet but he was then out of range so I pulled up. I then rejoined my section.

We were immediately jumped by two Fw 190s from astern and from the port side. The section broke. I lost my No 4 when I broke and had been orbiting looking for my section for about 5 minutes when I saw a number of Do 217 bombers approaching from the north. I was then at about 4,500 feet and I closed on one of the Dorniers and fired several bursts of cannon and machine-gun from dead astern, closing to 200 yards. I saw smoke coming from the port engine and did not experience any return fire. The enemy aircraft went into a shallow dive. I followed him but could not fire as I had expended all my machine ammunition and my cannon had a stoppage. I saw the Dornier crash in a field about 5 miles south of Dieppe.'

Richard L. 'Dixie' Alexander – American Volunteer Fighter Command pilot

Stalag VIIIF in Germany. In August 1942 he escaped with two fellow pilots and eventually returned to England via Poland, France, Spain and Gibraltar almost a year later, to become the first American to escape captivity and return to operational flying. P/Off Don J. Blakeslee joined 1 (RCAF) at Digby in April 1941 when it was renumbered 401 (RCAF) Sqn.

The first of the RAF's 'Eagle' squadrons was No 71 Sqn, formed at Church Fenton on 19 September 1940 and equipped with a single Magister trainer. Most of its pilots had been assigned to No 5 Service Flying Training School (SFTS) at RAF Sealand on their arrival in Britain. To oversee the American students' training USAAF Col Charles Sweeny acted as a liaison officer and was made an honorary Group Captain in the RAF.

The raw recruits were joined by Battle of Britain veterans 'Andy' Mamedorff, 'Shorty' Keough and 'Red' Tobin, who were all transferred to the new unit a week after it was formed, while P/Off P. H. Leckrone joined a month later. The first operational fighters for the 'Eagles' were two inadequate Brewster Buffalos, but these were quickly replaced by nine former 85 Squadron Hurricane Is in November. After working up at Martlesham Heath, 'Shorty' Keough failed to return from a coastal patrol on 9 February 1941 and was officially pronounced 'missing in action'.

After the squadron moved to North Weald and re-equipped with Spitfire IIs, P/Off William R. Dunn claimed two Bf 109s on 27 August, which, added to his three on Hurricanes, made him the first 'Eagle' squadron 'ace'.

On 7 September disaster struck again when four pilots, including 'Red' Tobin, were lost during a sweep over France, and before the year was out his two Battle of Britain colleagues, P/Offs Mamedorff and Leckrone, were also to lose their lives. In the meantime, a second 'Eagle' squadron was formed as 121 Sqn at Kirton-in-Lindsey on 14 May 1941 equipped with Hurricane Is. Although most of its pilots were raw recruits, they were joined by the Texans P/Off Mize and P/Off Scudday, who had learned their trade during six months' experience with 43 Sqn at Drem. After a shaky start to operations at the end of the year with its recently delivered Spitfire VBs, the squadron had to wait until 23 March 1942 before it opened its score when P/Off Mooney downed an Fw 190 over the Channel. Three months later he claimed another two over St Omer, while Californian P/Off Jackson B. Mahon destroyed two more on the same mission.

The third 'Eagle' squadron, No 133, had been formed at Coltishall on 1 August 1941 with

Hurricane IIBs. Only a week after it was declared operational at Duxford on 26 September, the squadron flew to Eglinton in Northern Ireland, but lost four of its aircraft when they crashed en route on the Isle of Man. After re-grouping at Kirton-in-Lindsey in January 1942 and re-equipping with Spitfire VA/Bs, the squadron moved south to Biggin Hill in May to begin Wing sweeps over France in earnest.

It was during this period that the squadron came of age and, with the likes of P/Offs Goodson and Gentile on strength, soon drew first blood escorting bombers across the Channel. Top poker player and aggressive Flight Commander Carroll W. 'Red' McColpin, from New York State, opened 133's score on 26 April when he claimed a Bf 109 over Abbeville. Another Flight Commander was F/Lt Don Blakeslee, who had left the Canadians to join his compatriots when the third 'Eagle' squadron became part of the Biggin Hill Wing.

The squadron's greatest successes were to be gained during Operation *Jubilee* over Dieppe on 19 August 1942, during which Spitfire VBs of 71 (Eagle) Sqn were some of the first to tangle with German fighters. Operating from Lympne, 133 Sqn's pilots claimed six enemy aircraft destroyed, two 'probables' and eight damaged, with F/Lt Blakeslee and F/Sgt Richard L. Alexander claiming one each and P/Off D. D. Gudmundsen, another pre-war private pilot, credited with two. 'Dixie' Alexander, a former professional baseball player, had joined the RCAF in 1940 to become one of the original members of 71 Sqn, and opened the squadron's score card when, flying a Hurricane, he claimed a possible Do 17 in May 1941.

By mid-September 1942 133 (Eagle) Sqn, now commanded by F/Lt 'Red' McColpin, received its first Spitfire IXs, but nearly all were lost when they had to force-land in Brittany after running out of fuel over Brest while on 'target cover' escort to USAAF B-17s. It was a sad end to the Eagle squadrons' operations, which, despite objections by many of their pilots, were transferred to the newly formed US 8th Air Force. At Debden on 29 September, Nos 71, 121 and 133 (Eagle) Sqns of the RAF became the 334th, 335th and 336th Sqns of the USAAF's 4th Fighter Group.

By the end of the war in Europe several former 'Eagles' were to become the 8th Air Force's leading 'aces', including Col Donald S. Gentile, christened 'Captain Courageous' by President Roosevelt, with 21.8 victories in the air, Col Donald J. Blakeslee, who flew over 400 missions as leader of the 4th Fighter Group, known to the Germans as the 'Blakesleewaffe', and scored 15.5 victories, and Col

James A. Goodson, whose score stood at 15 when he was shot down over Germany and captured in July 1944.

Although the pilot who would become the USAAF 8th Air Force's leading 'ace', with 28 victories, never served in the RAF, he was briefly attached to a British squadron on his arrival in England. Francis 'Gabby' Gabreski's parents were Polish immigrants to the USA and his fluent command of the Polish language led to his being posted to 315 (Polish) Sqn flying Spitfires at Northolt for a month in early 1943. His 13 operational sorties, mainly *Ramrods* over France, taught him valuable lessons in air combat over occupied Europe prior to taking command of the 56th Fighter Group's 61st Squadron flying P-47 Thunderbolts.

Despite the move to the USAAF, a large number of the 300 'Eagles' chose to turn down the considerable pay increase involved to stay with their comrades in the RCAF or RAF. F/Off Arthur G. Donahue from Minnesota had learned to fly before travelling to Canada to join the RAF in 1940. Initially joining 64 Sqn, he was posted to the Far East and, after his New Zealand Buffalo squadron had been withdrawn following the fall of Singapore, he returned to England to join 91 Sqn. He was lost when he ditched over the Channel in September 1942 having been shot down by a Ju 88 that he was attacking.

Most of the non-'Eagle' Americans who fought with Fighter Command had joined the RCAF. One of them was Claude Weaver III, son of Oklahoma's Assistant Attorney General, who dropped out of high school in 1941 to join the RCAF. Posted to Britain with 412 (RCAF) Sqn in April 1942, he joined 185 Sqn in Malta where he scored ten victories, including two-in-one-day three times. After being shot down, F/Sgt Weaver escaped from an Italian PoW camp and made his way back to England. Posted to 403 (RCAF) Sqn, F/Off C. Weaver DFC lost his life over France on 28 January 1944, having claimed the last of his 12½ victories the previous day.

Equalling Weaver's number of victories was S/Ldr David L. Fairbanks DFC, who joined the RCAF in 1941 and, after being posted to 501 Sqn flying Spitfires, was to become the RAF's only American Tempest Squadron Commander. In February 1945 'Foob' Fairbanks was appointed as CO of 274 Sqn based at Volkel in Holland flying Tempest Vs, after claiming a dozen victories in as many weeks, but before the end of the month he was shot down over Germany and taken prisoner.

Another American who proved to be an outstanding Squadron Commander was S/Ldr John Danworth Browne RCAF. New Jersey-born 'Danny' Browne had learned his trade as wingman to Fighter Command's top scoring pilot, 'Johnnie' Johnson, in 1943. He subsequently commanded 441 and 421 (RCAF) Sqns to survive the war with four confirmed destroyed.

Typical of the American volunteers was P/Off John Gillespie Magee Jnr. Son of a US senator, he had joined the RCAF in 1941 and was posted to 412 Sqn at RAF Digby flying Spitfires. Although he died in a flying accident in December 1941, before he had time to make his mark as a fighter pilot, he will ever be remembered for writing the fighter pilot's prayer, 'High Flight' ('Oh! I have slipped the surly bonds of earth. And danced the skies on laughter-silvered wings...'), only a few days before his death at the age of 19.

Irish eyes

Apart from Irish American pilots in the 'Eagle' squadrons, such as P/Offs Doyle, Doorly and Mooney, who considered that fighting the British was Ireland's prerogative, not Germany's, many pilots of Irish descent fought in RAF Fighter Command.

One of a number of top-scoring pilots who had joined the RAF as war clouds gathered over Europe was William Riley from Manorhamilton, Co Leitrim, who gained a short service commission in 1935. Bill Riley opened his score in the Norwegian campaign flying a 263 Sqn Gladiator and went on to claim eight enemy aircraft destroyed with Hurricanes and Beaufighters before being killed in a flying accident over the Mediterranean in June 1942.

Riley became one of more than a dozen Irish pilots to participate in the Battle of Britain, only one of whom was killed. The casualty was County Cork-born James Meaker, who had been a reporter on the *Chichester Observer* before joining the RAF in 1939. P/Off J. R. B. Meaker claimed seven enemy aircraft destroyed, including two Bf 109s on one day, plus one probable and another damaged over a period of six weeks flying a 249 Sqn Hurricane before losing his life on 27 September 1940.

Rupert Frederick Smythe from Killiney, Co Dublin, had joined the RAF on a short service commission in 1937. Posted to 504 Sqn on the outbreak of war, he moved to 32 Sqn in May 1940 to score six victories during the Battle with the same squadron before he was shot down and severely wounded on 24 August. Frederick Desmond Hughes from Doughdee, Co Down, who served in the Cambridge University Air Squadron (UAS) in 1938 before joining the RAF in October 1939, was posted to No 264 Sqn equipped with Defiants.

Above W/C Victor Beamish, third from right, with S/Ldr Teddy Donaldson, OC 151 Sqn, at North Weald in 1940. Beamish had claimed 10 destroyed and 11 probables when he was shot down over the Channel in March 1942.

Below Irish 'ace' Desmond Hughes, flying his 264 Sqn Defiant I N1801, gained most of his 18 victories at night between 1940 and 1944.

Credited with three daylight victories in 1940, the then P/Off Hughes began his successful night-fighting career with the Defiant. Subsequently flying on Beaufighters with 125 and 600 Sqns and eventually Mosquitos of 614 Sqn, Wing Commander Hughes finished his war with a score of 18½ kills.

Serving with Hughes in the Cambridge UAS was Charles Michael Miller, born in Curragh, Co Kildare. He later attended Cranwell, and was initially posted to Bomber Command flying Wellingtons in Malta. In 1942 he was posted to 54 OTU to become a night fighter and ended the war commanding 85 Sqn flying the Mosquito NF.XIX, with a score of four victories.

North Weald's charismatic Station Commander, Francis Victor Beamish, was an unlikely Battle of Britain 'ace' who joined in the fighting with various Hurricane squadrons based at his station. A former Harlequins rugby star and oldest of four Irish brothers serving in the RAF, Victor Beamish attended Cranwell in 1925 and commanded the pre-war 64 Sqn and 504 Sqn during the 'Phoney War'. He was promoted to Wing Commander at the age of 37 prior to taking command of North Weald in June 1940 where, despite his age and rank, he took every opportunity to follow his squadrons into action. By the time he was promoted to Group Captain and posted to No 11 Group as OC Training in

March 1941, he had claimed six destroyed and three probables.

On the morning of 12 February 1942 Beamish, then Station Commander at Kenley, took off for a *Jim Crow* with his Wing Leader. Over the Channel they found themselves above a large German battle fleet. The feared battlecruisers *Scharnhorst*, *Gneisenau* and *Prinz Eugen* had slipped their moorings at Brest and were making a dash to Germany through the English Channel. Returning safely to Kenley, Beamish was able to report his sighting, which began a massive, and costly, air assault on the German Fleet. Group Captain Beamish continued to take every opportunity of flying with the squadrons under his command despite warnings from his superiors, and this practice led to his death in 1942 while flying with 485 (RNZAF) Sqn when his Spitfire was shot down near Calais by an Fw 190.

Other 'aces' included F/Off A. D. J. Lovell, who was born in Ceylon to Irish parents and joined the RAF on a short service commission in 1937. Tony Lovell, who would fly more operational tours than any other pilot in the RAF, scored a total of 16 victories between 1940 and 1944. Dublin-born 'Paddy' Barthropp served with 602 Sqn during the Battle of Britain and

Paddy Finucane (centre), the Irish Flight Commander with 452 (RAAF) Sqn, at Kenley in September 1941, with Australian pilots 'Bluey' Truscott (left), who ended the war with 14 victories, and James Smith.

1940: 'Molotov breadbaskets'

'Coming back from collecting the CO from hospital in Maidstone, we get to the Blackwell Tunnel when the trouble starts raining down all around us – no time to get to a shelter. We stand under an arch and watch the German bombers approaching in waves, hear the bombs whistle down, then explosions. "Molotov breadbasket" showers incendiaries round us, several in the gasworks, which fortunately does not go up. We watch cockneys put out one incendiary, and discover a gloomy type leaning against a lamp-post, who discloses he is waiting for the pub to open!

The CO feels a bit hard done by as he has been shot down and wounded yesterday, then gets bombed today. P/Off Loweth drives like a demon along a street and skids to a halt. We all have stiff whiskies in the Russell Hotel. Head back to North Weald in the dark via Hampstead Heath, fires light up London and fire engines are coming from all suburbs into the docks. Stop at a pub outside Edmonton and get a riotous reception and lots of beer from excited public bar. I shake hands with everybody and get quite merry.'

James Reginald Bryan Meaker – Irish Fighter Command pilot (249AW)

had claimed three destroyed and one probable before he was shot down over France in May 1942. He later took part in the 'Great Escape' from *Stalag Luft III* in 1944 but was recaptured.

John Ignatius Kilmartin from Dundalk also joined the RAF in 1937 and was first posted to No 43 Sqn

flying the Hurricane I. His first 'victory' came a week after war was declared when, on 8 September 1939, he shot down a stray barrage balloon over Portsmouth. After being transferred to 1 Sqn, P/Off 'Killy' Kilmartin attained 'ace' status flying with the Advanced Air Striking Force (AASF) during the Battle

No 1 Sqn's 'United Nations' of 'aces' in France in 1940. From left: 'Billy' Drake, Australian Leslie Clisby, Laurie Lorimer, 'Prosser' Hanks, 'Boy' Mould, 'Bull' Halahan, Frenchman 'Moses' Demozay, Johnnie Walker, Adjutant 'Doc' Mould, Paul Richey, Irishman 'Killy' Kilmartin, New Zealander 'Stratters' Stratton, and American 'Pussy' Palmer.

of France. He rejoined 43 Sqn in the Battle of Britain and survived the war with a score of 14 confirmed destroyed, having commanded Nos 128 and 504 Sqns and a Typhoon Wing.

One of Fighter Command's most successful fighter pilots was Brendon 'Paddy' Finucane. Born in Dublin, his family moved to England in 1937, where a year later Brendan applied and was accepted for an RAF short service commission. Posted to No 65 Sqn in June 1940, P/Off Finucane soon proved to be a 'born' airman. Although he only scored two victories during the Battle of Britain, he also showed that he was a natural leader. After being posted as Flight Commander to the newly formed 452 (RAAF) Sqn in April 1941, he soon impressed the sceptical Australians with his easy-going charm and his excellent eyesight. On 11 July 1941 he opened 452 Sqn's score with a Bf 109 over France, and between August and October, his 21st birthday, claimed 18 more, including three-in-one-day twice!

At the end of the year Finucane was lucky to survive when he was 'jumped' by an Fw 190 off the French coast. After coaxing his damaged Spitfire back to Redhill, he made a perfect landing just before losing consciousness. His leg had been shattered by a German cannon shell. However, he was soon back in action and by January 1942 was leading 602 Sqn in the Kenley sector. There followed a hectic period of sweeps and escorts over France during which Finucane raised his score to 32. By the end of June he had been promoted to Wing Commander, one of the youngest in Fighter Command, but less than a month later he was dead.

Leading a fighter sweep from Hornchurch on 15 July, Finucane's aircraft was hit by ground fire while at low level over Le Touquet. Too low to bale out, he turned his stricken Spitfire out to sea and prepared to ditch. Although he was unhurt, he may have been knocked out when his aircraft hit the water and sank like a stone. His body was never recovered. At the time of his death he was Fighter Command's top-scoring pilot.

An Irish pilot who opened his score while attacking the German battlecruisers *Scharnhorst* and *Gneisenau* spotted by Victor Beamish during their Channel dash was Michael Plaistowe Kilburn. Having joined the RAFVR in 1940, 'Slim' Kilburn was posted to 124 Sqn flying Spitfires, and claimed 6½ destroyed, the last in April 1945 while flying a Tempest V with 80 Sqn. In the last month of the war he took command of No 56 Sqn at Fassberg in Germany.

Chapter 5
Battle of Britain

Preparation

After the fall of France, Fighter Command had a short month to regroup before it was committed to the defence of Britain. Many lessons had to be learned from its nine months of air combat, ranging from communications to protection and operational training.

When the Air Ministry negotiated the rights to build a modified version of the US Colt-Browning .300in machine-gun in 1935, eight of which were to be fitted to the new Hurricane and Spitfire fighters, it was considered to be the equal of any potential adversary. A total of 2,000 guns were built every week by the Birmingham Small Arms company (BSA) in 1940, modified to use the British standard rimmed .303in (7.7mm) calibre round with corresponding alterations to the ammunition feed system. After initial snags, the gun proved to be a first-class weapon.

The 44.5-inch-long gun weighed 22lb, had a muzzle velocity of 2,660 feet per second and carried 300 rounds, which fired at a rate of 1,200 per minute. This meant that Hurricane and Spitfire pilots using eight guns could fire 160 rounds in a 1-second burst. A full burst of eight guns could scrub almost 25mph off the flying speed and lower the nose as though the landing flaps had been extended. RAF regulations at the outbreak of war stated that the eight guns should be set up to converge at 400 yards, although many experienced combat pilots such as 'Al' Deere and 'Sailor' Malan soon calibrated their guns to converge at only 250 yards. Before radiator heat was ducted into the gun bays, the Brownings were prone to jamming in icy conditions, but this was prevented by the simple expedient of taping over the gun ports until the guns were fired.

The ammunition used was a mix of armour-piercing, tracer and incendiary. Following a last-minute deal in 1939, for £30,000 the Air Ministry purchased the rights to manufacture the Belgian-designed De Wilde combined armour-piercing and incendiary bullet, which became widely available during the Battle of France.

Access to the Hurricane's gun bays was by only two panels and 32 turnbuttons, while the Brownings installed in the Spitfire I were widely spaced and staggered to enable them to be fitted within the thin elliptical 'A' wing. When re-arming a Spitfire armourers had to open a total of 22 gun bay and ammunition panels held by 150 turnbuttons, but despite this a team of four experienced armourers could complete the job and re-tape the gun ports in less than 30 minutes.

Although many Browning guns were converted from the Mark II to Mark II Star with a slightly increased rate of fire, and plans to fit the Hurricane with four 20mm Oerlikon cannon were prepared in 1936, many considered that the Hurricane and Spitfire were being outgunned by the Bf 109E, which was armed with two 7.9mm MG 17 machine-guns each carrying 1,000 rounds, together with two 20mm MG FF cannon, each with 60 rounds.

A few operational fighters were fitted with a cine camera gun in the starboard wing root in time for the Battle of France. These were designed to be used to verify 'kills', but even when they were subsequently fitted they were prone to malfunction during the stresses of air combat.

Protection for the pilot was fairly basic in the early Hurricanes and Spitfires, restricted to only a 2-inch-thick glass windscreen and a ¼-inch-thick stainless steel plate behind the pilot's seat. Following battle damage suffered during the Dunkirk evacuation, during the Battle of Britain armoured glycol coolant tanks and self-sealing lower fuel tanks – located in front for the pilot's legs – were fitted in the field. Fireproof bulkheads behind the pilot and jettisonable canopies were also designed, but not fitted until after the Battle.

The slower but more robust Hurricane could absorb a lot more punishment, especially to its fabric-covered fuselage, and was consequently easier to repair in the field. Early examples also had fabric-covered wings, and although metal stressed-skin wings were introduced to the Brooklands production lines in 1939, many of the Hurricanes deployed to France retained fabric wings.

More importantly, they also retained the original two-bladed wooden propeller, as did the first

Right A vital part of Britain's air defence in 1940 were the 350-foot Chain Home Low (CHL) masts, each with a rotating aerial mounted on the top to search for low-flying enemy aircraft.

Below Radar masts of a Dover Chain Home Station under attack at the height of Battle of Britain.

production batch of Spitfires delivered to the RAF. These were replaced by first the de Havilland three-bladed variable-pitch metal propeller on both types, then the Rotol three-bladed constant-speed airscrew with magnesium blades, which both reduced the take-off run and increased the maximum speed and service ceiling, despite the added weight.

During the Battle of France ACM Dowding was putting the finishing touches to his air defence system. He had established his network of Operations Rooms, which collated the information from radar stations and observers sent down dedicated telephone lines. Sector Operations Rooms had two separate parts. In the DF rooms the positions of the fighters were obtained from the 'Pip-Squeak' bearings and RDF stations, while in Sector ops the situation map was similar to that at Group ops but smaller.

The Sector Controller had executive authority over the fighters until the enemy was spotted, then on the 'Tally-ho' the command passed automatically to the leader in the air. At the end of combat the command came back to the Controller. Sectors could only handle four squadrons because there were only that number of transmissions available on 'Pip-Squeak'. However, by a great deal of dead reckoning and smart thinking many Sector controllers in the Battle of Britain handled up to six squadrons.

All the reports were fed to the 'filter' room at Fighter Command's headquarters at Bentley Priory, in the North London suburbs. All unidentified aircraft reports, known as 'X-raids', were plotted, numbered and displayed on coloured markers, which were moved across the large map table by WAAF plotters using long rakes. As soon as an enemy formation's size, bearing and altitude was confirmed, the information was passed to the Sector Operations Rooms by landline.

Above An Observer Corps post in 1940 with the observers using binoculars and a device for measuring the altitude and heading of unidentified aircraft.

Left In the receiver hut of a Chain Home (CH) station a WAAF radar operator watches for tell-tale 'blips' on a cathode ray tube (CRT), which might be a radar return from an unidentified aircraft.

Controllers in No 12 Group's Sector Operations Room at Duxford in 1940.

There these 'X-raid' plots were tracked on a map table showing the Sector, its fighter airfields and the squadrons at 'Readiness' and 15 minutes 'Available' at each one, and their status. As soon as the plot was identified as an enemy formation, the Sector Controller, himself an experienced former or resting fighter pilot, would 'scramble' one or more squadrons by telephone to intercept the raiders.

Squadrons were divided into two flights of six aircraft which in turn were split into two sections of three. Each squadron had a codename, each flight a letter 'A' or 'B', each section a colour, and each section pilot a number. For example, the Controller might 'scramble' 'Diamond Squadron', 'Red' and 'Green' sections, 'B' flight. He would communicate with the Flight Commander – 'Diamond leader' – by radio telephone (R/T); this was a high-frequency (HF) radio that had a limited range and was subject to interference and distortion. Very-high-frequency (VHF) radio with a range of 100 miles would not be fully developed and in quantity production until after the Battle was over.

Once the aircraft were scrambled, the Sector Controller would watch the plotters moving the markers across the map table and give the Flight Commander an altitude to climb to ('angels') and a heading to steer ('vector') to intercept the unidentified aircraft ('bogeys'). The heavy but vital IFF equipment fitted to the aircraft enabled the Operations Rooms to identify friendly fighters with greater accuracy, although they were only in the process of being fitted when the Battle of Britain began. The Flight Commander would be in direct communication with his pilots, identified as 'Red One', 'Blue Two' and so on. When the formation was sighted and identified as hostile ('bandits') he would call 'Tally-ho' and the fight would be on.

Sector airfields were therefore of great importance, and the other fields, which were often literally that, grass fields, were smaller. There were no all-weather runways until after 1937, and during the first few months of the war personnel still had tents, even at Hornchurch, or other spartan accommodation. To cope with extra squadrons being moved towards the Battle

An airmen takes a message
from Sector Control in a
squadron's dispersal hut, with
the readiness board in front of
him.

SQUADRON

READINESS	
AVAILABLE	
30 MINUTES NOTICE	
STANDING-BY	
ON PATROL	
LANDED AND REFUELLING	
RELEASED	

Former New Zealand First World War 'ace' Air Vice-Marshal Keith Park replaced AVM Gossage as OC of the vital No 11 Group in February 1940, and flew his own Hurricane to visit his Sector stations.

Career officer Air Vice-Marshal Trafford Leigh-Mallory became the first commander of No 12 Group when Fighter Command was established in 1936, and remained in the post during the Battle of Britain.

front, or when under attack, many of these Sector stations had one or more 'satellite' airfields, and squadrons shuttled to and from the main Sector fields as required, often with only one flight going because of space or because shortage of pilots and aircraft might mean leaving the main field undefended. For example, No 74 Sqn shuttled to and fro between Hornchurch and its satellite at Rochford 13 times between 22 October 1939 and 27 May 1940, sleeping on camp beds in what had been the civilian flying club's dance hall.

When the first phase of the Battle of Britain began on 10 July 1940, under Air Chief Marshal Dowding, Fighter Command was divided into three groups. The most important of these during the Battle was No 11 Group, which covered the South East of England – the front line – with No 12 Group controlling Central and Northern England. No 13 Group, formed in January 1940, was headquartered at RAF Newcastle; commanded by Air Vice-Marshal Richard Saul, its area stretched from Yorkshire to Scotland. No 10 Group, commanded by the pioneer night-fighter, Air Vice-Marshal Sir Christopher Quintin Brand, was formed two days before the Battle commenced; based at Rudloe Manor in Wiltshire, it covering South East England.

While Dowding was an austere and remote figure to his young fighter pilots, who nicknamed him 'Stuffy', the No 11 Group commander, Air Vice-

Marshal Keith Park, was popular and approachable. A tough New Zealander, Park was a First World War RFC fighter pilot who had shot down 20 enemy aircraft. Promoted over the head of No 12 Group's commander, Air Vice-Marshal Trafford Leigh-Mallory, an ambitious career officer who would come into conflict with Dowding as the Battle progressed, Park made regular and informal visits to front-line units flying his own Hurricane.

Dowding was, however, able to establish a crucial relationship with Churchill's new Minister of Aircraft Production, William Maxwell Aitken, Lord Beaverbrook. A confirmed anglophile, the 61-year-old Canadian self-made millionaire owner of the *Daily Express* was an unlikely ally of Hugh Dowding, but they turned out to be an inspired team. Dowding had long been at loggerheads with the Air Staff, and Beaverbrook, who had little love for military red tape, virtually ignored them as he set about imposing mass-production methods on Britain's aircraft factories. Both men had sons who were RAF fighter pilots.

Beaverbrook recruited top executives from the motor industry and research scientists from universities, established the Civil Repair Organisation (CRO), and persuaded many of his wealthy friends to contribute large sums of money to the 'Buy a Spitfire' fund and the public to give up their

pots and pans to be turned into warplanes, coining the phrase 'From the frying-pan into the Spitfire'.

In April 1939 an order was placed for 1,000 Spitfires to be produced at a brand new 'shadow' factory at Castle Bromwich, Birmingham, the first deliveries of which were scheduled for January 1940. None had been delivered when Beaverbrook came into office, but following his decision to replace the management and re-organise production practices, the first Castle Bromwich Spitfire Mk II, which featured a more powerful Merlin, took to the air on 6 June. It was followed by 125 more by the end of September. During the same period AA gun production was almost doubled, radar chains were completed, and Rolls-Royce increased production of Merlin engines at its Derby and Crewe factories to 400 a week. The output of the CRO, which was responsible for repairing battle-damaged aircraft and returning them direct to operational units, also increased from 20 a week in June to 160 a week two months later.

While Beaverbrook was involved in a whirlwind clean sweep through the traditional corridors of power, upsetting civil servants and military 'brass hats' in the process, his only son, Squadron Leader the Honourable J. W. 'Max' Aitkin, was leading 601 Sqn into action over Belgium and France during the weeks

Hurricane Is of 601 (County 0f London) Sqn are re-fuelled and re-armed at Tangmere in July 1940, while the squadron's CO, S/Ldr 'Max' Aitken, stands by the wing of the aircraft on the left.

preceding the Battle of Britain, shooting down eight German aircraft in the process.

The real strength of Beaverbrook's relationship with Dowding was illustrated by the fact that the Minister phoned the Commander-in-Chief of Fighter Command on an almost daily basis to ask how the Battle was progressing and how he could be of help. By ruthless red-tape cutting and simplification of production methods, combined with charm and cunning, Beaverbrook succeeded in keeping replacements ahead of losses during the Battle of Britain.

After the Battle was over, Dowding paid tribute to the Canadian's contribution to its outcome by saying that 'the country owes as much to Beaverbrook for the Battle of Britain as it does to me'.

Let battle commence

For the first weeks of Phase One of the Battle, which officially began on 10 July 1940, three *Luftwaffe* Air Fleets, *Luftflotte* 2 in north-west France and the Low Countries, *Luftflotte* 3 in east and central France, and *Luftflotte* 5 based in Norway and Denmark, concentrated on attacking British shipping to clear the Straits of Dover. During this phase of the Battle only six Spitfire squadrons were assigned to No 11 Group, three of which were based at RAF Hornchurch, while there were 13 Hurricane squadrons and two Blenheim units.

Although the British fighters enjoyed considerable success against the Ju 87 'Stukas', used to attack coastal convoys in the Channel, and their Bf 110 escorts, the Spitfire units had no easy time, with 39 lost in combat compared with 32 Hurricanes. No 54 Squadron flew a total of 504 sorties during the period, and lost five pilots with another three wounded, and 12 Spitfires destroyed. One of the first pilots to be shot down was 85 Sqn's CO, S/Ldr Peter Townsend, who baled out of his Hurricane off Harwich after attacking a Do 17 on 11 July. He was quickly rescued by ship.

However, it was the Defiant and Blenheim squadrons that fared worst. No fewer than seven Defiants from 141 Sqn, almost one-third of those on the RAF's strength, were shot down on 19 July with the loss of ten aircrew, while No 236 Sqn lost six of its Blenheims and 13 aircrew during Phase One. Already there were serious doubts about these types' suitability as front-line fighters.

Phase Two of the Battle began on 8 August when the *Luftwaffe* decided to switch its attacks to coastal airfields and radar stations. There were now eight Spitfire squadrons in No 11 Group, but it was again the more numerous Hurricanes that bore the brunt of the fighting, their primary task now being the destruction of German bombers, while the Spitfires would attack their fighter escorts.

As a build-up to *Adler Tag* (Eagle Day) – the planned destruction of Fighter Command scheduled for 13 August – the *Luftwaffe* flew more than 1,000 sorties a day, carrying out a series of low-level attacks on convoys in the Thames Estuary and off East Anglia, radar stations at Dover (known as 'Hellfire Corner') and Ventnor on the Isle of Wight, and the airfields at Hawkinge, Lympne and Manston. In response, squadrons from Nos 10, 11 and 12 Groups were thrown into the action and losses on both sides began to mount.

Weather on *Adler Tag* led to a number of the *Luftwaffe*'s attacks being cancelled, although by the end of the day it had mounted 1,485 sorties against Fighter Command's 700. One of the highlights of the day for the defenders was Spitfires of 609 Sqn based at Middle Wallop shooting down six out of nine Stukas attacking the Ventnor radar station.

However, two days later the *Luftwaffe* could have succeeded in inflicting a mortal blow on Fighter Command when it committed all three Air Fleets to the Battle. He 111s and Ju 88s of *Luftflotte* 5 attacked airfields in Nos 12 and 13 Groups, while *Luftflotten* 2 and 3 mounted large raids on targets in Nos 10 and 11 Groups. In more that 1,700 sorties the *Luftwaffe* caused considerable damage to airfields, radar stations and the Short Brothers aircraft factory in the south, but their bombers suffered badly from No 13 Group's fighters over the North Sea. The day's action resulted in the transfer of *Luftflotte* 5's remaining bomber strength to the Air Fleets in France, and the withdrawal from the Battle of Stuka units, which had suffered unacceptable losses.

On 16 August Fighter Command won its first and only Victoria Cross. Flight Lieutenant J. B. Nicholson of 249 Sqn was leading Red Section on a patrol between Southampton and Poole when he was attacked by a Bf 109. His Hurricane was hit and set on fire, and a cannon shell injured him in the leg and eye. As he prepared to abandon his stricken Hurricane an Me 110 appeared in front of him. He remained in the cockpit long enough to shoot down the enemy aircraft before baling out. As Nicholson floated down on his parachute, in great pain from his wounds and burns, he was fired at by a Home Guard Sergeant with a shotgun, the pellets hitting him in the backside. After nearly three months in hospital, Nicholson was invested with the VC by King George VI at Buckingham Palace on 25 November, as a representative of 'The Few'.

Heavy raids on airfields continued for another week, with fighter squadrons having to fly up to five patrols a day during the long daylight hours of August. As a general rule the Hurricanes were tasked with intercepting the bomber formations, which typically flew between 12,000 and 20,000 feet, while the Spitfires attacked the protective layers of Bf 109s typically flying 5,000 to 10,000 feet above the bombers.

When bad weather provided a lull in the battle, the cost of the previous six weeks of fierce fighting became clear. Almost 100 Fighter Command pilots had been killed or were missing, and another 60 were wounded and temporarily out of action. In response to the death of many pilots who baled out over the sea, an RAF co-ordinated air-sea rescue organisation was established using RAF launches, Lysander Army Co-operation aircraft and a few Walrus amphibians borrowed from the Royal Navy.

As a short-term measure to combat a lack of pilots, Lysander and Battle light bomber pilots were transferred to Fighter Command and sent on a six-day course at the Harwarden OTU before being posted to front-line fighter squadrons. In the same period six airfields, including Kenley, Croydon and Biggin Hill, were badly damaged and hundreds of airmen and women killed or wounded in the air raids.

The *Luftwaffe*, meanwhile, had lost over 200 aircraft, mostly bombers, and decided to change its tactics in an all-out effort to bring the RAF to its knees. Its attacks would now concentrate on No 11 Group airfields that formed a protective ring around London. Also, the escorting Bf 109s would henceforth fly much closer to the bomber formations

to enable them to fight off the RAF interceptors before they had a chance to shoot down the raiders. Both of these measures were to produce immediate and positive results for the *Luftwaffe*. On 24 August Manston was almost put out of action after being attacked by more than 100 bombers. At the same time Hornchurch and North Weald airfields were accurately targeted by high-flying *Luftflotte* 2 bombers. On the same day RAF losses included four 264 Sqn Defiants, to which three more were added on 26 August. This effectively ended the type's day operations. All available No 11 Group squadrons were committed on that day to intercept German raids on Biggin Hill, Debden and Hornchurch airfields and lost a total of 30 aircraft in the process.

This pattern of heavy raids by large formations of well-protected bombers continued throughout August. On the 30th Fighter Command flew over 1,000 sorties for the first time, but the following day it suffered its worst losses to date. The *Luftwaffe* mounted a total of 1,300 sorties, leaving Hornchurch and Biggin Hill extensively damaged, while in the battles in the skies overhead 39 RAF fighters were shot down, including 28 Hurricanes, and 14 pilots were killed, with another six Spitfires destroyed on the ground. Forty-one German aircraft were lost on the day. Squadrons in No 11 Group were now at full stretch, while the opportunities for them to rotate with those in other groups to rest and replace lost pilots and aircraft were becoming fewer by the week.

At the beginning of September Dowding was forced to re-classify Fighter Command squadrons. All those in No 11 Group, Duxford in No 12 Group and Middle Wallop in No 10 Group were now 'A'

Spitfire Is of 66 Sqn are refuelled and re-armed at No 12 Group's Sector station at Duxford in June 1940.

squadrons, and the remainder in Nos 10 and 12 Groups became 'B' squadrons. All other units were designated as 'C' squadrons to be used as advanced OTUs preparing newly qualified pilots for posting to 'A' squadrons.

In the two weeks from 24 August, 466 RAF fighters were destroyed or damaged, nearly 200 more than were delivered from the factories or CROs. Potentially more serious was the fact that 103 pilots had been killed or were missing, with only 190 new pilots available to replace them.

Typical of No 11 Group's Spitfire squadrons were 603 Sqn, which lost 16 aircraft and 12 pilots, and 616 Sqn, which lost 12 aircraft and five pilots and had to be withdrawn from the Battle. On 30 August alone 222 Sqn at Hornchurch lost no fewer than six of its Spitfires.

As many as 750 German bombers attacked British airfields on every day of the first week in September, and although more than 100 of them were shot down during this phase of the Battle, they managed to inflict heavy damage on six of the seven Sector stations and five satellite airfields. During Phase Two of the Battle Fighter Command had lost 467 aircraft,

276 Hurricanes, 167 Spitfires, 10 Defiants and 13 Blenheims, and was now struggling to keep the *Luftwaffe* at bay. Unexpectedly, *Reichmarschall* Hermann Goering, First World War fighter ace and *Luftwaffe* Commander-in-Chief, was about to come to its rescue. Despite its apparent success in recent weeks, the *Luftwaffe* had patently failed to annihilate the RAF's fighter force, and the scheduled date of Operation *Seelowe* – the invasion of Britain – was looking less credible as the weeks of fighting wore on. It was now postponed until 17 September.

Goering blamed his fighter units for failing to gain air superiority over Fighter Command. In reality, the fact that the capable Bf 109s were tied to the slow and unwieldly bomber formations and were at the limit of their range when they met the defending fighters, seriously reduced their effectiveness.

Phase Three of the Battle commenced on 7 September, when Goering decided to commit all the Air Fleets in France and the Low Countries to a massive attack on one key target – London – rather than the expected airfield targets. More than 300 bombers escorted by no fewer than 600 fighters

A fitter, clearly expecting an air raid, helps S/Ldr R. H. Leigh to strap into his 66 Sqn Spitfire I at Duxford in the early months of the Battle of Britain.

Above Sections of 222 Sqn
Spitfire Is taking off from
Gravesend over a parked
Spitfire of 610 Sqn during a
Battle of Britain scramble.

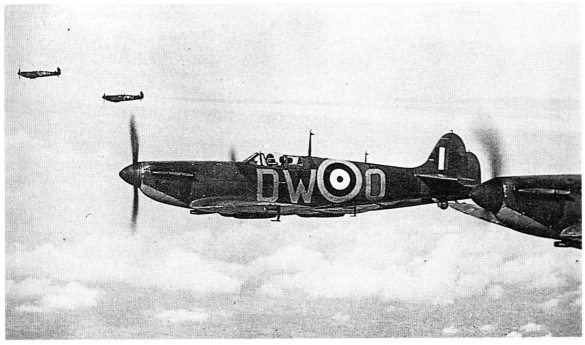

Left No 610 (County of
Chester) Sqn Spitfire Is from
Gravesend patrol over Kent
in July 1940.

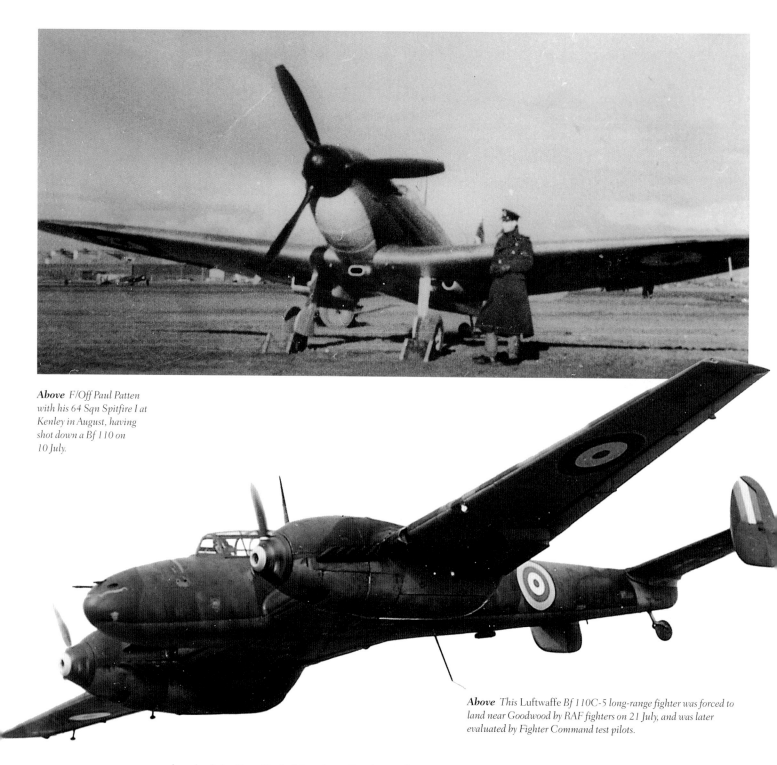

Above F/Off Paul Patten with his 64 Sqn Spitfire I at Kenley in August, having shot down a Bf 110 on 10 July.

Above This Luftwaffe Bf 110C-5 long-range fighter was forced to land near Goodwood by RAF fighters on 21 July, and was later evaluated by Fighter Command test pilots.

bombed the East End of London. Combat in the air was as fierce as ever, with both sides suffering heavy losses, but significantly Fighter Command's airfields remained intact and its groundcrews could service the fighters without air raid sirens interrupting their vital work.

London was not the only British city to be attacked in September 1940 – Southampton, Portsmouth,

Bristol and Plymouth were all targeted by German bombers. But it was a series of heavy raids on London on 15 September that would prove to be a decisive turning point in the Battle.

The weather was clear and sunny, and the German formations flew higher than usual, but on the day more than 300 RAF fighters were thrown into action. Although there were problems co-ordinating the large

A team of 'erks' dismantles a 609 Sqn Spitfire I that has made a 'heavy' landing at Middle Wallop in July 1940.

numbers of aircraft from two different Groups, Nos 11 and 12, some 60 German aircraft were shot down for the loss of just 29 RAF fighters. Seven of these were Spitfires, but eight new or repaired aircraft were delivered to squadrons the same day.

Typical of the squadrons fighting to protect the capital on 15 September was No 504. Deployed to Hendon airfield, which was acting as Northolt's satellite, the squadron was bought to readiness at 1100hrs as a party of US Generals and an Admiral arrived to see something of the life of an operational RAF fighter squadron. At 1123hrs, just as the pilots were being introduced to their distinguished visitors, the squadron was scrambled. Twelve Hurricanes took off in an impressive 4min 50sec scramble, with orders to rendezvous with 249 Sqn over North Weald at 15,000 feet. At about 1210hrs the Hurricanes intercepted a formation of Do 17s at 20,000 feet over south-east London. In the ensuing battle, 504 Sqn claimed to have shot down five enemy bombers.

One of the Dorniers had been attacking Buckingham Palace when it was brought down by Sgt R. T. Holmes in his first aerial combat. During the chase Holmes's Hurricane collided head-on with the stricken bomber, which crashed in Victoria station yard, while Sgt Holmes was forced to bale out over Chelsea, landing on a rooftop before sliding down into a neighbouring garden without serious injury. The engagement was witnessed by Queen Wilhelmina of the Netherlands from her London home. She sent a message to the Under-Secretary of State for Air, Sir Archibald Sinclair, congratulating the squadron concerned and the pilot who shot down the German aircraft.

However, two of 504 Sqn's other pilots failed to return from the morning's action, and it was subsequently confirmed that one of them, P/Off J. V. Gurteen, had been shot down and killed near Hartley in Kent. Soon after the last Hurricane had returned to Hendon, the squadron was again called to action against more raiders between South London and Hornchurch, during which another three enemy aircraft were claimed for the loss of F/Off M. Jebb, who died of his wounds after baling out over Kent.

Groundcrews 'walk out' two Spitfire Is of 609 Sqn to make sure that they are clear of other aircraft before taking off from Middle Wallop in 1940.

Two days later, Operation *Seelowe* was postponed indefinitely…

The weather was now becoming a factor in the Battle. Heavy bomber raids were replaced by 'hit and run' attacks by smaller formations of Me 110 and Bf 109 fighter-bombers, which met with limited success. At the end of the month the Ju 88s and He IIIs returned in force to attack aircraft factories in southern England. On 25 September the Bristol aeroplane works at Filton was put out of action for some weeks by a raid that killed or injured more than 250.

The following day the *Luftwaffe* turned its attention to Supermarine's Woolston factory. A precision raid by 75 bombers devastated the works and killed 30 of its staff in the process. As the Germans turned for home they were attacked by Spitfires from three squadrons, 152 and 609 in No 10 Group and 602 in No 11 Group, but in the ensuing fight only three of the raiders were shot down for the loss of five Hurricanes

and two Spitfires. Although only three complete Spitfires were destroyed in the raid, a number of others on the production lines were badly damaged and production was bought to a halt for more than a week. Total Spitfire production dropped from 133 in August to 59 in October.

Despite the ferocity of the aerial combats during Phase Three, Fighter Command lost only half as many aircraft as in Phase Two – 156 Hurricanes and 89 Spitfires. The Defiants and Blenheims had been almost completely withdrawn from day operations.

Meanwhile, serious splits in Fighter Command had surfaced during September, and between the commanders of Nos 11 and 12 Groups. While the *Luftwaffe's* attacks had been focused on the South of England, with Park's No 11 Group forming the front line of the Battle, Air Vice-Marshal Leigh-Mallory resented the fact that his No 12 Group was effectively held in reserve until such time as it was required by

Irish Battle of Britain 'ace' P/Off Rupert Smythe in his 32 Sqn Hurricane I P3522 at the Advanced Landing Ground (ALG) for the squadron's main base at Biggin Hill, in August 1940.

A nearly new Hurricane I of 17 Sqn, with artwork on the cockpit door, at readiness at Debden in August 1940 with the accumulator trolley lead plugged in for a quick start.

No 11 Group. On several occasions Leigh-Mallory, encouraged by some of his frustrated squadron commanders, committed a number of his units in 'Big Wing' formations to patrol his Sector airfields. These 'Big Wings' took a long time to assemble in the air, and Park considered that this was time wasted, particularly when he required No 12 Group's assistance at short notice when his Group was under severe pressure.

With no love lost between the two Group commanders, Dowding's confidence in Park was total, while Leigh-Mallory was gaining the support of the Deputy Chief of the Air Staff, Air Vice-Marshal Sholto Douglas; the rift was widening with serious consequences for the future.

However, in the air the worst was over, and although the Battle of Britain entered Phase Four on 1 October, which officially continued until 31

1940: Paying a debt

'We had plenty of Spitfires, Hurricanes and Gladiators on test work at Farnborough, but were forbidden to arm them. My outlook on this inactivity was not helped by the news of the death in action over the beaches of Dunkirk of my younger brother, Flight Lieutenant Falcon Nelson Clouston, who was serving with a Hurricane squadron, and I was feeling particularly low the day a Heinkel flew in at 2,000 feet in a clear sky, and dropped bombs in the direction of Aldershot. I had just returned from a test flight and was standing on the tarmac near the watch office. The fact that the bomber should have the audacity to fly over 100 miles inland on such a clear day made me hopping mad.

I ran to the Spitfire that I had just landed, and started up as the Heinkel passed over my head. I climbed up after him in a matter of seconds. He had turned towards the Continent, but I was gaining on him rapidly and was only a few thousand yards away when he gained the cover of a thin layer of cloud.

I jumped above, dived below, then climbed up above again. The cloud was so thin that I was sure he could not hide in it for long. The Spitfire was unarmed, so I had decided, once I had given chase, that I would fly slowly up behind him and chew into his tail with my propeller, hoping to do enough damage to force him down. I would then make a forced landing, or take to my parachute. Perhaps I was fortunate that I did not get the chance of putting this plan to the test. Although I kept looking above and below the cloud layer until I reached the Channel, I could find no trace of the Heinkel.

I returned to base. My Commanding Officer was furious and grounded me. I pleaded for our guns to be loaded, but without success.

Some weeks later, however, the order did come through that our fighters were to be armed. Once the sirens sounded, the first pilots to reach the fighters were to take off and patrol the airfield. I saw to it that I invariably won the scramble for one of the fighters, but there was little satisfaction in flying round and round Farnborough. After some weeks of it the inactivity began to get me down, and the day came when I decided I had had enough of it.

The sirens had gone. I had won the race for a Spitfire and was circling round Farnborough without the smell of a Hun. Away towards the east over Guildford I could see shell-bursts in the sky, and making sure once again that there were no enemy aircraft around Farnborough, I went over to investigate.

A tight formation of Heinkel bombers was on its way home after bombing London. Three or four Hurricanes were slowly and methodically shooting them down. Every now and then one of the Heinkels would spiral down in flames or out of control, while what was left of the formation flew on.

They looked like perfect sitting ducks, then, several thousand feet above, I noticed that they had an escort of eight or ten Me 110s. Curiously enough, they appeared to be making no attempt whatever to defend the Heinkels. I was trying to decide how I could best have a crack at them without interfering with the Hurricanes' methodical attack, when a Messerschmitt left his formation.

I thought he was making an attack on me, but he passed in a screaming dive towards the ground. At the last minute he pulled out and ran at full throttle towards the coast. I gave chase and was closing behind him when a Heinkel, twisting and turning a few hundred feet above the ground, appeared almost in my sights. I turned a few degrees to give him a long burst. The Heinkel rolled over and crashed down in flames into a field.

It took me some time to catch up with the Messerschmitt again. He was flying dangerously low, following the contour of the ground. I knew Kent was covered with high-tension cables and expected him to crash at any moment. Staying at a safe height, I decided to take him as he rose out of the valleys.

He started firing first. While I was still well out of range his rear gunner opened up and tracers screamed in my direction. I closed in quickly, and as he lifted to clear a ridge of high trees I gave him a burst with my right machine-guns. The rear gunner was silenced at once. The Me 110 was at my mercy.

I poured in lead at almost point-blank range. Flames flared up from his starboard engine and his speed fell away by half, but he still kept flying. I realised that my ammunition must be running low, and changed to short bursts. We were passing over the Channel when my guns stopped. The Me 110 limped like a bird with a broken wing, ready to drop into the water at any moment. He kept going, but very, very slowly. A Hurricane appeared alongside me. I veered away from the Me 110's tail to let the Hurricane move in for the kill. Instead, he flew in close on the other side of the Me 110. He, too, must have been out of ammunition. We waved to each other and turned for home, leaving the Hun to his fate.

I felt much better as I returned to base. I had paid the debt for my brother and I was exhilarated. In a burst of high spirits I put the Spitfire into two rolls over Farnborough, the recognised procedure by which the fighter boys indicated the number of aircraft they had shot down.

My CO was not amused. When I landed, I was grounded again.'

A. E. Clouston – New Zealand RAE test pilot attached to Fighter Command (Pan)

Fighter Command's only Victoria Cross was awarded to 23-year-old F/Lt James Brindley Nicholson, a 249 Sqn Flight Commander who, despite painful wounds, stayed in his stricken Hurricane to press home an attack on a Bf 110 before baling out on 14 August 1940.

A No 32 Sqn pilot climbs into his Hurricane I while a member of the groundcrew refuels the aircraft before a patrol from Biggin Hill.

October when the *Luftwaffe* turned its attention away from daylight raids to the night 'Blitz' tactics, the RAF had won a close-run and costly victory. During October 325 German aircraft were shot down, but Fighter Command lost 80 pilots with another 35 wounded. On 12 October Hitler postponed Operation *Seelowe* until 1941.

Of the nearly 3,000 Allied pilots from 14 different nations who took part in the Battle of Britain, more than 530 were killed and another 450 wounded. A total of 535 Hurricanes, 326 Spitfires, 31 Blenheims and 18 Defiants were destroyed in the four-month Battle, with another 589 damaged – 1,600 new aircraft were delivered from the factories. Although Hurricanes bore the brunt of the fighting during the Battle by virtue of the fact that there were more of them available, the Spitfire was undoubtedly the 'star of the show' in the public's mind, with 521 confirmed victories, but at the end of the day it all came down to the outstanding flying and leadership qualities of Fighter Command's pilots.

Many of the Battle's leading aces did not become household names at the time, despite their high scoring in a relatively short time, in some cases during less than four weeks in action. The highest-scoring British pilot was P/Off Eric Lock of 41 Sqn, with a confirmed score of 16 enemy aircraft shot down and one shared. He was followed by Battle of France 'ace' Sgt 'Ginger' Lacey and P/Off Bob Doe, each with 15, and Scots 'ace' F/Lt Archie McKellar, who claimed 14 destroyed before he was killed on 1 November.

Fighter Command's top-scoring pilot was the Czech Sgt Josef Frantisek of 303 (Polish) Sqn, who died in a flying accident on 8 October having scored 17 victories. The highest-scoring Commonwealth pilots included New Zealander F/Off Brian Carbury of 603 Sqn, who shot down 15 enemy aircraft, and Australia's F/Lt Pat Hughes, who claimed 14 destroyed plus three shared before being killed in action on 7 September. The top scoring squadron was 303 (Polish) Sqn, flying Hurricanes, which claimed a total of 126½ aircraft destroyed, while the top Spitfire squadron was No 602, with 102 kills. Five other squadrons, Nos 3, 41, 92, 501 and 603, claimed more than 90 enemy aircraft destroyed.

Within days of the end of the Battle the team that engineered Fighter Command's victory was abruptly broken up. Air Vice-Marshal Keith Park was 'relieved' of the command of No 11 Group, posted to Flying Training Command and replaced by his long-time rival, Leigh-Mallory. His boss, Air Chief Marshal Sir Hugh Dowding, was summarily 'retired' from his post and the RAF. At the end of the year Lord

Beaverbrook, who had been accused of causing disruption to established procedures, was moved to the Ministry of Supply, although it would be another five years before Winston Churchill would suffer a similar fate to Lord Dowding – being summarily dismissed from Office by the British electorate.

1940: Who do they think they are?

'Those halcyon days of the 1930s, the sun always shining, and on a Friday evening after a day's work, off to Hendon Aerodrome, through the gates, a walk across the grass to "our" hangar and 604 Squadron's dear old Demons. For those few hours we'd fly – someone always scrounged a lift in the rear cockpit, airborne for an hour or so, return, stow away the aircraft, then look forward to the weekend, for those two days we devoted ourselves to both flying and aircraft maintenance, rifle drill, forming fours, etc. Annual training took us, in "best blue" uniform, to Tangmere in lovely countryside with a feel of peacefulness and the South Downs in the background.

Suddenly a piercing shriek of air raid warnings, massive explosions, the sound of aircraft overhead. In that split second the image of Tangmere disappeared. I was here at Middle Wallop and back to reality. Lunch time – a mad dash for the shelters and suddenly I was consumed with anger. I walked up to the hangars. More aircraft overhead – who do they think they are? And what did I think I could do? I arrived at the hangars – huge bomb craters around our shattered hangar, its door flat on the ground, aircraft still overhead. A solitary airman appeared from somewhere and jumped into a huge crater, taking shelter under the gushing torrent of water from a shattered water main. Devastation lay all around. Still angry. A Ju 88 flew low overhead. I took a shot at it with my service-issue .45. Missed!

Back into the hangar, the very first time in my life I helped lift a torso on to a stretcher. Three Blenheims destroyed and one damaged.'

John 'Dave' Davis – Fighter Command Engineering Officer

Above *On the evening of 15 August, 30 Ju 88s attacked No 10 Group's Sector station at Middle Wallop, scoring a direct hit on one of its hangars and destroying three Blenheim IFs of 604 (County of Middlesex) Sqn.*

Left *Another victim of the Luftwaffe bombing raid on Middle Wallop on 15 August was this 609 Sqn Spitfire I. Two days earlier the squadron's Spitfires had destroyed 13 German aircraft for no loss.*

Opposite above *This 65 Sqn Spitfire I made an emergency landing at Middle Wallop in August bearing the scars of combat with a Bf 109 – at least six bullet holes can be seen.*

Opposite below *This KG 2 Ju 87B, the fearsome 'Stuka', was brought down near Chichester by Hurricanes of 43 Sqn on 16 August, its two-man crew dying of their wounds.*

Above *A KG 76 Do 17E-2 was shot down by 615 Sqn Hurricanes near Biggin Hill after a low-level raid on Kenley airfield on 18 August.*

Left *This corrugated-iron garage served as 64 Sqn's dispersal hut at Kenley in August 1940. The squadron's CO, S/Ldr Donald MacDonnell, sitting on the right, was credited with shooting down nine enemy aircraft in the Battle of Britain.*

Right One of 264 Sqn's most successful Defiant crews was Sgts Ted Thorn, pilot, and gunner Fred Barker, who shot down two Do 17s and a Bf 109E on 26 August.

Below 264 Sqn at Kirton-in-Lindsey lost four Defiant Is on 28 August, and after mixed success over Dunkirk these aircraft were subsequently withdrawn from day operations.

1940: No lights

'As the Battle of Britain reached its climax, I was invited to Buckingham Palace with my Commanding Officer, S/Ldr A. G. Malan, to receive my DFC. Our Squadron, No 74, was based at Kirton-in-Lindsey in Lincolnshire, and we arranged to fly down to Northolt on the outskirts of London in the Squadron's Miles Master trainer. Our departure was delayed several times by the CO, and by the time we eventually took off darkness was already falling. I therefore asked that a message be sent to Northolt requesting that the runway lights be turned on prior to our estimated time of arrival (ETA).

As that approached, I found that we were flying in among the balloon barrage that surrounded London, but still could see no lights from Northolt. I decided that we should put down as soon as possible before we hit a balloon cable, and we were lucky enough to land on the unobstructed fairway of Becontree Golf Club.

It was after I had retrieved the aircraft and finished the flight to Northolt early the next morning that I learned that the request for Northolt's runway lights had been sent to North Coates – an airfield only a few miles from Kirton-in-Lindsey!'

John Connell Freeborn – Fighter Command pilot

Spitfires were difficult to land at night as 'ace' Sgt 'Titch' Havercroft of 92 Sqn found on the night of 31 August while attempting to land at Pembrey.

1940: A very fine club

'As time went by you learned not to make close friends because they were likely to be killed. One of my best friends was killed by a '109 after he had baled out, shot while coming down by parachute.

They tried to do the same thing to another friend, Johnnie Cock, an Australian fellow pilot in 87 Sqn. He had baled out of his Hurricane and I saw an Me 109 have a go at him. So I shot the '109 down, chased off another and circled Johnnie all the way down to make sure he was all right.

Of course we were as scared as anybody else would have been, but we knew that we had the whole country behind us. Fighter Command was like a very fine club, a wonderful crowd. It was the greatest honour to be part of that Battle of Britain crowd – lovely people!'

William Dennis David – Fighter Command pilot (DT)

A No 504 Sqn rigger helps P/Off Blair 'Crasher' White, a veteran of the Battle of France, into his parachute at Filton in September 1940, the month he shot down a Do 17 and a Bf 110.

Above A British soldier
inspects an He III H-2 of
KG 1 from Luftflotte 2 shot
down by a 253 Sqn
Hurricane near Redhill
on 30 August.

Left Hurricanes of 56 Sqn
operating from North Weald
were heavily involved in the
defence of No 11 Group
airfields, losing two of the
'Punjab' Squadron
commanders before being
withdrawn to No 10 Group
in September 1940.

1940: Harmonisation

'Beyond No 74 Squadron's hangar was the stop butt for aircraft gun testing. We were equipped with Mk 1 Spitfires – eight in each flight, with five in the hangar that were part of the Fighter Command Reserve. We had about six armourers to each flight and two of us Fitter Armourers were mostly engaged in aircraft periodic inspections – at the time the first was after 30 hours flying, which was changed in the spring of 1940 to 40 hours. The armament inspection involved the removal of all guns, their servicing and replacement, which was followed by harmonisation and butt testing. The pneumatic gun-firing system was also checked, as was the gunsight.

The harmonising was done by aligning the Spitfire on a series of spots painted on the hangar door in a pattern approved by Command to give the best spread of bullets. Once the Spit was up on trestles and adjusted to flying position, the eight Brownings, gunsight and camera gun were adjusted on to the spots and locked into position. This was required to be checked by the pilot – preferably the one who used this particular Spit the most. I used to stick my head into the crew room and invariably one of the Sergeant pilots was "volunteered" for the job. The only exception was F/Lt Malan. He was "A" Flight Commander – the other flight was commanded by F/Lt "Paddy" Treacy, and those two were undoubtedly the best and most efficient pilots we had.

"Maxie" Malan, which was his universal nickname within the squadron until the press christened him "Sailor", always had his harmonisation done in his own way. We ignored the hangar door spots. A single disc on a pole was taken out to a measured 250 yards, the aircraft was levelled to flying position and all eight guns, gunsight and camera gun were fixed on the same spot – and he checked it. No wonder he survived so well. He was a real gentleman and took a great interest in our job as well as his own.'

Derek Morris – Fighter Command Fitter (Armourer)

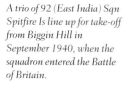

A trio of 92 (East India) Sqn Spitfire Is line up for take-off from Biggin Hill in September 1940, when the squadron entered the Battle of Britain.

Above Luftwaffe Bf 109E-3 fighters of JG 451 taking off from a forward airfield in Eastern France during the summer of 1940.

Left This JG 3 Bf 109E-3, shot down over Kent on 5 September by F/Lt Pat Hughes of 234 Sqn, the Australian's 11th victim of the Battle, belonged to Lt von Werra, the only Luftwaffe pilot to escape back to Germany.

Above *A Fighter Command engineering officer inspects a JG 51 Bf 109E shot down on the outskirts of London during the latter phase of the Battle of Britain.*

Above right *A captured Luftwaffe Bf 109 being paraded through the streets in Kent on a Queen Mary transporter escorted by British soldiers.*

Right *Likewise a captured RAF Spitfire, possibly from 54 Sqn, which force-landed at Dunkirk, was used by the Luftwaffe for a series of propaganda photographs published during the Battle of Britain.*

Above left *A 504 Sqn pilot climbs into Hurricane I P3774 at Hendon, one of the City of Nottingham Squadron's aircraft that intercepted the raid on Buckingham Palace on 15 September.*

Left *Hurricane P3878, the regular mount of 17 Sqn 'ace' F/Off Harold Bird-Wilson, was shot down by Adolf Galland near Chatham on 24 September. Bird-Wilson baled out but suffered severe burns.*

Above *F/Lt Frank Rimmer of 229 Sqn was shot down and killed by Bf 109s at Burwash on 27 September after having claimed one destroyed and one shared 12 days earlier.*

1940: Wing-tipped

'When on patrol with No 501 Sqn I followed "Red 1" attacking a Bf 109. He emptied his guns and damaged the enemy aircraft, hitting its glycol tank. He broke to the right as the Messerschmitt entered low cloud at 4,000 feet. I flew above "Red 1", who was below the cloud bank as the Bf 109 came out above it a right angles. I was above it at between 6,000 and 6,500 feet and attacked it from astern.

He quickly lost height and went into the sea off Hythe from 3,000 feet. The enemy aircraft sank slowly, the tail being visible for some time. I circled twice before the machine sank, and flew back towards the coast, climbing to 23,000 feet.

On reaching this altitude I could not see any sign of my squadron but heard the position of enemy aircraft over the R/T and decided to patrol between Dover and Folkestone about 8 to 10 miles inland.

At about 1335hrs I saw eight Bf 109s coming across the coast from the east about 1,800 feet above me. I attacked the three rearmost machines in vic

formation from beneath when a fourth enemy aircraft doing rear-guard flew across my line of fire. He developed a leak from the glycol tank. He half-rolled and dived towards the coast. I followed him – his aircraft was only about 200 yards ahead so was easy to catch. I emptied the rest of my ammunition into him from 200 yards but he still flew on, coming down to 80-100 feet.

I flew around him and signalled him to ditch, which had no result. I therefore attempted to ram his tail with my undercarriage, but when I lowered it it reduced my speed, which was too low to hit him. So, flying alongside, I dipped my starboard wing-tip on to his port tailplane. The tailplane came off and I lost the tip of my starboard wing.

The enemy aircraft spun into the sea and partially sank. I did not wait to see the final plunge as two Bf 109s were attacking me from above and behind. I weaved my way back towards Folkestone at 20-30 feet above the sea with them emptying a lot of machine-gun and cannon fire into my machine, damaging the engine, which belched oil and smoke into the cockpit.

They broke off the engagement about a mile from the coast and I managed to reach the coast and force-landed on a hill between Folkestone and Hawkinge. My Hurricane was pretty badly damaged and shot up, while I split my jaw and broke some teeth on the gunsight.'

Kenneth W. 'Mac' Mackenzie – Fighter Command pilot

P/Off Ken Mackenzie crash-landed his 501 Sqn Hurricane V6799 on 7 October 1940 after downing a Bf 109, his second of the day, by using his wing-tip to break off the German's tailplane.

Left *Pilots of 229 Sqn with one of their Hurricanes at Northolt in October 1940. From left to right, standing: Belgian 'ace' P/Off Vicky Ortmans, Sgt J. Arbuthnot, F/Off R. Berry, Rhodesian F/Lt J. Holderness, and F/Lt William Smith; front: Sgt F. J. Twitchett, Sgt G. F. Silvester and Sgt W. Hodson.*

Below *S/Ldr Don Finlay, OC 41 Sqn, surrounded by his pilots at the end of the Battle of Britain; the group includes the New Zealand 'ace' P/Off John Mackenzie immediately behind him and, next to him, F/Off Tony Lovell with F/Lt Norman Ryder standing second from left.*

P/Off 'John Willie', on the
wing of his 54 Sqn Spitfire I
at Hornchurch, finished the
Battle of Britain with a score
of four and one shared
destroyed.

Two of 74 Sqn's Battle of
Britain 'aces', P/Off
Harbourne Stephens and
F/Off John Mungo-Park,
sitting in his Spitfire I, were
credited with eight and ten
'kills' respectively.

Surviving members of the 'Few' surround the former AOC-in-C
Fighter Command, Air Chief Marshal Sir Hugh Dowding, at a Battle
of Britain reunion in September 1942. Left to right: W/C 'Sailor'
Malan, S/Ldr Al Deere, Dowding, F/Lt Richard Hillary, F/Off
Elspeth Henderson MM, W/C Johnny Kent and W/C Brian
Kingcombe.

1940: Sincere appreciation

'In handing over command of No 11 Fighter Group, I
wish to express sincere appreciation for the loyal
support of all ranks of Fighter Squadrons, Sector
Stations and Forward Aerodromes during the past
eight months hard fighting. The squadrons operating
under the control of No 11 Group have soundly
beaten the enemy, the German Air Force, in the
spring and summer, and finally autumn of 1940.

The following enemy aircraft have been accounted
for in combat against heavy odds: destroyed 2,424,
probably destroyed and damaged 2,161, total 4,585.

The outstanding successes were due to the courage
and skill of our fighter pilots who have been so ably
supported by the operational and ground staffs at all
aerodromes in spite of casualties and some damage
caused by enemy bombing attacks by day.

The German Air Force may again launch heavy
attacks by day against England in 1941, and I feel
confident that the units of 11 Group will again
defeat the enemy bombers and fighters, however
numerous.

I am proud to have commanded No 11 Fighter
Group throughout the heavy fighting of 1940, and
wish all ranks good luck in 1941.'

**Air Chief Marshal Sir Keith Park,
17 December 1940**

King George VI and Queen Elizabeth with Air Chief Marshal Lord
Dowding outside Buckingham Palace before the second anniversary
Battle of Britain parade on 26 September 1943.

Chapter 6
Auxiliary services

From the first day that Lord Trenchard formed the Royal Air Force, it included women as serving members. At the end of The First World War the Women's Royal Air Force (WRAF) had 32,000 members, but, as the RAF fought for its life, it was disbanded on 1 April 1920.

Nineteen years later, as war clouds gathered over Europe, the Women's Auxiliary Air Force (WAAF) was

WAAFs had to compete with their male counterparts to qualify for most RAF trades, including the servicing of front-line aircraft such as this Spitfire.

formed, and at its head was a close friend of Lady Trenchard, Jane Trefusis-Forbes, who became its first Director. Formed on 28 June 1939 from women members of RAF companies within the Auxiliary Territorial Service (ATS), the WAAF had a complement of 7,690 at the outbreak of war three months later.

In the months that followed the Duchess of Gloucester became the Commandant-in-Chief, and as thousands of women volunteered for service the RAF was hard put to cope with the influx. In January 1940 some 50 WAAFs arrived unannounced at RAF Hendon, then a Fighter Command station. There was no accommodation for them and their duties were the responsibility of the Station Commander. However, they were soon integrated into station routine, manning admin offices, driving motor transport and playing a crucial role in Command, Group and Sector Control Rooms and at radar stations.

It was during the desperate evacuation of British troops from Dunkirk that a WAAF was awarded the service's first George Medal when Cpl Joan Pearson rescued two members of the crew of a blazing aircraft that crashed at Detling on 31 May 1940.

At the start of the Battle of Britain more than 25,000 WAAFs were in service sharing the front line with their male colleagues at Fighter Command stations in the South East of England during the summer months of 1940. During August and September WAAFs were killed and injured by *Luftwaffe* attacks, while many others continued to carry out their duties irrespective of the danger.

Two WAAFs on duty in the Biggin Hill control room were awarded the Military Medal for staying at their posts when the station was heavily bombed on 18 August. One was killed at Kenley on 7 September, and many others were injured at Middle Wallop and Hornchurch. WAAFs had become part of Churchill's immortal 'Few'.

At that time those serving in the WAAF were all volunteers – conscription for women was more than a year away – but they were already being considered for trades other than dishwashers or glorified secretaries. An essential but less glamorous element of Britain's air defence was the balloon barrage that was operated by 47 Auxiliary Air Force squadrons, in which a great many WAAFs served as balloon operators. They were required to drive the lorry, operate the winch, splice ropes and manhandle 120lb blocks and sandbag ballast. They lived 'in the field' as part of a team of eight crew and two NCOs. The first WAAF-operated barrage balloon was named 'Romeo'.

When all women between 19 and 30 became liable to call-up in December 1941, the ranks of the WAAF swelled to over 100,000, and more and more trades were opened to women. By the service's peak in 1943, 182,000 WAAFs were serving in 22 branches of the RAF working at 75 trades ranging from photo-recce interpreters and met forecasters to engine mechanics and signals officers.

Intelligence analysis was another field that had a high percentage of WAAF personnel. One of them, Assistant Section Officer Noor Inayat Khan, became the first woman agent to be sent into Occupied France in 1943. She was betrayed to the Gestapo and spent almost a year in prison being interrogated before being shot at Dachau in September 1944. She was awarded a posthumous George Cross for her courage.

In October 1943 Dame Trefusis-Forbes was replaced by Lady Ruth Welsh, who, after driving ambulances in France during the First World War with the Women's Army Auxiliary Corps, married an RAF pilot, S/Ldr, later Air-Marshal, W. L. Welsh in 1922.

Two years after the Battle of Britain, London and South East England was again the target for German bombs. This time it was the unmanned and unpredictable V-1s, christened 'doodlebugs' by Londoners. More by luck than judgement, several fell close to RAF stations, causing much damage and many casualties. WAAF sick quarters at Biggin Hill and the WAAF headquarters building at Hendon were both severely damaged by V-1s in July 1944. Although the war had by this time moved to Europe, a large number of WAAFs, 157,000 of them, remained in the service on VE-Day.

Serving alongside WAAFs throughout the Second World War were members of Princess Mary's Royal Air Force Nursing Service, which had been established in 1923 when nurses became a permanent branch of the RAF. They were expected to drive ambulances on 'drome duty' as well as nurse badly injured aircrew or those injured in bombing raids on RAF stations. Many worked with the

WAAF Sgt Joan Mortimer and Cpl Elspeth Candlish-Henderson were awarded the Military Medal for staying at their posts at Biggin Hill throughout a heavy bombing raid on the station by German bombers in the summer of 1940.

1939: First arrivals

'A week or two after we had arrived at RAF Digby in December 1939, I went to a Camp dance held in the Sergeants' Mess; it seemed the thing to do apparently, so I went along. I had never been to a dance without an escort – and without really knowing who would be there or what it would be like.

However, I remember standing in the doorway of the hall, in the shadows, taking stock of my surroundings before venturing in. It all looked great fun. The music was playing merrily and everyone seemed to be dancing happily. I remained where I was.

Then someone came over and asked me to dance with him. What joy – he was tall, and danced beautifully. I loved dancing. We danced and chatted,

and then he called across to one of his friends, "Tubby, guess what, I'm dancing with a WAAF who is asking about centrifugal force!" I had asked him. I wanted to know. I had been reading an article – which I didn't understand – about it in The Times that morning in Ops.

I learned that many of the pilots belonged to 46 Squadron. Later the squadron disappeared, but before they left I got to know my first dancing partner, Jack Lawson [later OC 19 Sqn, who claimed five destroyed and three probables in the Battle of Britain], quite well. I found he never fussed me, and danced beautifully – completely to my liking. And, above all he was great fun and made me laugh.'

Margaret Balfour – Fighter Command WAAF

Air Commandant Lady Ruth Welsh, who took over from the first WAAF Director, Dame Jane Trefusis-Forbes, in October 1943, seated at her desk with Deputy Director Group Officer I. M. Campbell.

1940: Tense times

'During September and October, after all the summer activity, we were kept busy in the Ops Room – the Battle of Britain was just over, but the sweeps never seemed to stop. We heard of many losses, both aircraft and pilots – so many I had known. I felt I'd never get used to it – each time someone went missing it made me feel more than just sad. I knew I was not supposed to worry about things like that, but I did. I hoped no one noticed.

We constantly heard of raids on inland cities, and there we sat in Ops, and sometimes it seemed that we were of so little use. I can remember one day, a strange feeling – things were not going on like this for much longer – I think I was in need of a longer leave than just 48 hours.

However, in spite of everything we still remained cheerful – there were still parties and dances, and we all had as much fun as we could.'

Margaret Balfour – Fighter Command WAAF

1941: Grand Hotel

'On a Saturday afternoon in April I arrived at HQ
Fighter Command at Bentley Priory, a raw recruit
straight from Initial Training at the Grand Hotel and
Panal Ash in Harrogate. I was not expected!

The Sergeant SP directed me to the WAAF Admin
Office and I had my first encounter with F/Sgt
Swaffam, a large imposing lady of whom I was
immediately in awe. However, having established that
I had an aunt in Streatham, she made me ring to ask if
I could stay there until Monday 0900 and, mercifully,
she agreed.

I was allocated to Dr R. E. Watson, Senior Met
Officer, Fighter Command, and spent my time between
his office in a hut near the entrance to the "Hole" and
the Foresters' office down the "Hole", overlooking the
plotting table and gallery where the Filter Room was
situated, and where the Army, Navy and, later,
American Service Liaison Officers had their desks.
Visitors such as David Niven and Robert Young caused
great excitement, and there seemed to be more WAAF
on duty at those times! My first duty each morning was
to take the Met report directly to the AOC-in-C, Air
Chief Marshal Sir Sholto Douglas, initially an awe-
inspiring experience that soon became enjoyable.

My first billet was "The Briars", halfway up
Stanmore Hill, where the seasoned Sergeant told all
the rookies on arrival that if Air Commandant
Trefusis-Forbes could take off her jacket, roll up her
sleeves and scrub floors, which apparently she did
when "The Briars" was requisitioned, we need not
think it beneath us to do likewise!

While at "The Briars" conscription came into force,
and those WAAF personnel who had volunteered were
given the option of leaving the service. However, we
were irrecoverably locked in "for the duration" and
glad to be so. We volunteers never lost our pride in
wearing an "A" on our sleeves, and resisted any
attempts to outlaw it.'

Frances Philip – Fighter Command WAAF

1941: Backseat driver

'In 1941 my husband Christopher was posted to 256
Squadron at Colerne as a Flight Commander flying
Defiant night fighters; in partnership with his New
Zealander air gunner Jack Scott, he shot down four
German bombers in a single month. He was later
awarded a DFC and, after moving to Squires Gate
near Blackpool, was promoted to Squadron Leader to
become commanding officer. I was a serving WAAF
on the airfield at the time and was able to see quite a
lot of Christopher during that period. I even
managed to fly in a Defiant's gun turret on a number
of occasions. Strictly illegal of course, but we
managed to get away with it.'

Kuni Deanesly – Fighter Command WAAF

pioneering plastic surgeon Sir Archibald McIndoe as
he attempted to rebuilt the faces of badly burned
Battle of Britain pilots known as the 'Guinea Pigs'.

RAF nurses also manned Air Ambulance aircraft
attached to No 24 Sqn at Hendon, one of which was
named 'Nurse Cavell' and another 'Women of Britain'.
These were some of the first non-combat aircraft to
land in France on D-Day plus 7, and by the end of July
more than 10,000 patients had been flown home from
Normandy by the RAF.

Apart from releasing thousands of men for front-
line duties, both WAAFs and RAF nurses did their bit
to raise the morale of RAF personnel, so much so that
in fact many married serving airmen during their time
of service.

However capable the 'Girls in Blue' proved to be in
all the branches of the RAF, the one thing they were
not permitted to do was to fly service aircraft. The
only women who were qualified to fly operational
RAF aircraft were members of the Air Transport
Auxiliary (ATA). Formed in February 1940 at
Whitchurch with the encouragement of the Under-
Secretary of State for Air, Captain Harold Balfour, the
ATA was administered by BOAC and manned by
former experienced civil pilots and RAF aircrew

1942: Life at Bentley Priory

'When I was made up to Corporal I was transferred to work for W/C Ops, W/C Thompson, an early pioneer of ACC/CHL, the beginning of radar. It was during that period, in May 1942, that I was one of the team of WAAF Clerks/General Duties involved in the typing of plans for an operation so secret that large sections were left blank, and we could not leave camp. The operation turned out to be providing fighter cover for the first thousand-bomber raid over Germany on the night of 30/31 May.

Also at that time the Duke of Kent was well known at Bentley Priory, where he was stationed until his untimely death in an air crash in Scotland. I was on leave with a friend of mine in Scotland in August and we were walking down the hill in Colinton, Edinburgh, when we saw the news on a poster outside a newsagent. We were stunned.

Richard Hilary was also at Fighter Command HQ upon returning to ground duties after sustaining dreadful burns when his Spitfire was shot down during the Battle of Britain. He gave me a copy of his book The Last Enemy, which he autographed – a prized possession until someone borrowed it and failed to return it. He waged an ongoing battle to return to flying duties, which he eventually won. He was posted to No 10 Group but later died in a training accident. He was such a modest man and hated being saluted because he was aware of his dreadful scarring.

I was posted to RAF Gravesend in December 1942, then to RAF Colerne, where the RAF Admin S/Ldr gave me the job of doing all the station announcements. No one ever got to know the real identity of the announcer who was called "Vera Belfridge"!

Then I was posted out of Fighter Command for ever. It was very difficult to get used to never wearing the top button of my jacket open (off duty!), and I could never lose the feeling of pride in being in Fighter Command, as a small cog, but a cog none the less.'

Frances Philip – Fighter Command WAAF

1942: A whole new field

'I joined the WAAF because I really wanted to do something with my hands, to learn a trade, a mechanical trade. I chose engines and I was actually on Spitfires, and used to service the whole thing.

When I was on the mechanics course it was like an amazing dream. I could not imagine how I'd got to the age of 20, jumping on and off buses, without understanding the marvellous theory about how things worked. Suddenly there was this whole new field of work and thought. On one occasion I got into trouble for not being at a make-up lecture, and being instead in the library swotting up on mechanics.'

Nina Hibbin – Fighter Command WAAF (RD)

1943: Gradually trusted

'We were expected to complete the course in the same time as our male counterparts, which seemed a bit unfair as none of us had any mechanical knowledge. In fact, all I knew about my father's car was that he put water, petrol and oil in three different holes, swung a handle and with luck it started.

On our first morning we were demoralised and threatened that failure incurred re-mustering, which seemed an attractive option at the time. We progressed through the workshop digesting the lessons on carburettors, magnetos, generators and so on, working long hours, but gradually we were trusted and allowed to do the jobs.'

Stella Burgess – Fighter Command WAAF (RAFN)

deemed over the age for operational service. Of the initial 52 pilots accepted for the ATA, ten were women, and they were tasked with ferrying operational RAF and Fleet Air Arm aircraft from factories and Maintenance Units to Flying Training Schools and operation stations. By 1942 the ATA had established six Ferry Pools operating from 14 airfields, and ran its own elementary and advanced Flying Training Schools at Luton and White Waltham respectively.

The aircraft they ferried were classified in six categories: Class 1, Single-engined light aircraft; Class 2, Single-engined service aircraft; Class 3, Twin-engined light aircraft; Class 4, Twin-engined service aircraft; Class 5, Four-engined aircraft; and Class 6, Flying boats. The ATA's Flying Training School, which moved to Thame as No 5(T)FP, used Tiger Moths and Magisters for elementary training, and Masters, Martinets, Harvards and, later, Hurricanes and Spitfires for advanced training.

The Auxiliary also had a fleet of Fairchild Argus

and Anson taxi aircraft for moving ferry pilots around the country. By 1944 the ATA operated 16 Ferry Pools, with 658 pilots, including 108 women, 100 flight engineers and more than 3,000 groundcrew. Pilots came from an astonishing variety of backgrounds. The Officer Commanding the No 5(T)FP was Derek Pickup, a former RAF pilot who had seen service with the AASF in France, while the instructors came from a mixed background of service and civil flying. Some had failed to be selected for operational flying despite their experience; for example, F/Off Dutton had only one arm, while F/Capt Keith-Jopp, who was over 50 and had only one eye and one hand, both flew Spitfires and Hurricanes for the ATA. Many others had flown with the pre-war Civil Air Guard, but new recruits were RAF student pilots transferred to the ATA having received their basic training in Canada as part of BCATP or in the United States with the BFTS or Arnold Schemes.

Typical of these was George Lewis, who graduated

Six pilots assigned to the women's section of the Air Transport Auxiliary (ATA) No 5(T) Ferry Pool at Thame, where new recruits gained experience of basic ferrying duties.

1942: Down a bolt-hole

'The Air Transport Auxiliary (ATA) had decided that recruits such as I should not be taught to fly on instruments. And as we sometimes did several different deliveries in different types of aircraft in a day, it wouldn't have been practical to carry a radio and have to waste time tuning in and testing before each flight.

The night before I was to deliver Spitfire IX BS148 from Hanworth to Cosford, I had been taken out in London by some former 601 Squadron pilots. In the "400 Club" in Leicester Square Max Aitken and Billy Clyde had drawn a lot of diagrams on the tablecloth and lectured me on what to do if I ever got into cloud.

"Straighten the aircraft up first," said Max, "and think. You usually go into cloud sideways."

"Always watch your safety height," said Billy. "Get back on your original course, then turn slowly and gently – a steady Rate 1 turn – back on to your reciprocal heading, and retrace your steps. Leave your throttle setting where it was when you entered the cloud, and let down in as shallow a dive as possible."

The next day was one of those exceptional days when the dew point had risen dramatically. With the variation in temperature the whole of Central England was shrouded in cloud, much of it right down to the deck. After setting out in lovely sunshine, I flew straight into the muck as I headed north-west over the Cotswolds. The options were now few.

I couldn't bale out because I was wearing a skirt! The wartime black stockings were a bit short and left off just above my knees. My wartime panties, made out of silk from old parachutes, didn't come down to meet the stockings so there was a large gap of me in between. And, anyway, the 'chute straps chafed the insides of my legs. But I knew I had passed Little Rissington on the way up. That was 750 feet above sea level and was presumably still in sunshine. I would turn on my gyro compass as Max and Billy had said and try to put down there. I would give myself a break-off height of 800 feet – madness only having 50 feet to spare, but I knew no better then.

The altimeter began to fall alarmingly to 600 feet. At that moment I broke cloud at tree-top level. The

First Officer Joan Taylor ATA in the cockpit of a presentation Spitfire V 'Adele Astaire', which she is about to deliver from the factory to a Maintenance Unit.

trees flashed by with cloud just resting on the tops, and the rain pelting down.

Then, momentarily, I caught a glimpse of an aircraft on a small stretch of grass. Little Rissington, I thought, and turned tightly, keeping the little bolt-hole in view. It looked more like a pond that a landing ground as the rain cascaded down.

I landed – splosh! And at once I wondered whether the Spitfire would go up on its nose. But I skidded through the puddles and eventually came safely to rest. A tall RAF man came out of a Nissen hut with a camouflaged rain cape held aloft over his head. As he

came up to the aircraft I got out on to the wing – and my knees collapsed.

"I say, Miss, you must be good on instruments."

I did not want to disillusion him, nor did I want to give the game away that I was lost. Just then I saw a large notice board: "RAF Station Windrush. Navigation and Blind-Flying Establishment. Altitude 560ft". My knees began to give way again, and I was glad of the mug of steaming tea that the RAF man brought me.'

Diana Barnato Walker – Air Transport Auxiliary (ATA) pilot (OOTB)

Second Officer Helen Harrison ATA delivers at Spitfire IX in style in November 1943, by which time there were almost 100 women pilots in the ATA.

1944: Typhoon shuttle

'In June 1944, shortly after D-Day, Group Support Units (GSU) were set up to keep the 2nd Tactical Air Force (2TAF) supplied with aircraft, but No 83 GSU based at Redhill was directly under the track of the V-1 flying bombs. The decision was therefore made to move it to a field near Bognor. On 24 June, after taking a Halifax from Radlett to Linton-on-Ouse and a Whitley from Honeybourne to Llandow, my final task of the day was to fly a Mustang from St Athan to Redhill.

There, before I had even switched off the engine, a man climbed on to the wing to tell me that I must take the aircraft on to Bognor. The following day, Sunday 25 June, a team of No 1 Ferry Pool (FP) pilots descended on Redhill to move the remaining aircraft. My stint in this operation was:

Typhoon JP371	*Redhill-Bognor*	*15 minutes*
Typhoon MN919	*Redhill-Bognor*	*20 minutes*
Typhoon MN309	*Redhill-Bognor*	*15 minutes*
Auster MT366	*Redhill-Bognor*	*30 minutes*
Spitfire BS499	*Redhill-Bognor*	*16 minutes*
Hurricane KZ610	*Redhill-Bognor*	*20 minutes*

Some pilots moved more than this six, and the taxi pilot who ferried us back and forth in the Anson recorded 7 hours 35 minutes flying.'

Lettice Curtis – Air Transport Auxiliary (ATA) pilot (FP)

WAAF plotters in the No 12 Group Sector Control Room at Digby in 1943 tracking aircraft over The Wash.

WAAF Dorothy Turner updates the Digby Sector Control Room, with details of all the headings listed on the right-hand side of the notice board.

1944: Sheared

'You could do anything with a Merlin-engined Spitfire. For example, I had a complete engine failure – the only one ever from Castle Bromwich – "shearing of the fuel pump drive", my log book says. But what I didn't tell them was that I had been flying mainly upside-down to give the new American Flying Fortress gunners some practice for about 15 minutes!

I got down at Edgehill with no other damage whatsoever, and that was Mark IX MJ889 that later went to 349 (Free French) Sqn.'

John Jordan – Air Transport Auxiliary (ATA) pilot

from No 5 BFTS run by the Riddle-McKay Aero College at Clewiston, Florida, in December 1943 with 240 hours flight training. The following year he was posted to the ATA's 1FTS at Barton to fly another 100 hours on Magisters, Proctors and the Fairchild Argus. By the end of 1944 he transferred to No 5(T)FP at Thame to convert to the Spitfire after 50 hours on the Harvard. For the remaining months of the war T/Off Lewis, now authorised to fly Class 2 aircraft, ferried Spitfires, Seafires and Fireflies to and from 23 different British airfields.

Many of the female pilots were married to serving RAF pilots, such as Charlie Willis and Derek Walker, the latter's wife Diana being the daughter of the business magnate Woolf Barnato. All were expected to fly anything the men flew, from a

Typhoon to a Stirling bomber, often having never seen the type before they were ordered to ferry it to an airfield into which they had never flown. The ATA pilot's only aids were a map and brief Ferry Pilot's Notes, which only covered the bare essentials of the type they were to fly. They were supposed to fly only in clear weather, but taking off under such conditions did not mean that it would be the same at their destination, and as they were prohibited from using the radio to check, many had to put down at any airfield they could see. This often meant long waits on the ground with no food or accommodation. Nevertheless, ATA pilots ferried a total of 308,567 aircraft, including 57,826 Spitfires, before the service was disbanded on 30 November 1945, by which time 143 pilots had lost their lives.

1944: Ladies first

'In August, 247 Sqn converted from Spitfire IXs to Tempests to chase "doodle-bugs". My pilots were a little anxious about flying the new Tempest. However, the first aircraft was delivered to West Malling by the Air Transport Auxiliary (ATA), and the pretty young lady who piloted it powdered her nose and put lipstick on before she got out of the cockpit, so they decided that the Tempest was not that difficult to fly.'

James F. 'Eddie' Edwards – Canadian Fighter Command pilot

Chapter 7
Night fighting

On 5 August 1917 a London Air Defence Area (LADA) was established in response to raids on the capital by German airships and Gotha bombers. All the 16 Home Defence Group fighter squadrons of the RFC and RNAS were put under the control of LADA, and a policy of aircraft patrols and a screen of anti-aircraft guns surrounding London caused the Gothas to switch to night attacks. The first heavy night raid took place on 24 September when 13 Gothas attacked London. None were intercepted but five LADA fighters were lost on the night, mainly due to landing accidents.

The first Gotha was shot down on the night of 28 January by two Sopwith Camels of No 44 Sqn based at Hainault Farm. Its commanding officer was a Major G. W. Murlis-Green, who would finish the war with 20 confirmed victories. Another Gotha was attacked without result by a Bristol fighter of 39 Sqn, the squadron that had shot down no fewer than four German airships in 1916. However, one of the squadron's Bristol fighters flown by Lt A. J. Arkell finished off a Gotha that had been damaged by a 78 Sqn Camel on the night of 19/20 May, the last Gotha attack on London. Altogether, 24 Gothas were shot down by aircraft or AA fire during night raids on London and the basic principles of aerial night fighting had been established.

However, with no navigation or communications aids it was a hazardous occupation, as many pilots found to their cost, including one of the RFC's top 'aces', the Australian Capt Robert A. Little, who was credited with the destruction of 47 German aircraft over the Western Front. He lost his life on the night of 20 May attacking Gothas over London while on leave in England. One who survived, and would become a leading proponent of night-fighting aircraft, was Major C. J. Q. Brand, who was promoted to Commanding Officer of 44 Sqn in 1919.

A few days before the start of the Battle of Britain Air Vice-Marshal Sir Christopher Quintin Brand KBE, DSO, MC, DFC was appointed Air Officer Commanding (AOC) No 10 Group, tasked with the defence of South West England. His fellow First World War night-fighting exponent, Group Captain Murlis-Green, was then the station commander of

RAF Aston Down, and the two men had seen little progress in the art of night fighting in the intervening 20 years. The development of the radio telephone (R/T) had solved the fighter pilot's communications problem, but it was the research into Radio Direction Finding (RDF) systems led by Sir Robert Watson Watt and Henry Tizard in the late 1930s that would revolutionise night-fighting tactics.

Although the emphasis had been centred on establishing a network of ground RDF stations, at the outbreak of the Second World War the new technology was being used to develop Ground Control of Interception (GCI) radar and, more crucially, Airborne Intercept (AI) radar.

At that time Fighter Command had no dedicated night-fighting units, and night defence was still the responsibility of day-fighter squadrons. Pilots were given limited night-flying training to be able, in co-operation with searchlights, to shoot down enemy bombers. During the 'Phoney War' little of or no attempt was made to intercept the occasional night raid over the British Isles, and even during the German *Blitzkrieg* of Scandinavia and the Low Countries few night sorties were flown by either side.

An experimental version of airborne radar, which could locate aircraft from 2 miles down to 300 yards, was installed in a Battle aircraft in June 1939, and by October early production versions of AI were being provided for a flight of Blenheim IVFs of Nos 25 and 600 Sqns. At the same time 604 Sqn at RAF Northolt was informed that its Blenheims would be used exclusively for night-fighting operations in the future, although it did not receive any AI radar equipment.

The twin-engine Blenheim had the space for the cumbersome and heavy AI together with a radar operator, who was in the main an air gunner undergoing AI training at RAF Manston under S/Ldrs Walter Pretty and John Tester. However, the added weight reduced the Blenheim's top speed to below that of most of the *Luftwaffe*'s bombers. None the less, a Blenheim made the first successful radar-controlled night interception of an enemy aircraft on 5 February 1940 when F/Lt Smith shot down an He 111 off the Suffolk coast.

Above The Bristol Blenheim IF was the first of Fighter Command's aircraft to be tasked specifically in the night-fighting role, but for the first year of the war was operated without any night-fighting aids.

Below Early night sorties by Blenheim IFs led to a number of accidents such as this 604 Sqn example, which crash-landed at North Weald while being flown by Sgt Woolley on 29 February 1940.

1940: 'Blood Orange'

'I was in our hut at Bawdsey Manor on 5 February 1940. This was a completely blacked-out building that housed the Chain Home (CH) Radio Direction Finding (RDF) equipment and cathode ray tube. The four airmen technicians were on duty on the morning shift. Suddenly the airmen scanning the tube reported an aeroplane at 50 to 60 miles range. The best bearing we could get was south-south-east. We suspected the aircraft was German, looking for targets in the shipping lanes off the East Coast.

Bawdsey's calibration aircraft was a Bristol Blenheim based at Martlesham Heath, the historic home of the RAF's development flying. Its pilot was a F/Lt Smith – his personal callsign was "Blood Orange". "Blood Orange" Smith was always at readiness, armed up, refuelled and ready to scramble. I alerted him at once and within 5 minutes he was airborne and setting course. I knew that if there was a lot of chatter on the VHF, the German's control station in France would pick it up and he would be recalled. But I needed to get "Blood Orange" beyond the ground effect and interference of Bawdsey, and far enough seawards both to identify him and work out the track of the enemy aircraft. After we picked up our aircraft on the Trace, I gave "Blood Orange" the briefest of directions and a course to steer to ensure that I put him south and up-sun of the target, and well above it. We had tracked our adversary to a point 40 miles or so east of Aldeburgh, off the Suffolk coast, when Smith transmitted his excited

"Tally-ho!" He had sighted an He 111 below and was going in to the attack.

Some 2 or 3 minutes later (it seemed an age) "Blood Orange" called again. He was clearly distressed. He urgently requested an emergency course to steer for base. I gave him the answer: "Steer Two Five Zero for base."

Luck had taken a hand again, this time badly for Smith. He had followed the enemy aircraft down to confirm his kill, and the rear gunner of the Heinkel, courageously, had opened fire, hitting "Blood Orange" in the chest and upper arm. He just made Martlesham where he crash-landed the Blenheim; the emergency crews were ready to remove him from the aircraft and transfer him to an ambulance. He recovered in hospital.

"Blood Orange" had made history. He was the first pilot to destroy an enemy aircraft many miles from land as a result of a controlled interception. I had the good fortune to be the chap who helped him do it and to prove the theories of S/Ldrs Tester and Pretty, which could be turned to practical advantage in the future development of the direct radar control.'

Bill Farnes – Fighter Command Controller (OOTB)

AI Operator LAC Dennis Moody with members of a 604 Sqn Blenheim IF's groundcrew after an early Airborne Intercept (AI) sortie in March 1940.

Right *After being withdrawn from day operations during the Battle of Britain following unacceptable losses, 264 Sqn Defiant Is moved to Kirton-in-Lindsey to begin night patrols.*

Below *When night fighting became the predominant role of 151 Sqn at the end of 1940, it operated both Hurricanes and Defiant Is, one of which, AA436, is seen here.*

Prior to the Battle of Britain 25 Sqn Blenheims shot down three enemy aircraft on the night of 18 June for the loss of one Blenheim. Although the squadron had been involved in radar calibration exercises with CH stations, the Mk III AI equipment installed in its Blenheims in early 1940 was prone to give wavering and flared images on the early cathode ray tube (CRT) scopes, and it was not until Phase Two of the Battle of Britain that the first successful AI interception was made. This was by a Blenheim of the Fighter Interception Unit (FIU) using one of the first advanced Mk IV AI sets, which was vectored on to a Do 17 by the CH radar at Poling on the night of 23 July. When radar contact was established, the operator steered the pilot, F/Off G. Ashfield, towards the bomber, but it took P/Off G. E. Morris, who was in the nose acting as an observer, to catch sight of the Dornier, which was promptly shot down over the Channel.

The night-fighting Blenheim squadrons were also some of the first Fighter Command units to be fitted with VHF radio, which was vital for clear long-range communications, and by the end of the Battle of Britain six Blenheim squadrons had been equipped with AI equipment.

During the Battle itself several day-fighter squadron pilots had successfully intercepted enemy aircraft during 'Fighter Night' operations. These entailed the use of single-engined fighters on clear nights when the Germans were operating in strength. Moreover, Fighter Command always hoped that, when improved methods of searchlight control came into operation, single-engined fighters, even though they were not equipped with AI, would be able to operate effectively at night.

This proved to be the exception rather that the rule. The likes of F/Lt Adolph Gysbert 'Sailor' Malan shot down two He 111s on the clear moonlit night of 18 June 1940 flying a 74 Sqn Spitfire from Hornchurch, and F/Lt Allan Wright shot down another Heinkel near Bristol on the night of 29 August flying a Spitfire of 92 Sqn, although the AA gunners tried to claim it as theirs.

However, as the Battle of Britain entered its last phase Germany resorted to night raids on London, as it had some 23 years earlier. On 14 September a Night Air Defence Committee was convened under the chairmanship of the Marshal of the Royal Air Force, Sir John Salmon, to report to the Air Council. Although the committee acknowledged that it was still on AI, and on improved methods of controlling night fighters from the ground, that Fighter Command relied for the answer to its night-fighting problems, one of its members, AVM Sholto Douglas, recommended that there was a role for single-seater fighters as well.

Dowding did not agree, but the Air Council agreed with the argument for single-seaters and ordered him to allocate three Hurricane squadrons for night fighting. The real problem was suitable aircraft. The Blenheim was already obsolete, and two Defiant squadrons, already outclassed in the day battle and transferred in September to night fighting, were only a stop-gap. No 141 Sqn did, however, have some success by shooting down two He 111s on the night of 15/16 September during a 'Fighter Night' operation. In the event, two Hurricane Squadrons, Nos 85 and 151, were also trained for night operations in November.

There had been high hopes for the Blenheim's successor, the Bristol Beaufighter, which had made its maiden flight in July 1939. As fast as a Spitfire, the Beaufighter was armed with four 20mm cannon in the nose, considerably more firepower than the Blenheim's four .303in machine-guns. Unfortunately, it had more that its fair share of teething troubles and did not become fully operational until the end of 1940. Dowding best summed up Fighter Command's night-fighting position when he recorded, 'In nine cases out of ten, something would go wrong with the aircraft, or with the AI set, or with the RO Direction Finding System, or with the communication system, before an interception could be made.'

Air Chief Marshal Sir Hugh Dowding was retired as AOC-in-C on 24 November 1940. The fact that new aircraft, new AI equipment and new techniques of interception were coming into operation also raised the question of the proper training of pilots and operators for night fighting. All these problems had to be solved while the London Blitz was in progress. In those circumstances rapid improvement in the scale of fighter success at night was hardly to be expected. In response to these problems a specialist night-fighting Operational Training Unit, No 4 OTU, was established at Church Fenton in November, and new Defiant squadrons were formed to join the night-fighter force.

A series of Ground Control of Interception (GCI) stations were opened along the South and East coasts of England. Working directly from the GCI radar screen – or Plan Position Indicator (PPI) – the controller could see the relative positions of the night fighter's IFF blip and the target. Using this information he could direct the night fighter close enough to the target for its own AI radar to take over. However, the AI Mk IV radar was limited by the attacking aircraft's altitude due to the fact that the radar transmitted in all directions, so ground returns blotted out part of the CRT image. Consequently, a night fighter flying at 5,000 feet could not detect targets beyond a range of 5,000 feet.

1940: 'Mutton' Ops

'*After finishing a course on Blenheims with No 5 OTU at Aston Down, I was posted to No 420 Flight at Middle Wallop in October to fly Harrow bomber/transports as "night fighters"!*

This secret unit under the control of Farnborough RAE was formed to develop aerial mining. This consisted of towing 168 parachute mines along a 2,000-foot cable in front of an approaching enemy bomber formation as it crossed the southern English coastline. Known as Long Aerial Mines (LAM), the sorties were codenamed Mutton *operations, for obvious reasons. With the lumbering twin-engine bombers stripped of all but essential equipment and flown by a single pilot, we would climb to 20,000 feet and wait for the radar station to pick up any enemy bombers. Most nights nothing happened and the most exciting part of the 3½-hour sortie was dropping the mines without hitting any habitation below, which was difficult in the blackout.*

Dowding's response to the use of LAMs was, "It might be all right as long as you hit the enemy pilot in the eye."

Despite a certain lack of enthusiasm for aerial minelaying, two of our pilots, "Pat" Burke and "Tinker" Hayley-Bell, were each credited with destroying an enemy bomber with aerial mines in the winter months of 1940/41. The Flight, expanded into No 93 Squadron in December 1940, was now equipped with the first American Havocs, which had tricycle undercarriages, in addition to the five Harrows. The squadron also had a General Aircraft Cygnet light aircraft for tricycle landing practice, but this proved more difficult to handle than the heavier Havoc. "Pat" Burke and "Tinker" Hayley-Bell also claimed a probable each with LAM-equipped Havocs in April 1941, but aerial mining was abandoned soon after.'

William 'Will' Hoy – Fighter Command night-fighter pilot

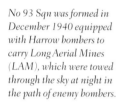

No 93 Sqn was formed in December 1940 equipped with Harrow bombers to carry Long Aerial Mines (LAM), which were towed through the sky at night in the path of enemy bombers.

Another aid in the battle against night raids was No 80 (Signals) Wing, which opened at Radlett in October 1940. Its task was to detect radio beams and other navigational aids used by the *Luftwaffe*. These beams were then 'bent' from their original course and other radio devices were mutilated by interference. Some 80 Wing units masqueraded as German beacons to give inaccurate 'fixes' to enemy raiders.

By early 1941 most of the Beaufighter's problems had been ironed out and the type began to build up a respectable score rate. The first confirmed kill by a Beaufighter was achieved by Sgts Hodginson and Benn of 219 Sqn when they shot down a Do 17 on 25/26 October 1940, by moonlight, but it was not until February 1941 that the type's first AI kill was registered. F/Lt John Cunningham of 604 Sqn had already shot down a Ju 88 by moonlight the previous November and an He 111 in December, but on the night of 15/16 February he and his radar operator, Sgt Jimmy Rawnsley, shot down another He 111 in bad weather using the AI. In April 1941 the same team destroyed seven enemy aircraft, three in one night, and damaged two more during April.

Another 604 Sqn pilot, Roderick Chisholm, destroyed four He 111s and damaged a Ju 88 during the same period. The Beaufighter 1F equipped with Mk IV AI was now Fighter Command's principal night fighter. Another pilot who was making his mark flying the Beaufighter IF was a certain F/Lt Guy Gibson, who shot down three enemy bombers and damaged another while flying with 29 Sqn between March and July 1941.

In the meantime those night fighters without the benefit of airborne radar soldiered on into 1941. There were now no fewer than seven Defiant night-fighter squadrons, but their successes were few. The leading exponents of night-fighting Defiants included Eric Barwell, who had shot down six German aircraft in day operations with the Defiant and was very critical of the waste of the type's potential. When 264 Sqn transferred to night fighting he increased his score by three in April 1941. The New Zealander Irving 'Black' Smith also scored at night with a Defiant of 151 Sqn, and he claimed at least one night victory flying one of the same squadron's Hurricanes.

However, it was a fellow pilot on 151 Sqn who was by far the most successful Hurricane night-fighter pilot. Richard Stevens was a pre-war commercial pilot who joined the RAF in 1939 at the age of 32. He was posted to 151 Sqn as it was about to be become a night-fighting unit at the end of 1940 and claimed his first two enemy aircraft in January 1941. It was rumoured that his wife and children had been killed in a German raid on Manchester, which may have

explained his single-minded determination to destroy *Luftwaffe* bombers whenever the opportunity came his way. By July 1941 he had become the RAF's top-scoring night-fighter pilot, and when he was killed over Holland chasing an enemy bomber in December, Stevens's score stood at 15 destroyed, two probable and one damaged, all at night flying Hurricanes without the benefit of AI.

New aircraft and night-fighting techniques were under trial in the early months of 1941, including the towing of aerial mines from Harrow, Wellington and Havoc bombers in the paths of enemy formations. No fewer than ten Air Target Illumination Units were formed with AI-equipped Bostons and Havocs fitted with high-powered Turbinlites in the nose; these would be accompanied by Hurricanes, which would move in to kill the enemy aircraft that had been intercepted and illuminated by the searchlight aircraft. These units were later formed into squadrons but, like the aerial mining experiment, failed to live up to expectations. Only two enemy aircraft were destroyed by this method in two years of Turbinlite operations, all falling to the same Squadron, No 538, which was commanded by S/Ldr E. J. B. Nicholson VC.

The American Douglas Havoc had more success as a pure night fighter equipping Nos 23 and 85 Sqns, the latter commanded by Battle of Britain 'ace' S/Ldr Peter Townsend, who scored one night victory with a Hurricane and another with a Havoc, known at the time as the Moonfighter, in April 1941. No 23 Sqn used the Havoc to great effect in night *Intruder* raids over enemy airfields in France, which Fighter Command had initiated in December 1940 using Blenheim IFs.

Nos 85 and 151 Sqns were joined by seven other Hurricane units, Nos 3, 43, 87, 96, 111, 245 and 257, most of which had either 12 .303in machine-gun-armed Hurricane IIBs or four 20mm-cannon-armed IICs, to concentrate on night *Intruder* patrols. The Blitz on Britain eased when Germany turned its attention to the invasion of the Soviet Union on 22 June, initially committing four *Luftflotten* to Operation *Barbarossa*.

More emphasis was then placed on *Intruder* missions, during which pilots had to seek out enemy aircraft over their own bases instead of waiting for them to come to them. During the following 12 months a number of pilots were able to rack up impressive scores, including 1 Sqn pilots S/Ldr James Maclachlan and the Czech F/Lt Karel Kuttelwascher, who claimed nine and 18 destroyed respectively. But these operations could be costly, as 418 (RCAF) Sqn flying Bostons was to find out, losing 18 aircraft and nearly 50 crew during 1942.

Far left After the
introduction of Ground
Control of Interception
(GCI) radar in early 1941,
which guided an aircraft
close enough to a target for its
own AI radar to take over,
night-fighter success rates
multiplied.

Left At Wellingore F/Lt Guy
Penrose Gibson of 29 Sqn
with his observer Sgt Richard
James and their Beaufighter
1F RO-C, R2250, named
'Admiral Foobang III',
celebrate the first of two
night victories on 14 March
1941.

Above *Roderick Chisholm scored his first AI victory flying a 604 Sqn Beaufighter IF on 13/14 March 1941 and claimed a total of nine destroyed and one probable by the end of the war.*

Below *604 Sqn Beaufighter IF NG-R R210, the personal mount of the squadron's CO, S/Ldr John Cunningham, at Middle Wallop in May 1941.*

Left *John 'Cats Eyes' Cunningham, who only had 'average' night vision, and his AI operator, Jimmy Rawnsley, formed Fighter Command's top-scoring night-fighter team; they had both joined 604 Sqn before the war. Cunningham finished the war as Fighter Command's leading night-fighter 'ace' with 20 destroyed and three probables.*

Below *A famed wartime cartoonist's caricature of Cunningham and Rawnsley in 1940.*

Below *Cunningham became a household name after shooting down three He IIIs on the night of 14/15 April 1941.*

The first successful Intruder aircraft of one of Fighter Command's first night-fighter units, No 23 Sqn, was the American Boston I, which entered service at Ford in March 1941.

1941: Dead ahead

'I took off from Middle Wallop at 2344hrs in a 604 Sqn Beaufighter 1F under Sopley Control. About 10 miles south of Bournemouth at 16,000 feet I was given a final vector of 310 degrees. My radar operator, F/Off Joll, had a contact ahead about 3-4,000 feet above. An AI chase ensued that lasted for 10-15 minutes owing to the enemy aircraft's alterations of course and height.

During this pursuit I climbed to 21,000 feet at 110-130mph, Sopley having warned me of the enemy aircraft's slow speed. Coming into minimum range without sighting the target, I had to drop back to about 5,000 feet and come in again. My operator told me that the enemy aircraft was above us and appeared to be diving. He told me to look dead ahead! I dropped the nose slightly and sighted the target silhouetted against the centre of a dark cloud at the same height, which was now 19,500 feet.

The enemy aircraft was about 800 yards ahead and was still weaving. I closed in gradually from dead astern and identified it as an He 111 with its flaps down. When 150-200 yards astern and slightly to starboard, I fired a 1-second burst, which caused instantaneous explosions in the fuselage. I broke off to port, noticing as I did so two shorts bursts of return fire from the top rear gun. The shooting was high and well to the rear.

As I had overtaken quickly and as the Heinkel was maintaining height, with only a small amount of flame visible, I made a complete turn to port in order to attack again. Before I had completed the turn several explosions occurred, followed by a long trail of brilliant sparks, and the bomber began to lose height before finally bursting into flames and crashing on the outskirts of Frome.'

Hubert Paul Patten – Fighter Command night-fighter pilot

Left *Another doyen of night-fighting pilots was Eric Barwell, who shot down six enemy aircraft over Dunkirk while flying Defiants. After converting to night fighting he flew Defiants, Beaufighters and Mosquitos, claiming a total of nine aircraft and one V-1 destroyed.*

Left *Leading night-fighter 'ace' Bob Braham, seen here in his 29 Sqn Beaufighter IF, pioneered the Serrate system and finished the war with a total of 29 destroyed and two probables.*

1941: Bus drivers

'After flying Spitfires with No 64 Squadron since April 1940, I was posted in November to 307 Squadron, the first Polish night-fighter squadron, which was being formed at Kirton-in-Lindsey.

Equipped with the Defiant, an "old gentleman's aircraft", the squadron's Commanding Officer, Flight Commanders, Engineering and Intelligence Officers and a few of the gunners were British. I think I was selected because I spoke fluent French, my mother being French, and, having fought in the Battle of France, most of the Polish pilots spoke better French than English. To begin with we had to teach them the basic radio calls phonetically. Most of them had fought their way across Europe to become RAF fighter pilots and strongly objected to being turned into "bus drivers" for gunners. After heated appeals to the Air Ministry, the first batch of Polish pilots was replaced by a more docile intake.

However, during a practice alert at night one of these insisted on landing despite repeatedly being shown a red light. In the event he overshot, hit a pillbox, shedding a wing in the process, rolled over, shed the other wing and ended up in a haystack. Luckily there was no fire and he was pulled out of the wreckage alive, which showed how strong the Defiant was. At the subsequent enquiry the pilot was found to be colour blind. All the pilots were then tested for colour blindness, and most of them failed.

The third batch of Polish pilots posted to 307 Squadron were mostly pre-war airline pilots, test pilots and record-breakers, and the squadron became operational at Jurby on the Isle of Man in February 1941 before moving to Exeter.'

Hubert Paul Patten – Fighter Command night-fighter pilot

F/Lt Paul Patten was a British Flight Commander with the first Polish night-fighter unit, No 307 (Polish) Sqn, during its work-up at Jurby.

Above *1458 Flight was formed in July 1941 as part of 93 Sqn, with Douglas Havoc Is equipped with Turbinlites to illuminate targets for accompanying Hurricanes to shoot down. They were not a success.*

Below *Members of 604 Sqn on the steps of the Officers' Mess at Middle Wallop on 15 July 1941 celebrating the Squadron's 50th victory. The group includes, from the left, P/Off Derek 'Professor' Jackson RO, married to heiress Penelope Mitford, F/Lt Olliffe-Lee (Adjutant), F/Lt Corbic Gomm (with dark glasses), past CO S/Ldr M. F. Anderson, present CO W/C Appleton, and, looking over his shoulder, F/Lt Hugh Speke, who would lose his life two weeks later.*

Defiant II crews of 125 Sqn at Fairwood Common in October 1941. Left to right: P/Off 'Prune' Matthews, P/Off Johnny Surman, P/Off Morgan (Adjutant), P/Off 'Col' Colmore, F/Lt James Bailey, Sgt 'Walt' Walters, P/Off 'Morg' Morgan, and Sgts Tom Sharpe, 'Dicky' Bastow, 'Jonah' Jones, 'Tiki' Allen, 'Bren' Lacey, John Newton and 'Paddy' White.

Aircrews of 125 (Newfoundland) Sqn at Fairwood Common in December 1941. Left to right: P/Offs 'Pat' Boyd, John Turnbull, Ron White and John Bentley, CO S/Ldr 'Auntie B' Barwell, P/Offs 'Lofty' Youings and Dan Shephard, Adjutant P. Morgan, 'Gabby' Gavegan and 'Knobby' Hall.

A small number of General Aircraft Owlets were issued to Nos 23 and 605 night-fighter squadrons to help pilots convert to American Bostons and Havocs, which had tricycle undercarriages.

1941: No trade

'On 29 August the day culminated in a long Mandolin, intruder at night, with 247 Sqn Hurricane IIBs, the long-range jobs, covering reconnaissance of Lannion and Morlaix airfields down towards Brest, a look at Brest, to Rennes and home.

With Sgt Doherty as my Number 2 we flew around at 2,000 feet in open formation, visibility good after taking off at 2200hrs and making landfall at Ile de St Batz and thence to Lannion where there was no activity. Several lights were seen, some vehicles on the road from Lannion to Morlaix, which we followed towards Brest. Nothing at Morlaix, but approaching Brest our presence was noted by some flak-firing towards us. Though we were quite a distance from them, the bursts were very high and they obviously thought we were bombers.

Skirting the town, which was clearly visible, we turned inland flying east towards Rennes. Several beacons were visible but little activity of any kind seen. As we were approaching Rennes at 1,800 feet the lights of the town were quite bright and could have been mistaken for runway lighting, or a dummy flare-path.

From there we turned west again and made our way to the French coast, passing near Lannion. We landed back at Predannack at 0130hrs after 3hr 30min of uneventful but pleasant flight, but no trade.'

Kenneth W. 'Mac' Mackenzie – Fighter Command pilot

On the night of 30/31 May 1942 Bomber Command launched its first thousand-bomber raid with the support of Fighter Command's night fighters. Two squadrons of Bostons, Nos 23 and 418, with Nos 1 and 3 Sqn's Hurricanes, were tasked with *Intruder* patrols over *Luftwaffe* night-fighter bases in Holland along the bombers' projected track. The Hurricanes could only claim two probables and three damaged enemy aircraft during the operation, while a 23 Sqn Boston was shot down over Schipol and two of its crew killed. Bomber Command lost 41 aircraft that night.

Sir Quintin Brand's No 10 Group controlled six night-fighter squadrons in 1942 and made it clear to their commanders that 'if the Hun is flying … so can you!' There were also five radar stations in No 10 Group, which gave the local units more accurate and efficient controlling and better chances of successful

interceptions. By mid-year updated variants of the Beaufighter were being delivered along with the latest Mk VII AI radar, but the biggest boost to Fighter Command's night-fighter force had come at the beginning of 1942 when the first DH Mosquito entered service with 157 Sqn. Powered by two Rolls-Royce Merlin engines, the light and manoeuvrable all-wood-construction Mosquito had a maximum speed of almost 400mph and a range of more than 1,700 miles with underwing tanks. With the two-man crew seated side-by-side under a well-glazed armoured canopy and carrying the punch of four 20mm cannon and four .303in machine-guns, the Mosquito proved to be an outstanding night fighter and intruder, flying its first night sortie on 27/28 April 1942.

On 29 May S/Ldr G. Ashfield, who had made the first AI-assisted interception nearly two years earlier,

A black-painted 87 Sqn Hurricane IIC night intruder named 'Cawnpore I' and flown from Charmy Down by its CO, S/Ldr Dennis Smallwood, in early 1942.

Above *No 247 Sqn flew its Hurricane IICs flying night intruder and Roadstead sorties with No 10 Group throughout 1942 before converting to Typhoons and returning to day operations in 1943.*

Left *604 Sqn night-fighter 'aces' relax in the Pheasant inn near Middle Wallop in the spring of 1942. Left to right: Micky Phillips, John Cunningham, Jeremy Howard-Williams, Norwegian Johan Rad, Bob Wright and another Norwegian, Per Bugge.*

Left *Beaufighter IIF R2270, the unloved Merlin-engined variant that entered service with 604 Sqn for a brief period before being passed on to 406 (RCAF) Sqn in 1942.*

Below left *Mosquito NF.II DZ238 YP-H, named 'Babs', was delivered to 23 Sqn at Bradwell Bay in late 1942.*

Above *A Fighter Command Mosquito NF.II shows off its firepower by firing tracer from its four 20mm cannon and four .303in machine-guns.*

scored a probable Do 217, but 157 Sqn's first confirmed night victory was claimed by the CO, W/C R. G. Slade, on the night of 22 August. The worst night of the year for Fighter Command's night fighters occurred on 8/9 September when three Mosquitos of 23 Sqn on *Night Intruder* sorties over Holland and two Beaufighters on interception patrols failed to return.

More advances in radar technology emerged the following year with the introduction of the first British centimetric radar, the Mk VIII AI, which was fitted into the Mosquito NF.XII and the Beaufighter VIF; by mid-1943 Fighter Command had ten Mosquito squadrons and nine Beaufighter squadrons so equipped. All night-fighting Hurricanes, Defiants and Havocs had now been replaced.

One of the new technologies was *Serrate*, a radar countermeasures device that homed in on the *Lichtenstein* AI radar used by *Luftwaffe* night fighters and which was first issued to Beaufighter IVFs of 141 Sqn. By the end of the year the Squadron's CO, S/Ldr Bob Braham, and his radar operator, F/Off W. J. 'Sticks' Gregory, had overtaken John 'Cats Eyes' Cunningham as Fighter Command's top-scoring

night fighter. A second *Serrate* Squadron, No 239, was later formed with Mosquito NF.IIs to provide fighter support for Bomber Command night raids.

Throughout the year pressure on German-occupied Western Europe was increased both day and night culminating in the division of Fighter Command to create the Air Defence of Great Britain (ADGB) and the 2nd Tactical Air Force (2TAF) in November. Six Mosquito squadrons were assigned to 2TAF while nine Mosquito and two Beaufighter squadrons were retained by the ADGB.

As the Allies prepared for the invasion of France, the *Luftwaffe* launched Operation *Steinbock*, a 'Baby Blitz' at the end of January 1944. Twenty-one raids of between 100 and 200 German bombers attacked London and the southern counties over the next three months. RAF night fighters flew 1,850 sorties during this period, accounting for some 120 enemy aircraft.

For some time prior to D-Day *Intruder* patrols increased, although during the days immediately preceding Operation *Overlord* night-fighting squadrons carried out 'normal patrols' in order not to forewarn the Germans of the impending invasion of

Beaufighter VIF V8324, with a dihedral tailplane for added directional stability, served with 29 Sqn in 1943 before being issued to 51 OTU.

1943: Some bastard's firing at us!

'Four lines of tracer streaked over the canopy, and almost simultaneously we heard the rattle of cannons. There was a shout from the navigator: "Some bastard's firing at us!"

"I know." I had already pushed everything – stick, rudder, throttles – into the bottom right-hand corner. As night intruders, No 141 Squadron's remit that night was for one flight to escort Lancasters, which were to attack Peenmunde, out as far as the limited range of our Beaufighters would allow. Our other flight was, later, to meet the returning bombers as deep into Germany as possible and escort them home. Our targets were the enemy night fighters that ranged along the bomber's route.

Mike Allen and I were approaching Hamburg at about 16,000 feet on a clear but very dark night. Mike had picked up a contact on his radar. Normally we would know from the type of contact whether it was hostile or not. This time we did not. I suppose that was why I was less alert than I should have been. I presumed it would be "one of ours".

Using our radar we closed rapidly from 2 to 3 miles, and had to lose height to put our target slightly above so I could identify it visually against the rather lighter sky. Going "downhill" we had built up a fair overtaking speed. At 500 feet I realised that this shape was an Me 110, a twin-engined German night fighter.

I swore. I was closing too fast to open fire. I eased back the throttles. I dared not snap them shut – if I did there would have been sheets of flame from the exhaust and we would be seen. To help lose speed I turned hard to port, then to starboard. It was at that precise instant that we became the target. The Me 110 must have seen us slip from underneath him and then, slowing down, turn to port and starboard in front of him. A gift!

If it had not been for the momentary glimpse of four lines of tracer streaking past, I would not have had that split-second lead, which I needed to get the hell out of it. If he had not used tracer – and only some German night fighters did – he would have had time to correct his aim before I knew I was being attacked. Chastened, breathing deeply, but having evaded, we climbed back to our operating height.

But neither Mike nor I was in the mood to let matters rest, and 20 minutes later, using our radar, we were closing slowly on a known enemy aircraft. Even at full throttle it took an age. Our opponent was obviously on his way towards our returning stream of bombers. Mike read off the range: "1,500 feet … 1,200 feet … 1,000 feet." It looked like another Me 110. "900 feet." It was an Me 110. "Still 900 feet." And again, "Still 900 feet."

Even at full throttle we could not close the range further. I took aim. Nine hundred feet is not ideal on a dark night. I opened fire with our four cannons and six machine-guns. There were strikes, like fireworks – flecks of flame – flashes. The Messerschmitt dived steeply. It might have been destroyed but we could not be sure. We climbed to our operating height again and reset course to meet our returning bombers. On we went eastwards. Shortly there was another enemy radar contact.

"It's a Ju 88, Mike."

My navigator grunted and looked up from the radar. "Fix him properly," he said. "Don't bugger about this time."

Slowly I closed to 700 feet. I took careful aim and gave him everything. The fire flashed through the fuselage and engulfed the port engine. The Junkers was well alight. It spiralled down, shedding pieces of burning aircraft. Minutes later it blew up as it hit the ground.

With fuel now critical, we set course for base. We had made a hash of one attack, and had only survived to make two successful attacks that same night because our attacker had – by chance – been armed with visible tracer ammunition, which for Mike and me had been the difference between life and death.'

Harold Edward 'Harry' White – Fighter Command night-fighter pilot (OOTB)

The high-altitude Mosquito NF.XV was issued to only a handful of units in 1943, including the Fighter Interceptor Unit (FIU) and 85 Sqn at West Malling.

1943: A detached view

'It was less harrowing on night operations, when you went over the Low Countries for an hour looking for targets of opportunity for your Typhoon's four 20mm cannon and two 1,000lb bombs. It was fun shooting up trains, but although we must have killed some innocent railwaymen, it was more detached because of the darkness.

On operations there was an elation mixed with foreboding to which you never confessed and which you countered with banter and booze-ups in the mess.'

Richard Hough – Fighter Command night-intruder pilot (DT)

Normandy. On 6 June most night-fighter squadrons encountered very little opposition, and it would be some days before scores began to mount.

On the night of 14/15 June a Mosquito NF.XIII of 410 (RCAF) Sqn shot down an unusual *Mistel* composite aircraft off the Normandy coast. This was an unmanned Ju 88 filled with explosives and controlled by a manned Fw 190 fighter mounted on top. When it had acquired its target, the control aircraft would release the flying bomb and return to base.

It was another month before the first night squadrons moved to forward airfields in France, but before this happened they were to be heavily involved in the battle against the V-1 flying bomb. At 0407hrs on 13 June the Royal Observer Corps post at Dymchurch plotted a 'bogey' flying north-west at 1,000 feet. The unusual sound of its flight, and the fact that its white light and red glow could be seen, prompted the post to report it as a 'pilotless aircraft', which in fact it was.

A V-1 'doodlebug' carried under the port wing of a KG 53 He 111 H-20 'mother' aircraft that air-launched the flying bomb over the Channel some 50 miles from the English coast.

The ADGB's night fighters had a new and numerous target, and it was the following night that they opened their *Diver* score when a 605 Sqn Mosquito shot a V-1 down over the Channel and was seriously damaged by the debris as it exploded at close range. Although the pilots had not been briefed about these ultra-secret flying bombs, they soon became much-sought-after prey, particularly for the Mosquitos, which had the speed required to catch a V-1 flying at low level at almost 400mph.

Once interception tactics were worked out, and anti-*Diver* patrols became routine, they were destroyed in their hundreds. As Allied bombing also took its toll on V-1 launch sites in France and Holland, He 111s of KG 53 were used to air-launch flying bombs in ever-increasing numbers. One of these was intercepted by a 125 Sqn Mosquito NF.XVII flown by F/Lt Dick Leggett on the night of 22/23 December 1944. With his radar observer, F/Off 'Midi' Midlane, using the latest Mk X AI, he picked up some 'trade' over the North Sea and stalked the Heinkel for almost an hour before shooting it down over Holland.

At the end of the six-month V-1 campaign, which ceased in January 1945, RAF night fighters had destroyed 486 flying bombs with No 96 Sqn accounting for no fewer than 174, while 418 (RCAF) and 605 Sqns scored 90 and 72 respectively. The top-scoring pilot was F/Sgt Bryan with 61 destroyed,

closely followed by F/Off P. del Brooke of 264 Sqn with 53.

As the Allies pressed on throughout occupied Europe towards Germany, there was less 'trade' for the night fighters and a number of squadrons were disbanded at the end of 1944. Others became heavily involved in bomber support, and there were the occasional combats even in the last few weeks of the war. A Mosquito NF.XXX of 29 Sqn shot down an Me 262 on 24 April, but on the debit side a similar Mosquito of 25 Sqn was shot down by German night fighters on the last night of the war.

Fighter Command's top-scoring night-fighter pilot was John 'Cat's Eyes' Cunningham, who destroyed 20 enemy aircraft, all but four flying Beaufighters with 604 Sqn, and most of them with his radar operator, Jimmy Rawnsley. His close rival was Bob Braham, who claimed 19 destroyed at night, two probables and five damaged before being shot down on 25 June 1944 to spend the rest of the war as a PoW in *Stalag Luft III*. Desmond Hughes, who claimed his first night victories with the Defiant, finished the war with 12 destroyed.

No 85 Sqn was the top-scoring night-fighting unit with over 200 victories, closely followed by 600 Sqn with 180. The leading Commonwealth squadron was No 418 (RCAF), which accounted for 103 enemy aircraft at night, while another five squadrons, Nos 96, 151, 219, 264 and 604, scored more than 100.

Right 604 Sqn groundcrew,
Sgt Wilson third from left
with the pilot and navigator
to his left, pose in front a rare
'shark's mouth' Mosquito
NF.XIII at Hurn in
May 1944.

Below A Czech pilot and
navigator about to climb
aboard their 68 Sqn
Mosquito NF.XIX on a bleak
winter's night at Coltishall in
November 1944.

NIGHT FIGHTING

1944: Opposing bombers

'When flying Mosquito night fighters with 125 Sqn, my superb navigator, Egbert J. "Midi" Midlane and I were sometimes diverted through bad weather to a main bomber-stream airfield. After debriefing at their base we could always tell if the Bomber Command Pathfinder Force (PFF) had made a "cock-up" of laying their flare markers on the target. If this was the case the bomber crews were laughing and joking with us. However, if they were miserable and dejected, "Midi" and I knew that the Pathfinders had done a good job.

The enmity between "the opposing forces" was bizarre, but a fact of operational life.'

Richard W. 'Dick' Leggett – Fighter Command night-fighter pilot

Left F/Lt R. W. 'Dickie' Leggett with his navigator, F/Off Egbert J. 'Midi' Midlane of 125 Sqn at Coltishall, from where they shot down a He 111 H-20 V-1 air-launcher on the night of 23/24 December 1944.

Below A line-up of 125 (Newfoundland) Sqn Mosquito NF.XVIIs at Church Fenton a month before the end of the war, the Squadron having claimed 44 destroyed in four years of night fighting.

Chapter 8
On the offensive

A t the end of 1940 Fighter Command's new AOC-in-C, Air Chief Marshal William Sholto Douglas, had to take stock and plan for the next stage of the air war. No 9 and 14 Groups had been formed in November, headquartered at Barton Hall at Preston, covering North West England, and the Drunmossie Hotel at Inverness, covering the Highlands and Islands of Scotland. New OTUs were opening under the command of No 81 Group, which was headquartered at RAF Sealand.

Veteran combat pilots were posted to Group and Wing HQs while Fighter Command lost other experienced pilots to the rapidly expanding Middle East theatre. To replace them new inexperienced pilots were beginning to filter through from the Empire Air Training Schemes and the OTUs, which had returned to the full six-month courses that had been abandoned at the height of the Battle of Britain.

Improved variants of the Hurricane and Spitfire were being delivered. Apart from upgraded Merlin engines, the main advance was made in the armament. Many pilots considered that during the Battle of Britain the Spitfire and Hurricane were outgunned by the Bf 109, which was armed with two MG 17 7.9mm machine-guns together with two MG FF 20mm cannon. In response to this perceived disadvantage, the Spitfire's wing was redesigned to accommodate a 20mm cannon in place of two of its Brownings. Known as the 'B' wing, it was first fitted to 30 Mk 1 aircraft on the production line, and these were issued to 19 Sqn in August 1940. The gun selected was the Hispano-Suiza 20mm Oerlikon cannon, ironically the same gun as that used by the *Luftwaffe* Bf 109E, the Spitfire's opponent in the Battle of Britain. A licence agreement was purchased in 1937 and the first of the 45,582 Hispano cannons built during the Second World War was delivered from the BSA factory at Sparkbrook, Birmingham, in April 1940.

Shoehorning the 52.8-inch-long cannon into the thin wing proved a problem, and a blister fairing had to be fitted over the ammunition feed drums. The Hispano Mk I cannon was also plagued by frequent jamming caused by an unreliable feed mechanism and ejector. The Spitfire IBs were unpopular, their pilots thinking that a total firing period of only 6 seconds – if the gun did not jam – was too short for accurate aiming.

Although a prototype cannon-armed Spitfire had shot down a Do 17 in March 1940, the new gun's teething problems were not ironed out until the introduction of the Spitfire IIB, after the Battle of

Following the Battle of Britain, Fighter Command Spitfires and Hurricanes were identified by a wide band around the rear fuselage as seen on this 66 Sqn Spitfire II in late 1940.

Amongst those promoted to Wing Leader in 1941 was Douglas Bader, seen here with the Czech S/Ldr Anton Hess who scored his first victories with 312 (Czech) Sqn in September 1940.

Above *After landing upside down following a misjudged approach at Acklington in May 1941, this badly damaged 72 Sqn Spitfire I was rebuilt and served with a number of OTUs until 1950.*

Below *Spitfire II P7753 'Pampero I' was presented by the British Community in Buenos Aires and served with 616 Sqn at Tangmere in March 1941 before being shot down on 5 May when flown by P/Off Lionel Casson, who baled out over the Channel.*

1941: Tangmere days

'At the age of 18 years I enlisted in the RAF as a Clerk General Duties/Shorthand Typist and was attested and sworn-in at Penarth, South Wales, on 28 February 1941. After basic training at Melksham, Wiltshire, I arrived at Tangmere near Chichester, Sussex, on 4 April, having been posted to No 616 Squadron to work in the orderly room.

As the squadron had been formed in Doncaster, the original ground staff all came from Doncaster, Gainsborough and areas of South Yorkshire and Lincolnshire, but by 1941 some of these original members had been posted away and their places taken by men from all over the country. As a lad from Somerset, I was accepted into the presence of the original personnel and treated as one of their own.

The squadron's Spitfires were stationed at the far side of the aerodrome next to a Beaufighter squadron, and although this was some six months after the Battle of Britain, enemy planes were constantly coming across the Channel and over the southern counties. On the night of 8 April there were heavy air raids on Tangmere at 10.30pm and 6.00am the next morning, and No 5 Block had a direct hit with six killed and 16 injured. These were station personnel and not squadron, but after only four days with 616 it made me realise that ground staff were at risk from the dangers of air raids. There was also some machine-gunning by enemy planes during this period.

The following month 616 moved to Westhampnett, which was a satellite airfield of Tangmere close to Chichester. It had perimeter tracks but no runway. Our Orderly Room and Engineering Officer's Office, plus Adjutant and CO's Office, were in a marquee in the field just behind "A" Flight Dispersal. W/Cdr Douglas Bader was the Wing Leader at this time and his Spitfire was based with our "A" Flight. "Johnnie" Johnson and "Cocky" Dundas were also both members of "A" Flight.

More enemy aircraft attacked Tangmere and Westhampnett on the nights of 11 and 16 May. It was because of these raids that a number of 616 ground staff were sleeping in Goodwood House, situated on the top of the Sussex Downs, to be away from the airfield.

The squadron was involved in several sweeps and scrambles during this period. It was always an anxious time when the planes took off as we knew that they had to be back in 2 hours' time – the Spitfire's maximum endurance. At times during these flights we would look skyward to the south to see if we could spot the aircraft returning, and see if the cloth covering the guns had been torn, indicating that the guns had been fired.

When they came back in formation we knew that there had been no fights in the air, but when they came back in ones and twos we just waited to see if all 12 were back at base – if not, Casualty Signals would follow.'

Dennis J. Hill – Fighter Command Clerk/General Duties

Britain was over, and, in mid-1941, the Mk VB. The Hurricane IIB was fitted with 12 .303in machine-guns, while the IIC was armed with four 20mm cannon. New types being introduced into service included the Westland Whirlwind, a twin-engine single-seat long-range fighter armed with four 20mm cannon, and the heavyweight successor to the Hurricane, the Hawker Typhoon.

AVM Leigh-Mallory was, as AOC No 11 Group, now free to deploy his 'Big Wings' on offensive operations across the Channel. Known as *Circuses*, these operations were fighter-escorted daylight raids by Bomber Command aircraft against short-range

targets designed to bring German fighters into battle. They were not popular with the bomber crews, who were in effect acting as bait. More successful were the *Rhubarb* operations, small-scale freelance fighter raids on ground targets of opportunity.

In the first six months of 1941 Fighter Command flew almost 3,000 sorties on these operations and lost more than 50 pilots in the process. Following the German invasion of the Soviet Union on 22 June 1941, *Rhubarbs* were increased together with *Roadsteads*, *Ramrods* and *Jim Crows*, which were, respectively, low-level attacks on enemy shipping, escorting bomber raids, and fighter patrols over the Channel.

Above *This group of pilots of 501 (County of Gloucester) Sqn in the spring of 1941 includes Battle of Britain 'aces' OC Ken Holden seated centre, 'Ginger' Lacey seated far left, Ken Mackenzie second from right, 'Lofty' Dafforn second from left and the Pole, Stanislaw Skalski far right.*

Below *A flight of 501 Sqn's Spitfire Is soon after they replaced the squadron's Hurricanes at Chilbolton in June 1941.*

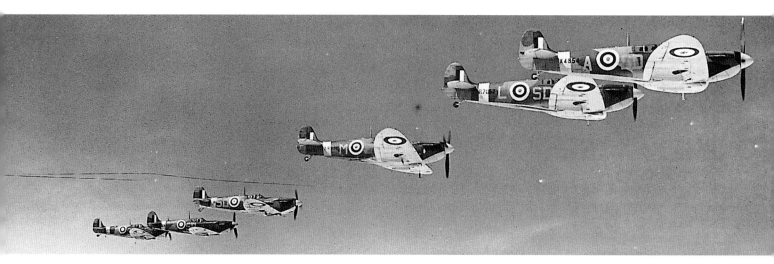

1941: Down but not out

'After putting my damaged Spitfire down in a farm near St Omer in northern France, I destroyed the radio and other secret items and began walking away from the area. As darkness fell I was on the outskirts of a small village. I walked in through the partially opened front door of one of the houses. It was occupied by a man and two women, one of whom immediately drew the curtain across the window. I stood there in my uniform and explained in my poor French that I was a British pilot, and hungry. I was told to sit down and was given some fried eggs on toast. With the help of an English/French dictionary we began a halting conversation.

The man told me he had a farming friend who, he believed, could help me to contact the French underground organisation. He promised to take me to him in the morning. That night I slept fully clothed with the window wide open, ready to slip out if necessary. In the morning the man produced a spare bicycle. He said I was to cycle a short distance behind him and he would give warning of German patrols.

We eventually arrived at a house where I was questioned closely by two other Frenchmen. I could not understand all the questions, and they seemed rather agitated. Finally, they left me and went into a back room. After a few minutes one of them came back. It was M Fillerin, who was to help more than 30 aircrew to join the escape route before being arrested

on suspicion of being a member of the underground, and put in the notorious Buchenwald concentration camp from which, happily, he was a survivor. He looked at me, then stubbed two fingers of one hand into the palm of the other. At the same time he gave the impression of an explosion.

I suddenly realised that he was trying to find out whether I recognised the action required to blow up the vital Identification Friend or Foe (IFF) radio on my Spitfire. I said I knew what he meant and that I had indeed set off the charge, by simultaneously pushing down two buttons alongside one another, and destroyed it. It seemed that at that moment he concluded that I could be genuine.

It was not until I visited M Fillerin after the war that I learned that they had decided to shoot me, believing me to be a German posing as a shot-down British airman. I had walked so far from the scene of my force-landing that they had not yet heard of any aircraft or parachute landing in their area. They had, therefore, thought that I must be a German. Fortunately for me, M Fillerin had decided to question me once more. He then gave me the benefit of the doubt.

I was subsequently fed into the escape route via Paris and Marseilles, and over the Pyrenees into Spain. Eventually I was transported back to Britain and was able to rejoin my old squadron, No 610, at Tangmere.'

Denis 'Crow' Crowley-Milling – Fighter Command pilot (OOTB)

However, although the *Luftwaffe* was weakened in numbers of units following Operation *Barbarossa*, it had the benefit of advanced ground radar equipment ranged along the occupied coastlines, a superior variant of the Bf 109, the 'F-Model', and a completely new fighter, the Fw 190. This aircraft outclassed both the Spitfire V and Whirlwind. Only the Typhoon could meet the Fw 190 on equal terms, but it was suffering from serious engine and airframe problems and would not be fully operational until the end of the year.

Two American fighters, the Bell Airacobra and the Curtiss Tomahawk, both of which had been originally ordered for the French Air Force in 1939, were

delivered to Fighter Command. However, neither proved very effective, especially against the German fighters, and in fact the Airacobra was withdrawn from service at the end of 1941, having only been delivered to one squadron.

With losses mounting, the development of the Spitfire IX was accelerated. Powered by a supercharged Merlin, which gave it a maximum speed of over 400mph and a range of almost 1,000 miles with external fuel tanks, it was a match for the Fw 190. The bad news was that it would not enter service until April 1942. From June to December 1941 Fighter Command lost more than 500 aircraft, with 17 Spitfires shot down on one day alone, 8 November.

Above A line-up of 72 Sqn Spitfire VBs at Biggin Hill in July 1941, including the presentation aircraft named 'Basuto'.

Right When the Luftwaffe's *Fw 190A first* appeared over the Channel with Adolf Galland's Jag in the summer of 1941, it was able to outperform Fighter Command's Spitfire V and was only equalled by the Spitfire IX, which entered service the following year.

Air Vice-Marshal Sir Christopher Quintin Brand, commander of No 10 Group, presents 501 Sqn's 'Ginger' Lacey with an Australian presentation parachute and scarf at Chilbolton in July 1941.

3 Sqn Hurricane IIC BD867 in day camouflage in mid-1941 prior to the squadron beginning a period of night-fighting duties from Hunsdon.

Above *Presentation Spitfire VB W3333 'Hendon Pegasus', one of four paid for by local donations from people living in the London Borough of Hendon, was issued to 601 (County of London) Sqn in August 1941.*

Below *Presentation Westland Whirlwind I P7116 'Bellows Argentina No 2' served with 263 Sqn, the RAF's first squadron to be equipped with the types, based at Filton in November 1941.*

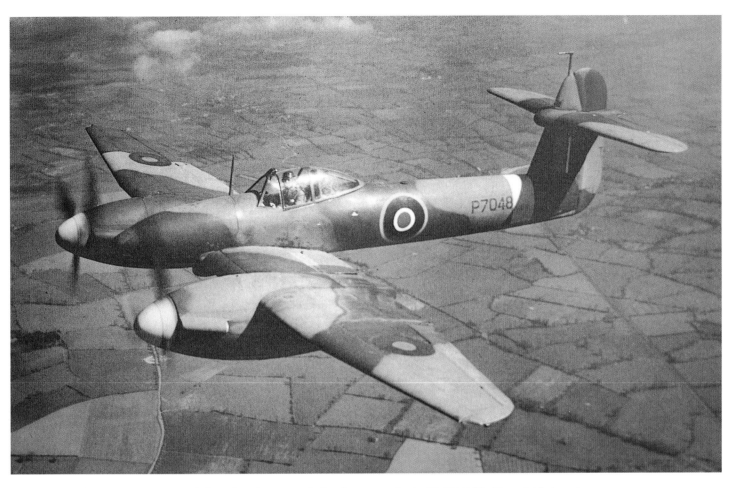

Above *Whirlwind I P7048 of No 137 Sqn, which was formed in September 1941 to be the second Fighter Command unit equipped with the twin-engined long-range fighter, at Charmy Down.*

Below *Presentation Spitfire VB AD381 'The Plessey Spitfire' served with six squadrons from December 1941, including 312 (Czech) Sqn, before being written off in an accident in June 1945.*

No 601 Sqn was the first and only Fighter Command squadron to re-equip with the American Bell Airacobra in late 1941 to replace its Hurricanes, but the type proved unsuitable for European operations and was in turn replaced by the Spitfire V six months later.

Channel dash

Another low came early in 1942 when the German battlecruisers *Scharnhorst*, *Gneisenau* and *Prinz Eugen* broke cover from Brest and steamed at high speed through the English Channel heading for Norway. After they were spotted in mid-Channel on the morning of 12 February by two Fighter Command Spitfires on a *Jim Crow* patrol, Operation *Fuller* swung into action. What followed was a confused and desperate combined operation involving the RAF's Fighter, Bomber and Coastal Commands, and the Fleet Air Arm.

Bad weather was a crucial factor, as was the lack of a co-ordinated command structure. In the event the German warships arrived at their German base on 13 February having only sustained minor damage from mines, despite 250 Bomber Command sorties and the loss of all six Fleet Air Arm Swordfish torpedo bombers sent to attack them – resulting in the award of a VC for their leader. Meanwhile, 20 fighter aircraft taking part in Operation *Fuller* on 12 February, including four 137 Sqn Whirlwinds, were also lost.

In April and May the *Luftwaffe* launched a series of *Baedeker* raids against historic British cities, including Exeter, Bath, Canterbury and Norwich, while Fighter Command Typhoons went into action for the first time against 'hit and run' attacks against coastal targets by German fighter-bombers.

The Dieppe Raid and after

By mid-1942 the first aircraft of the US 8th Air Force were arriving at British bases, America having entered the war on the previous 8 December following the Japanese attack on Pearl Harbor, and one of the first operations in which their fighter pilots were involved was another glorious failure – the Dieppe Raid.

This Combined Operation, an Anglo-Canadian seaborne assault on the Normandy port of Dieppe, and codenamed *Jubilee*, had been delayed by bad weather from June to 19 August. It would be Fighter Command's busiest day since the end of the Battle of Britain, involving no fewer than 65 fighter squadrons, including 48 Spitfire and 24 Hurricane units. Due to recent heavy loses, and high demand in the Middle East, Fighter Command was short of Spitfires, particularly the Mark IX, and this fact, combined with the late delivery of operational Typhoons, meant that once again it had to rely heavily on the veteran Hurricane. Defiants were tasked with air-sea rescue and Army Co-operation Command also provided four squadrons of the new Mustang I reconnaissance fighters and a few elderly Blenheims.

With AVM Leigh-Mallory as head of the Allied Expeditionary Air Force (AEAF), at first light Fighter Command *Intruders*, led by No 43 Sqn Hurricanes and 418 Sqn Bostons, attacked enemy positions and coastal defences. The German defenders appeared to be taken by surprise and it was not until 1000hrs that the *Luftwaffe* appeared over the area in large numbers. Fighter Command was maintaining constant air cover over the invasion fleet of 250 ships and the landing area, but the Germans were countering this effort with highly accurate flak and, from mid-morning, with standing patrols over the beachhead by ever-growing numbers of JG 2 and JG 26 Focke-Wulfs from Abbeville and St Omer.

By this time the decision to evacuate the 6,000 Canadian troops and Royal Marine Commandos, who were being decimated by German defences, had already been taken. The RAF fighters were now on the defensive and were hard put to protect the retreating troop landing ships from German bombers while being attacked by the superior Fw 190s. At the end of the long day almost half the invasion force had been killed or captured, while Fighter and Army Co-operation Commands, which had flown 2,471 sorties, lost 98 aircraft, including ten Mustangs.

The *Luftwaffe* lost only 48 aircraft, most of them bombers, nine of them falling to Fighter Command's top-scoring squadron, No 303. But Operation *Jubilee* emphasised not only the Fw 190's superiority over the Spitfire V – there being only a handful of Spitfire IXs in the battle and even fewer Typhoons – but also that a new command structure would be required to successfully support large-scale combined operations in the future.

Although the RAF's tactics during the Dieppe Raid had proved to be less effective than planned, Operation *Jubilee*'s commander, AVM Leigh-Mallory, succeeded Sholto Douglas as AOC-in-C Fighter Command in November 1942. No 11 Group was taken over by Air Vice-Marshal Hugh 'Dingbat' Saunders. With now almost 100 squadrons under Leigh-Mallory's command at the beginning of 1943, the tempo of operations increased accordingly.

In addition to *Rhubarbs*, which had a maximum radius of action of 150 miles for Spitfires, Hurricanes and Typhoons, 135 miles for Whirlwinds, 200 miles for Spitfires and Hurricanes fitted with long-range tanks, and 300 miles for Mustangs, Fighter Command had been escorting US 8th Air Force light bombers since their introduction to the European theatre in mid-1942.

The catalogue of various types of attacking targets in occupied Europe increased with the introduction of the Hurricane IV fitted with rocket projectiles (R/P). These proved to be so successful that a number of Typhoon squadrons adopted R/Ps as their main weapons and were particularly effective against shipping and railway targets.

From the beginning of 1943 RAF fighters had to contend with increasing numbers of low-level German 'tip and run' raids by bomb-carrying Bf 109s and Fw 190s on towns along England's South Coast. In January alone the *Luftwaffe* carried out 49 daylight raids and 31 night attacks, aided by bad weather and the use of 'Window', metallic foil dropped in bundles to confuse British radar. However, nine of the 28 German fighter-bombers that attacked London docks on 28 January were shot down.

While the daylight raids decreased as the weather improved and standing patrols by Typhoons became an effective deterrent – only one was carried out in July – night raids increased to a maximum of 47 in August. By the end of the year almost 500 'tip and run' raids had been carried out, but with losses rising they were scaled down, with only one daylight and 13 night raids being recorded in December.

With the increasing momentum of attacks by RAF and USAAF medium bombers, more of Fighter Command's aircraft from all Groups frequently operated away from their home bases. The stations most busily occupied during 1943 were Manston, Bradwell Bay and Tangmere, all in the South of England, the first two being particularly suitable for bad weather operations as they were equipped with 'Fido'.

Also, as more Fighter Command sorties operated over the sea, ranging from long-range *Instep* and *Lagoon* operations to sweeps and escorts across the Channel, air-sea rescued played an ever-increasing role. By 1943 the RAF operated a dozen dedicated ASR squadrons, many of which were formed from Group Anti-Aircraft Co-operation (AAC) flights, deployed around the British Isles. Equipped initially with Defiants, and later Spitfires, most had at least one rugged Walrus amphibian on strength. At least ten ASR aircraft were lost during the year, including at least one Walrus that was attempting to pick up a downed pilot off the French coast.

1942: Second time unlucky

'In June 1941 I was on a basic flying training course on the Stearman PT-17 at Macon, Georgia, as part of the Arnold Scheme. Having gained my "wings", I completed my advanced training on the AT-6A Texan at Craig Field, Alabama, before converting to the Spitfire at an OTU in England.

Almost a year after I began my flying training I was posted to "B" Flight of No 167 Sqn based at Peterhead. After only a few weeks the squadron began to convert to an all-Dutch flight, which was later to became the nucleus of 322 (Dutch) Sqn. I was then transferred to 602 Sqn, led by S/Ldr Peter Brothers and based at the same airfield.

In August 1942 the squadron moved to Biggin Hill for Operation Jubilee, the Anglo-Canadian raid at Dieppe. My first sortie, on 19 August, which was to provide an "umbrella" over the beachhead, took off at 0550 hours. This was uneventful although one Fw 190 was claimed by the squadron. I was airborne again at 1015 hours and, while on patrol over the beaches approximately 45 minutes later, my Spitfire VB was hit by ground fire.

I baled out, landed on "Blue" Beach at Puys and spent the next few days with the remnants of the Royal Regiment of Canada before being captured and interned in a camp built by the French in 1940 as a prison for the Germans.

I was eventually transferred to Stalag Luft III, where I remained until January 1945 when we walked to Lubeck to be met by members of the Cheshire Regiment before being repatriated by an RAF Lancaster in April.'

Mike F. Goodchap – Fighter Command pilot

By 1942 most of Fighter Command's ASR squadrons had an amphibious Supermarine Walrus, known as 'Shagbags', on strength.

Almost 850 Fighter Command aircraft were lost in combat during 1943, and some 550 aircrew killed. The increased intensity of operational flying meant that the chance of surviving one Fighter Command tour, fixed in general terms at 200 hours, was 43 per cent for day-fighter pilots, reducing to only 18½ per cent for two tours.

On 1 June 1943, following Exercise *Spartan* in

March when the Home Forces rehearsed the liberation of North West Europe, Fighter Command underwent its most radical re-organisation since 1936 with the formation of the 2nd Tactical Air Force (2TAF) in preparation for the invasion of Europe. This comprised No 83 Group with fighter and fighter-bomber wings, No 84 Group, which incorporated Army Co-operation Command whose AOC-in-C, Air

Spitfire VBs of 122 (Bombay) Sqn landing at Hornchurch after a sweep over France, one of which, MT-B, was shot down over Dunkirk in January 1942.

S/Ldr D. G. Smallwood, OC No 87 (United Provinces) Sqn (centre), with his night intruder Hurricane IIC 'Cawnpore II' at Charmy Down in March 1942.

Marshal Barratt, had headed the report on Exercise *Spartan*, and No 2 Group, which was transferred from Bomber Command.

No 85 Group, which would be responsible for the defence of Allied forces in Europe, was formed in November to coincide with the re-naming of Fighter Command as Air Defence of Great Britain (ADGB). Air Chief Marshal Sir Trafford Leigh-Mallory took command of the AEAF, of which 2TAF, commanded by First World War 'ace' Air Marshal Sir Arthur Coningham, was a part, while Air Marshal Roderick Hill, AOC of No 11 Group since 1942, when he had replaced Leigh-Mallory, was given the ADGB.

Hill's ADGB had its first challenge in January 1944 when the *Luftwaffe* launched Operation *Steinbock*, a series of heavy bombing raids on major British cities including London. Countering what became known as the 'Baby Blitz' was mainly the province of ADGB night fighters, which accounted for most of the 329 German bombers shot down during the four-month campaign.

ADGB fighters also continued to carry out offensive operations across the Channel, while 2TAF built up resources and deployed to new stations being built in southern England. Its main sector stations were Ford, Tangmere, Holmesley South and Hurn. Prior to any invasion, 2TAF Groups continued to operate from airfields and landing grounds in No 11 Group territory. By 1 April 1944 ADGB Order of Battle showed only 43 operational squadrons, while 2TAF had 91 squadrons including ten of Boston, Mosquito and Mitchell bombers. Secondary to the air defence of southern England, ADGB was also responsible for the protection of the vast Allied invasion fleets, comprising some 7,000 ships and landing craft, as they began to assemble at locations only a few minutes' flying time from the enemy-occupied coast; it was therefore vital to take the most careful precautions against German reconnaissance patrols. To deal with this threat ADGB flew high-level and low-level day patrols over certain coastal areas, and these were to extend as far out as 40-50 miles south of the Isle of Wight.

In the six weeks prior to the D-Day invasion, however, the *Luftwaffe* flew only 125 day sorties in the area and four over the Thames Estuary and East Coast. Although the Allied fighters rarely got a glimpse of these aircraft, a total of 167 German aircraft were shot down by ADGB squadrons in day offensive operations between November 1943 and 5 June 1944. The prerequisite for a successful combined-operation invasion – air superiority over the beachheads – seemed to have been achieved. The next few hours would tell.

Spitfire VB AD233 of 222 Sqn based at North Weald in March 1942 flown by the squadron's CO, S/Ldr Dickie Milne, who finished the war with a score of 14 destroyed and one probable.

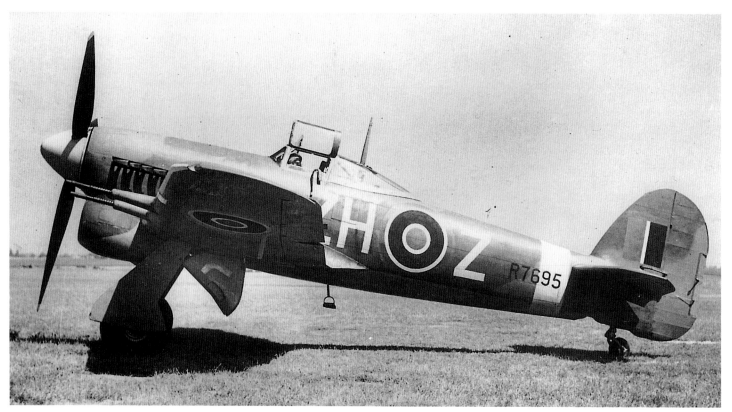

Left *An early Hawker Typhoon IA delivered to 266 (Rhodesia) Sqn at Duxford in March 1942; the squadron's first operation with the type was a Dutch coast sweep on 28 May.*

Below left *Cannon-armed Spitfire VB EN821, delivered to 243 Sqn in June 1942, ended its days as a Royal Navy trainer at Lee-on-Solent two years later.*

Right *S/Ldr Brian Kingcombe, OC No 72 (Basutoland) Sqn, introduces King George VI to his pilots at Biggin Hill in April 1942 during the King's tour of No 11 Group Sector stations.*

Below *Numerous accidents were caused by the unreliability of the Napier Sabre engine of the early Typhoons, such as R7646, which crash-landed at Cranfield in May 1942.*

The damage inflicted to the cannon bay of Sgt J. Lang's Spitfire at Debden after he was 'bounced' by an Fw 190 in June 1942.

A pilot and his rigger inspect the damage to their Spitfire's rudder after being attacked by five Fw 190s over St Omer, also in June 1942.

Above *Groundcrew hold down the tail of one of the newly formed 131 Sqn's Spitfire VBs during an engine test at Tangmere in the summer of 1942.*

Left *A close formation of three 243 Sqn Spitfire VBs based at Ouston in July 1942, four months before the squadron was moved to North Africa.*

Left *A formation of No 1 Sqn Hurricane IICs from Tangmere in July 1942, having relinquished their night-intruder role and about to be replaced by Typhoons.*

Above *In September 1942 No 137 Sqn's Whirlwinds were fitted with bomb racks and their pilots practised dive-bombing techniques for attacks on enemy shipping and Rhubarb operations.*

Right *No 137 Sqn groundcrew load 250lb bombs on to the underwing pylons of a Whirlwind I fighter bomber at Manston.*

Above *OC 137 Sqn, S/Ldr Hugh St John Coghlan, climbs aboard Whirlwind I 'Comrades in Arms', presented to the RAF by Mr and Mrs S. H. Ellis from Australia in 1942.*

Left *Two sections of 165 (Ceylon) Sqn Spitfire VBs take off from Gravesend over BL295 SK-D on a Rhubarb operation in October 1942.*

1943: Flak train

'My squadron, No 165, equipped with Spitfire VBs, was stationed at Tangmere during the winter of 1942/3, where we were employed on fighter sweeps, convoy patrols and shipping recces. During days when there was very low cloud cover, Rhubarbs – low-level targets suitable for attack – were sometimes permitted. On 16 January Sgt John Curry and myself carried out one of these sorties. We flew at nought feet over the Channel, crossing the French coast at Etretat and covering the area bounded by Montivilliers, Bolbec and Fauville.

We eventually spotted a freight train upon which we both made two attacks. During these the sides of one of the trucks opened up to reveal machine-guns manned by German soldiers, who returned our fire. This was the first time that RAF aircraft came across armed freight trains, and it was of sufficient interest to gain a mention in the BBC 9 o'clock news bulletin that evening, and a paragraph in the next morning's papers. This flight, the first of its type carried out by our squadron, turned out to be one of only four before the CO cancelled any more following the loss of three pilots, two killed and one missing, during the next three sorties. John Curry was the missing pilot, shot down on the second Rhubarb when I was on leave.

However, he managed to evade capture and walked home, returning to the squadron at the end of June 1943. Unfortunately he was shot down again and killed over Holland on his first offensive sortie at the end of July.'

Eric Shipp – Fighter Command pilot

From January to September 1943 No 616 (South Yorkshire) Sqn took on the high-altitude role with pressurised Spitfire VIs operating from Ibsley.

Typhoon pilots of 56 Sqn in early 1943. Their CO, S/Ldr T. Pheloung, is in the centre – he was killed in action on 20 June – and to his right is Flight Commander F/Lt Brian Haskin and another Flight Commander, F/Lt Pat Thorton-Brown, who was killed by 'friendly fire' on 21 December when OC 609 Sqn.

1943: False alarm

'Following a long period as a Controller, and frequent requests to be posted back to an operational squadron, I was posted as a supernumerary Squadron Leader to No 276 (ASR) Sqn at Harrowbeer. It was equipped with Spitfire IICs, an Anson ASR 1 and a Walrus ASR 2. I was looking forward to flying the Walrus, which was an aged amphibian biplane, but somebody pranged it before I got the opportunity.

However, one day in June the squadron received a call from the Ops Room at Exeter saying that the Typhoon wing was involved in a large sweep over France and one of their aircraft had gone down in the drink. I was down to fly that day, but before I could take off I was summonsed to the CO, who told me that I was to be posted to Malta and that I should prepare to leave forthwith.

In the meantime a pair of Spitfires had taken off to look for the missing Typhoon pilot, but it turned out that it was a false alarm. Both our Spitfires were shot down over the Channel and the pilots, one of whom had replaced me on the sortie, were missing.'

Hubert Paul Patten – Fighter Command pilot

OC 165 Sqn from August
1942 to March 1943 was
Battles of France and Britain
veteran S/Ldr Jim 'Darkie'
Hallowes, who completed his
tour having raised his score to
17 victories and four
probables.

This 167 Sqn Spitfire VB
VP-F EP350 returned to
Ludham on 2 March 1943
with its tailplane seriously
damaged by an enemy fighter
while escorting bombers
over France.

Above *Groundcrews get to work refuelling and re-arming 56 Sqn Typhoon IB DN374 at Matlaske after a sweep over France on 2 March 1943, 13 days before it was shot down over Holland.*

Below *Groundcrew at Manston watch their CO, S/Ldr 'Bee' Beamont, fly overhead in his 609 (West Riding) Sqn Typhoon IB in March 1943.*

Above *A close-up of 56 Sqn Typhoon IB US-A EK183 at Matlaske in April 1943, showing the yellow overwing identification stripe that was designed to prevent it from being mistaken for an Fw 190.*

Right *Two sections of 56 Sqn's Typhoons, including US-A, flying out of Matlaske on a cross-Channel patrol in May 1943.*

Forced down by RAF fighters at Dyce on 9 May 1943, NJG 3 Ju 88R-1 D5+EV later flew in RAF markings, serialled PJ867.

Above *Pilots of 257 (Burma) Sqn with Typhoon IB FM-M EK172 at Warmwell on 13 May 1943 with their CO, S/Ldr Ronnie Fokes, on the left and one of Fighter Command's few Burmese pilots sitting on the wing.*

Right *One of 257 Sqn's Sergeant Pilots in the cockpit of his Typhoon IB; note the port-opening 'car' door complete with wind-up window.*

Above *No 181 Sqn Typhoon EL-C DN421 overflies Tangmere in June 1943 carrying two 500lb bombs and wearing its pre-D-Day identification stripes.*

Below *The personnel of the newly operational 131 Sqn at Tangmere in June 1943 gather around Typhoon IB EL-G, named 'Cemetery Bait II', with their CO, S/Ldr Denis Crowley-Milling, in the centre without cap.*

No 118 Sqn operated the Spitfire VB for three years, with NK-H involved in Roadstead patrols in mid-1943 flying from Coltishall.

Two 611 (West Lancashire) Sqn Spitfire IXs, which were flying high cover escorts and patrols in June 1943 from Biggin Hill.

Clipped-wing Spitfire VB SZ-X BL479 of 316 (Warsawski) Sqn from Northolt was used for low-level operations and Ramrods in mid-1943.

Left New Zealander Sgt
Southwood surveys the
damage to the trailing edge of
his Spitfire IX after being
'bounced' by an Fw 190
during a sweep over France
in 1943.

Below This North
American Mustang I of 2
Sqn was transferred to
Fighter Command when it
absorbed Army Co-operation
Command in June 1943.

Pilots of 165 (Ceylon) Sqn playing poker outside the Ibsley readiness room in July 1943. Left to right: Eric Shipp, John Curry, 'Chalky' White, 'Walt' Disney and Marcel Jordain.

No 165 Sqn's name board in the readiness room at Gravesend in October 1942.

Above P/Off Eric Shipp
(left) at Ibsley with his
Spitfire VB and fellow 165
Sqn pilot, Australian Sgt Bill
Brown, who was shot down
over Holland in July 1943.

Left Eric Shipp with his
fitter, rigger and Spitfire IX
when flying from No 10
Group airfield at
Churchstanton in
November 1943.

Right *A No 131 Sqn pilot staggers from the wreckage of his Spitfire IX MA860 with only superficial injuries after crash-landing at Colerne on 4 February 1944, returning from a long-range escort.*

Below *This other 131 Spitfire IX, NX-A MA834, carrying a 45-gallon overload fuel tank, came to grief at Colerne on the same day when it swung off the runway avoiding the wreckage of MA860.*

Above *No 118 Sqn Spitfire LF IXC MJ271 was not delivered to the squadron until February 1944 when they began flying long-range escorts from Detling.*

Below *Typhoon IB EK497 was used by 183 Sqn for rocket projectile (R/P) trials in March 1944; it used R/P in operations from Thorney Island leading up to D-Day.*

A 183 Sqn Typhoon pilot checks the complement of 16 60lb 3-inch rocket projectiles carried by his aircraft.

1944: Tempest ditched

'Flying Tempests of No 486 (RNZAF) Squadron from Newchurch by Romney Marsh, we were on a routine cross-Channel patrol when my engine failed at about 6,000 feet. We had been told that it was inadvisable to try to ditch a Tempest in the sea as the radiator scoop at the front of the engine could make it tricky.

I tried to bale out, but couldn't remove the hood with the release toggle. After struggling to no avail, there was no option but to ditch and hope. Luckily, when I hit the water the hood flew off, so I quickly hopped into my dinghy and set sail for Folkestone.

After a while a Royal Navy destroyer came by and at once started manoeuvring alongside. Good, I thought, there'll be a few free drinks in the wardroom. Alas! An RAF air-sea rescue launch, which had put out from Dover, beat the Navy to it – and all I got was a cup of Bovril!

This was the first Tempest to be ditched in the sea, so I was ordered to go to London to tell the world about it.'

Bruce Lawless – New Zealand Fighter Command pilot (OOTB)

Above Late production Typhoon IB HF-L JP601, with clear-view 'bubble' canopy and whip aerial, belonged to 183 Sqn, which operated from Manston in the spring of 1944.

Left The only German pilot to fly in Fighter Command – until his brother joined him later in 1944 – was Sgt Ken 'Heinie' Adam, who flew R/P-armed Typhoons of 609 Sqn in the weeks preceding D-Day.

This group of pilots of 609 Sqn at Manston in the spring of 1944 includes the CO, S/Ldr 'Johnnie' Wells (seated centre), and Sgt Ken Adam (back row, second from right).

D-Day

Almost 2,200 aircraft from 51 2TAF and 21 ADGB squadrons were available for air operations on D-Day, 6 June 1944. The six tasks of the Allied Expeditionary Air Force were to attain and maintain an air superiority whereby the *Luftwaffe* would be rendered incapable of effectively interfering with the assault operations, to make continuous reconnaissance of enemy dispositions and movements, to disrupt communications and so interrupt the flow of the enemy's reinforcements and supplies, to support the Allied landing and subsequent advances, to attack enemy naval forces, and to provide an airlift for Allied airborne forces.

Although Leigh-Mallory had successfully instigated his 'Transportation Plan', whereby Bomber Command and the 8th Air Force concentrated on the bombing of German communications prior to Operation *Overlord* – the invasion of Normandy – he found that he could not count on the unconditional support of his fellow RAF D-Day air commanders, Tedder and Coningham. Air Marshal Sir Arthur Tedder had been appointed General Eisenhower's Army and Air Force Deputy Commander in North Africa to be responsible for co-ordinating the land and air operations during the invasion of Sicily and Italy in 1943. Following the success of these operations, he became Eisenhower's Deputy in the run-up to the D-Day landings. Meanwhile tough New Zealander and Desert Air Force commander AM Sir Arthur Coningham was not only C-in-C of 2TAF but also Commander of the Advanced Allied Expeditionary Air Force, and had built up a close relationship with Tedder. Together they mirrored the Battle of Britain-winning partnership of Dowding and Park, and thought that Leigh-Mallory was over-cautious and unwilling to take risks, as well as being too reliant on the opinions of his senior operational Wing Leaders.

This was the background to Operation *Overlord*, the largest and most complex single operation the world had ever seen. A total of 2,172 RAF fighters and

1944: Supreme sacrifice

'This period was a busy one for 125 Sqn as we helped to defend the D-Day launching area of the South Coast. However, the squadron was forbidden to get nearer than 10 miles from the enemy coast, as our Mosquitos' radar was classified as top secret. It was not until some time after 6 June that the annoying restriction was lifted.

Shortly before D-Day a team of Fighter Controllers visited us before embarking on a ship fitted out to be a floating GCI station, which was to be anchored in the Bay of the Seine. We were honoured to meet these brave people who were well aware of the extreme dangers that lay ahead. However, this tactical deployment was essential for the protection of the huge invasion fleet of naval and other supply ships bound for the beaches of Normandy.

The aircrews of the German Ju 88 mine-laying and torpedo aircraft were amazed to be presented with a stationary sitting-duck vessel that continually broadcast instructions to night fighters, thereby revealing its precise position. Nevertheless, before the supreme sacrifice of Flight Direction Tender (FTD) 13 was made, this team of expert Fighter Controllers, which included WAAF officers, were able to render magnificent assistance to us destroying the low-level Ju 88s that were creating havoc among the invading armada.

Many of our night-fighter crews benefited from this stratagem, but none more so than one of our pilots from 125 Sqn, Flying Officer "Taffy" Jones, who, with the help of his navigator, shot down three of the offending Luftwaffe aircraft within 21 minutes. It was right and proper that this crew was awarded immediate DFCs on their return to Hurn.'

Richard W. 'Dick' Leggett – Fighter Command night-fighter pilot

fighter-bombers together with 96 air-sea rescue aircraft took part in the first day's operations, flying 5,656 sorties. Total AEAF losses for the day were 113, while the *Luftwaffe* only managed to mount 319 sorties over the D-Day beaches. Almost 100 ADGB Spitfires flew top cover over the invasion fleet and provided escorts for troop-carrying aircraft and gliders. As the beachheads were established they flew escort cover for Bomber Command's heavy bombers, making daylight attacks beyond the battle front.

As Air Vice-Marshal Harry Broadhurst's No 83 Group Typhoons and Mustangs began pounding German defence positions and armour moving towards the invasion area, 85 Group's Hawker Tempests were in combat for the first time with German fighters in the Le Havre area. The fastest piston-engine fighter to enter RAF service during the Second World War, the Tempest V was also a formidable ground attack aircraft, and first entered squadron service a month before D-Day.

By 10 June AEAF Spitfires and Typhoons were being deployed to the first of 50 temporary air strips in Normandy, and within days Typhoon 'cab ranks' were established – these were aircraft briefed to attack pre-selected targets at regular 30-minute intervals, but would also orbit the area while in direct communication with a Forward Control Post, which would pass on updated information on the targets close to the front line.

Divers

As the Allied advance into France continued, ADGB was faced with another major German onslaught against South East England. This time it would not be intercepting bomber aircraft but unmanned flying bombs. The *Luftwaffe*-operated Fieseler Fi-103, *Vergeltungswaffe* (revenge weapon)-1, was first successfully ground-launched in December 1943 by *Flak Regiment* 155 from a site in the Pas de Calais. At least 13,000 V-1s were built, and 5,823 of the 8,564 (codenamed *Divers*) that were launched against Britain reached their target, the first on 13 June 1944.

Ordered at Hitler's behest specifically for use against 'non-military' targets, the V-1 was powered by a 670lb-thrust Argus pulse-jet and could carry a 2,000lb warhead at speeds of up to 470mph. V-1s killed more than 900 civilians and injured over 35,000. Fifteen ADGB squadrons were deployed to combat the V-1, and RAF bombers dropped a total of 16,000 tons of bombs on V-1 ground-launch sites, known as *Noballs*, in France. To compensate for the loss of these sites, built between Cherbourg and St

The Rolls-Royce Griffon-powered Spitfire XIV, the fastest RAF fighter, first entered service with 610 Sqn at West Malling in January 1944, which went on to destroy over 50 V-1s by September.

Spitfire XIIs of 41 Sqn were also used for anti-Diver patrols, claiming 52 V-1s destroyed, and sweeps using 500lb bombs.

Hawker Tempest V EJ743 entered service with 3 Sqn at Manston in March 1944, the RAF's top-scoring anti-Diver squadron with over 300 V-1s destroyed.

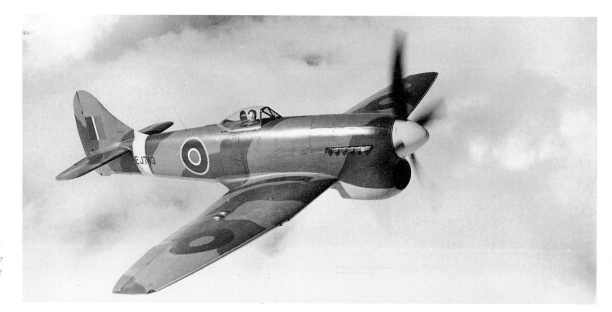

Omer, the *Luftwaffe's* KG 53 operated over 100 He 111s, which air-launched a single flying bomb from beneath the port wing. To avoid British air defences, the German crews had to operate their outdated and overloaded Heinkels at night and at low level. They flew over the English Channel at 300 feet, below British radar, then 'popped up' at 1,500 feet some 40 miles from the coast to launch the flying bomb. Some 1,200 V-1s were air-launched up to 14 January 1945, but fewer than half that number reached England and only one in ten arrived at its target.

As part of Operation *Crossbow*, which was controlled from RAF Biggin Hill, ADGB's 15 day-fighter and 10 night-fighter squadrons flew more than 20,000 anti-*Diver* patrols over a six-month period, and destroyed a total of 1,846 V-1s before they reached their targets, while another 1,867 fell victim to AA guns on the North Downs and 232 more were bought down by a balloon barrage between the guns and the capital.

The most successful RAF unit in the battle against the V-1 was No 150 Wing based at Newchurch near Dungeness in Kent. Two of the Wing's three squadrons, Nos 3 and 486 (RCAF) Sqns, were equipped with the 435mph Tempest V, whose four 20mm cannon claimed 638 V-1s, more than any other RAF type. No 150 Wing was led by Battles of France and Britain 'ace' W/C Roland Beamont, and his recommendations to the Senior Staff of No 11 Group, which controlled his Wing's Sector, were instrumental in the success of Operation *Crossbow*.

His report read: 'Fighter patrols should be concentrated between Eastbourne and Dover in a belt extending 7,000 feet high and 3 miles out to sea. Within that operational area, anti-aircraft guns should be restricted from firing, and all slow fighters should be withdrawn, leaving the field clear for the Tempests, some squadrons of special Spitfires, and Mustangs with increased boost. Observer Corps posts should be concentrated at half-mile intervals and equipped with rockets to be fired towards the position of the V-1 reported on the radar plot. The converging rockets should help the patrolling fighter to sight the target quickly.'

In clear weather conditions, codenamed *Flabby*, fighters had full freedom of action and the guns closed down. In medium *Fickle* weather conditions, the fighters were permitted to pursue flying bombs over the gun-belt to the balloon line, and, where a fighter was in close pursuit, the guns held their fire. In bad, or *Spouse*, weather the fighters had to keep clear of the guns, which had full freedom of action up to 8,000 feet.

The top-scoring night fighter was the Mosquito, which accounted for 486 V-1s, but it was the RAF's first operational jet fighter, the Gloster Meteor F.1, that caught the public's imagination. On 4 August 1944 a Meteor of 616 Sqn flown by F/Off T. D. 'Dixie' Dean scored his, and the Meteor's, first victory when he tipped a V-1 into a terminal dive after his guns had jammed. Dean subsequently shot down another two *Divers* adding to the Squadron's scoreboard of 16 V-1s in only one month.

The RAF's top V-1 'ace' was S/Ldr Joe Berry, who downed 60 *Divers* flying Tempests with the Fighter Interception Unit (FIU) and 501 Sqn. The Dutch pilot F/Off R. F. Burgwal of 322 (Dutch) Sqn, flying Spitfire XIVs, shot down 21, while F/Lt Desmond Ruchwaldy of 129 Sqn was the top Mustang pilot with a score of ten destroyed.

*A line-up of Gloster Meteor F.1s, the Fighter Command's first operational jet fighter, at Manston during anti-*Diver* operations from July 1944.*

Armourers, fitters and riggers
clamber over a 3 Sqn
Tempest wearing D-Day
'invasion stripes' at
Newchurch at the height of
anti-Diver patrols in
July 1944.

A 'vic' of Tempest Vs from
Fighter Command's Air
Fighting Development Unit
(AFDU) in mid-1944; some
of them took part in anti-
Diver patrols over southern
England.

1944: Deadly robots

'In August 1944 the German V-1 flying bombs were coming over fast and furious. I was with No 125 Squadron on Mosquito NF.XVIIs based at Hurn near Bournemouth. I was flying a standing patrol at night when radar vectored us to a target. I saw the distinctive flame from a V-1's rocket motor in the darkness some way off flying towards us at low level, no more than 500 feet.

As the V-1 flew straight and level at over 400mph and faster than the Mosquito, an attack had to be judged just right. The technique was to have a height advantage and to turn into the flying bomb's path. The speed in the dive should bring your aircraft to a position some 50-100 yards behind the flying bomb, and with enough speed to overtake it. If you turned in too early you would end up in front of the target, and if

you turned too late you would never be able to catch it up. I had attempted the manoeuvre four or five times without success before this occasion.

We had also been told to close one eye when attacking a V-1 at night to avoid losing our night vision when the flying bomb exploded, and to stop firing as soon as pieces flew off the target, because if you hit it anywhere, it would go down.

However, I was fed up with these deadly robots flying over England and I kept firing at it with both eyes wide open until it blew up in front of me – temporarily blinding me! I managed to climb sharply, avoiding most of the debris, although two pieces of shrapnel were found embedded in the Mosquito's nose after I landed at Hurn.'

Eric Gordon Barwell – Fighter Command night-fighter pilot

No 150 Wing leader, W/C 'Bee' Beamont, in a 486 Sqn Tempest at Matlaske in September 1944, by which time the Squadron had destroyed 223½ V-1 flying bombs.

The last lap

While ADGB was dealing very effectively with the V-1 menace, 2TAF was heavily involved in the Allied bridgehead breakouts in Normandy. Despite summer storms that seriously disrupted supplies, good progress was made in all sectors, with the exception of Caen, where the Anglo-Canadian advance ground to a halt. By the end of June ADGB and 2TAF had flown almost 46,000 sorties in support of ground operations, losing 740 aircraft in the process.

However, only 35 2TAF squadrons were operating

from 13 airstrips instead of the planned 81 squadrons from 27 temporary airfields. In order to take Caen, Leigh-Mallory proposed that a Bomber Command force of 450 Lancasters and Halifaxes, escorted by ADGB Spitfires, should bomb the outskirts of Caen ahead of an Allied attack on the city.

Operation *Charnwood* had General Montgomery's support, but Tedder and Coningham were less enthusiastic. In the event the operation, which took place on 7 July, blocked the Army's advance into the city with craters and rubble and it would take a series of heavy bombing raids on the city itself by Bomber

Command, the US 8th Air Force and 2TAF before Caen fell to the Allies in mid-August after claiming heavy casualties.

But the breakout had been established, and on 7 August German forces launched a counter-attack at Mortain in an effort to halt the Allied advance towards Paris. However, the German armour had no air cover and was a sitting target for 2TAF fighter-bombers, particularly the Typhoons that were protected by American fighters of the 9th Air Force.

Trapped in the Falaise Gap, more than 2,000 German tanks and an untold number of other military vehicles were destroyed by Allied tactical aircraft in less than two weeks of non-stop operations. By the end of August the German Seventh Army in France no longer existed as a fighting force and the Battle of Normandy was won, mainly by air power. It was not won, however, without considerable cost. Having flown 151,370 *Overlord* sorties, the ADGB and 2TAF had lost 829 aircraft with 1,035 aircrew killed or missing.

If the German Army in France was a spent force, the *Luftwaffe* throughout the Low Countries was now virtually non-existent. While the Allies raced towards Germany, remaining *Luftwaffe* units fell back to defend the Fatherland alongside the newly operational Me 262 jet fighter and Ar 234 jet bomber.

In an attempt to hasten the end of the war a massive Anglo-American airborne invasion of Holland was planned in order to seize bridgeheads over the Rivers Meuse and Lower Rhine. On 17 September ADGB Spitfires acted as escorts for 1,500 Allied transport aircraft and gliders that had taken off from British airfields. Most reached their objectives, although the British Airborne Division drop zone at Arnhem was unexpectedly heavily defended by German ground forces.

Operation *Market Garden* continued until 25 September, but with a combination of bad weather, which prevented 2TAF from giving full support, and poor communications and intelligence on the ground, it ended in failure. The British force was cut off at Arnhem and had to be evacuated after more than 60 per cent of its troops were killed or captured. The ADGB and 2TAF lost more than 50 aircraft and 50 pilots.

In October 1944 Fighter Command was reborn. With the end of the AEAF, Leigh-Mallory was appointed C-in-C Allied Air Forces in South East Asia Command (SEAC), while Air Marshal Sir Roderick Hill seamlessly transferred from ADGB to AOC-in-C Fighter Command. On 14 November Leigh-Mallory left for the Far East with his wife aboard an RAF York. Hours later, in bad weather, it crashed in the Alps near Grenoble. There were no survivors.

The rejuvenated Fighter Command was virtually unchallenged by the *Luftwaffe*, and its last victory over the British Isles was an Fw 190 that was shot down near Broadbridge Heath in Sussex on 30 November, but the battle against German V-weapons would continue.

On 8 September the first two V-2 rockets fell on London. A pure rocket that carried a 1-ton warhead, the V-2 was designed to travel to a height of 70 miles above the earth until its fuel was exhausted, when it coasted on a parabola towards its target at above the speed of sound. There was no defence.

All that Fighter Command could do was to carry out *Big Ben* operations with Griffon-engined Spitfire XVIs from No 12 Group to attack likely launch sites in the Hook of Holland with 250 and 500lb bombs. However, the V-2 mobile launchers were extremely difficult to find and the *Big Ben* operations could do little to stem the flow of V-2 launches before Allied ground forces overran the area.

No 401 (RCAF) Sqn took a small number of Spitfires PR XIs with its Mark IXBs to Europe after D-Day, one of which is seen here at Volkel (B.80) in November 1944.

1944: A fear of flying?

'I was often asked if during the Battle of Britain I felt fear. My answer to this was that being fired at on a daily basis when flying with Nos 266 and 41 Sqns was not a pleasant feeling, but as I was so committed to the task of trying to repel the Luftwaffe, that overrode whatever personal feelings I might have felt.

However, later, on my four operational sorties with 485 Sqn to Arnhem in support of the Allied airdrops during Operation Market Garden in September 1944, I did experience real fear for the following reasons.

First, the appalling weather conditions that prevailed, ie very low cloud, 1,500 feet at best, forced us to fly below that height, coupled with very poor visibility. These were extremely unsuitable conditions in which to be ordered to operate a high-level, high-speed aircraft such as the Spitfire.

Second, the pilot of a Spitfire sat behind a very long engine that prevented all forward view of the ground below for some miles ahead. This meant not being able to see where you were going when travelling at some 250mph at very low altitude, as was necessary in this case – a highly dangerous state of affairs with high-tension power lines, etc! An hour and a half of this type of sortie was extremely taxing.

Last, to make matters worse, we were subjected to fairly intensive fire from German anti-aircraft guns, in particular from 40mm Bofors, for much of this operation. It was very frustrating not to be able to return the Bofors' fire, but as Spitfire guns were fixed to point straight ahead, to attack a ground target you had to dive towards the ground and, starting from such a low altitude and travelling at such a speed, you would hit the ground in a matter of seconds!'

Edward Preston 'Hawkeye' Wells – New

The last of 1,054 V-2s fell on Britain on 27 March 1945, having killed 2,700 Londoners in six months. During the same period another 753 V-1s were air-launched from He 111s and sites in Holland at night. Only 79 reached and fell on London, and one on Manchester, Fighter Command accounting for 75 while 421 where brought down by AA guns.

As the Allies relentlessly closed in on Germany from all fronts, they were slowed by bad weather as winter approached. The *Luftwaffe* still had more than 2,000 fighters along the Western Front, including a few hundred Me 262s. On 16 December Germany attempted to break through the weakly held Anglo-American front in the Ardennes sector to recapture the vital Allied supply ports of Liege and Antwerp.

Initially aided by thick fog, which kept 2TAF fighter-bombers grounded, the German armour made good progress, but as the weather improved they were stopped well short of their objectives. On 1 January 1945 the *Luftwaffe* embarked on a last desperate effort to destroy 2TAF on its doorstep. Over 800 German aircraft took part in Operation *Bodenplatte*, attacking 13 RAF and four USAAF airfields in northern France, Belgium and Holland at dawn as the Allied pilots recovered from the previous night's celebrations. But not all of them were on the ground, as the Germans found out when they ran into 50

Below One of the few Fighter Command units to operate the high-altitude Spitfire VII with lengthened wings was 131 Sqn from Culmhead until October 1944.

Bottom One of the more unusual aircraft assigned to Fighter Command was Piper Cub J4 DG667 (ex-G-AFXS), used for liaison duties with No 10 Group from 1941 until 1944.

Spitfires of No 131 Wing as they returned from a dawn sweep over the Ardennes. This encounter resulted in the destruction of 18 German fighters.

In fact, by the end of the day the *Luftwaffe* had lost more than 220 aircraft, a total of 45 to 2TAF fighters and another 12 to Fighter Command aircraft. Nearly 100 fell to AA guns, including German flak batteries that had not been warned of the secret operation.

In return for their sacrifice, *Luftwaffe* pilots wrecked 135 Allied aircraft on the ground and severely damaged another 123. The biggest losers were 2TAF Typhoon squadrons in Holland with 162 aircraft destroyed or seriously damaged. However, all were replaced within a week, whereas there would be few replacements for the German aircraft lost in Operation *Bodenplatte*, while the many experienced pilots killed in the action were irreplaceable.

With the Allies poised on Germany's borders, several 2TAF squadrons returned to Great Britain and others were disbanded. One of the few to move across the Channel was 616 Sqn, which deployed to Melsbroek, Belgium, with the RAF's first jet fighters in Europe, the Gloster Meteor F.IIIs. Ten days later 2TAF Spitfires and Typhoons destroyed railway lines used by German forces in the Wesel region and attacked the Munster-Rhine group of airfields used by Me 262 and Ar 234 jets. More than 9,000 Allied aircraft took part in Operation *Clarion* on 22 February in an effort to destroy Germany's remaining rail, road and river transport networks.

In the first three months of 1945, a period that ended with Operation *Varsity*, the Allied airborne crossing of the Rhine on 24 March, Fighter Command flew a total of 15,398 sorties. These included 7,283 as escort and cover to Bomber and Coastal Command day raids, 3,681 on armed recce over potential V-2 launch sites, 1,354 on sweeps and patrols, and 1,806 night operations. To these were

added 33 ASR patrols, 234 weather and photographic reconnaissance flights, and 647 day defensive patrols.

The last major raid mounted by the *Luftwaffe* against RAF airfields in eastern England occurred on the night of 3/4 March when a force of 140 Ju 88s and Ju 188s destroyed 19 aircraft at 14 airfields for the loss of six Junkers, these being the last *Luftwaffe* aircraft to be shot down over English soil.

The last recorded *Luftwaffe* sortie over the British Isles took place on 10 April when an Ar 234 based in Norway flew a reconnaissance mission from Scapa Flow to the Firth of Tay, the same area over which the *Luftwaffe* had first flown in the days following the outbreak of war. The fact that the *Luftwaffe* no longer posed a threat to Fighter Command was reflected by the closure of No 10 Group, which was merged with No 11 Group within days after Germany's last violation of British airspace.

Typhoons and Tempests continued to smash their way into Germany in the last weeks of the war, sustaining heavy casualties from ferocious and accurate flak batteries in their last-ditch efforts to protect not only the failing German war machine, but also families and homes. Me 262 jet fighters were decimating Allied daylight bombers whenever they came into contact, but there were too few, too late. The *Luftwaffe* defenders were rapidly running out of pilots and, more importantly, fuel.

The *Luftwaffe* was virtually grounded when Tempests of No 122 Wing supported Operation *Enterprise*, the Allied crossing of the Elbe, during which they destroyed 14 aircraft and 110 armoured vehicles. Between 1 and 4 May, the last day of air operations in North West Europe, 2TAF fighters claimed the destruction of 141 Germany aircraft, but lost 29 of their own.

Three days later, all German forces surrendered unconditionally.

No 616 Sqn's Meteor F.IIIs were deployed to Melsbroek (B.58) in Belgium in January 1945, the first Allied jet fighter to operate from Continental Europe during the Second World War.

1944: I should have done better

'On 2 October we were sent from our base at Middle Wallop to Bradwell Bay on the Essex coast to refuel and patrol an area from the east of London, over the Channel and off the coast of Holland. Shortly after we neared the Dutch coast on our patrol we felt a "thud" on the port side of the Mosquito. There had been some light flak, but nothing to be alarmed about. We thought that we might have suffered a small strike, but there was no immediate indication of any trouble. Five minutes later the left engine started to surge from high power to low power, but there was nothing on the gauges to indicate the problem. We were at about 6,000 feet at the time, and as the surging continued to get worse, I shut down the left engine and returned to Bradwell Bay.

The next morning my mechanic, Ray Blackmore, from Newfoundland, Canada, found that the port engine had ingested something into the carburettor air scoop, damaging the automatic boost control. He felt that the aircraft would be OK for a ferry flight back to No 125 (Newfoundland) Sqn's base at Middle Wallop for repairs, provided we flew at a low altitude. Blackmore wanted to fly with us, but he would have to crouch down into a small space in front of the navigator.

For some reason he decided not to go at the last minute, a decision that probably saved his life. We were one of three 125 (Newfoundland) Sqn Mosquitos that took off to return to Middle Wallop. North of London the weather became very poor and we were flying very near the ground when our port engine began to surge again, so I shut it down. We also received word that the weather at base was very poor and, talking it over with the Flight Commander, I decided that we should land at nearby Northolt.

The weather was rapidly closing in and I was unable to contact the Northolt tower. However, when we circled the airfield they could see that we had a feathered engine, so we were given the green light to land. On the approach I spotted some construction equipment on the side of the runway, causing some concern and diverting my attention. The landing gear was lowered on finals and showed safe. On the Mosquito the undercarriage selector returned to the neutral position when the gear was down. It was recommended that the lever be held down manually for a few seconds to build up pressure. Being preoccupied with the equipment close to the runway, I did not hold the lever down long enough.

On touchdown everything was normal until the aircraft started to slow down. I got the feeling that it was settling down on the port side. I immediately knew what was wrong but was unable to overshoot with the left engine out. I tried to hold the port wing up as long as possible, but at 80mph it started to drag on the runway and the aircraft turned sideways.

We began to skid along the runway until the right wheel collapsed and penetrated the side of the aircraft, right where Ray would have been sitting. Without doubt he would have been killed instantly.

My navigator was not injured in the accident, although the wheel ended up inches in front of his legs. I smacked my head on the gunsight and was a bit woozy for a few minutes, but was otherwise OK. Although I was not blamed for the accident, I felt I should have done a better job.

We returned to Bradwell Bay that night in another Mosquito and did another patrol over the Arnhem sector, where the ground forces were being pounded very hard. The flak over the area was heavy, but we were not hit. Our patrol that night was 3 hours 45 minutes, which was cutting it pretty fine as the normal endurance of our Mosquito was 4 hours!'

Royal 'Roy' Cooper – Canadian Fighter Command night-fighter pilot

1944: Rescue the rescuers

'In November No 611 Sqn was in the Shetland
Islands, flying out of Sumburgh. Our primary task
was to intercept German planes that flew out into the
North Atlantic between the Shetlands and the Faroe
Islands. These flights were made to obtain
meteorological information and also report on convoy
activity. We were also responsible for flying east to seek
out Norwegian boats carrying escapers to the
Shetlands.

On this day the haar (sea fog) was thick and the
temperature was low so there was little activity.
However, two Spitfires were scrambled to go to the
assistance of, ironically, an air-sea rescue Warwick of
281 Sqn, which was out to the east and was having
trouble in one engine. Visibility was extremely poor
and the grey sea merged with the fog so that there was
no horizon.

I was fortunate to catch a glimpse of the disabled
aircraft as it passed near me heading for Sumburgh
airfield. I did a quick 180 and followed the
Warwick's course. I then saw it ditch! I called the
airfield tower and gave them as much information as
I could, given the difficulties in establishing their
position. Another Warwick came and dropped a
lifeboat – I had moved away and did not see the
outcome. Another aircraft, an Anson, arrived and I
believe another lifeboat or dinghy was dropped. By
now it was time for me to head for Sumburgh.

Later I learned that some of the crew had survived
the ditching and had made it to land after getting
into one of the lifeboats. Unfortunately, it capsized
and one of the Warwick's crew died from immersion
and hypothermia. The other five survived.'

John S. Bennett – Fighter Command pilot

1945: Whistling in the wind

'I was one of a 74 Sqn section of four that strafed a
landing strip near Ardoff airfield in Germany. We
saw the aircraft on the ground as we flew over, so we
turned to come in at low level line astern. I was No 3
and on my first run I concentrated on the gun
emplacements. On the second run I went down to
below 40 feet and got a lot of strikes. There was still a
lot of fire coming from the ground and on the third
run I got hit by a shell, which struck the armour
plating on the back of my seat, where it exploded.
Bits of shrapnel and fuselage flew around the cockpit
and there was blue smoke everywhere. The engine
and controls were not damaged and the flight back to
our strip was notable only for the noise of the wind
whistling through the hole!

On examination there was a large dent in the
armour plating. It was decided that it did not need
repairing, while the holes in the fuselage were fixed
by the ground crew, enabling me to fly the aircraft
next day on a bombing sortie during which I assisted
in the destruction of a train south of Wilhelmshaven.
The train blew up and was believed to be carrying
petrol.'

John S. Bennett – Fighter Command pilot

Pilots of No 74 'Tiger' Sqn, with Canadian F/Off John Bennett on the left, in front of a Spitfire LF IXE armed with 250lb bombs at Lille/Vendeville (B.51) in September 1944.

Chapter 9
Prisoners of war

Of more than 10,000 RAF aircrew, and some groundcrew, who became German prisoners of war, less than 1,000 belonged to Fighter Command. However, among this total was a high percentage of highly experienced and capable fighter leaders, including 19 Wing Leaders.

Two of the first Fighter Command pilots to fall into German hands, and who would become a long-term thorn in the authorities' sides, were both shot down and captured on the same day, 23 May 1940. F/Off V. G. 'Paddy' Byrne of 74 Sqn and 92 Sqn's CO, S/Ldr Roger Bushell, a flamboyant South African-born lawyer and sportsman who joined No 601 Sqn's famed 'Legionnaires' before the war, were flying Spitfires over the Dunkirk beaches when they were bought down.

Very few Fighter Command pilots became PoWs during the Battle of Britain, and it was not until RAF fighters went on the offensive the following year that the number increased at all significantly. Even by the end of 1941 fewer than 100 Fighter Command aircrew were in captivity, but three of them were Wing Leaders. One of the best known to both sides was Tangmere's Wing Leader, Douglas Bader, who was shot down on 9 August, only days after the same fate befell Hornchurch Wing Leader W/C Joe Kayll, who was sent to Spangenberg Castle. Two months later W/C Norman Ryder, Kenley's Wing Leader, joined Bader as a PoW in Germany.

All three were to prove difficult to keep behind the PoW camp wire. In *Dulag Luft* Bader met 'Paddy' Byrne, who had been shot down over Dunkirk, and made several attempts to escape despite his false legs. He was eventually sent to Colditz Castle. Kayll escaped in September 1942 but was recaptured and sent to *Stalag Luft III*. Norman Ryder also eventually managed to escape from his PoW camp, but was recaptured in Poland in 1943.

German flak claimed its biggest 'prize' of the war so far when W/C Stanford Tuck, Biggin Hill's top-scoring Wing Leader with 27 destroyed and six probables, joined Bader in a prison camp on 28 January 1942. A few weeks later yet another Wing Leader, North Weald's W/C Tony Eyre, was captured after he crash-landed his Spitfire in France after

combat with an Fw 190, and in August Portreath's Wing Leader, W/C 'Mindy' Blake, joined him in *Stalag Luft III*.

During the year of *Escorts*, *Intruders* and the Dieppe Raid, some 250 aircrew became PoWs, while many others evaded capture with the assistance of sympathetic French and Belgian men and women. Although some managed to escape from their captors, a few would ultimately return to England to carry on the battle.

Three who chose very different routes home were Sgt Philip Wareing of 616 Sqn, who struck north to neutral Sweden, while the Australian Sgt Keith Chisholm of 452 Sqn escaped from *Stalag VIIIB* with an American Sergeant Pilot, Charles E. 'Mac' McDonald, in 1942 and led a secret underground life in Poland before surfacing in Paris when it was liberated in August 1944. The naturalised American S/Ldr Whitney Straight had taken the more conventional route through Vichy France to Gibraltar a year earlier.

Three more Wing Leaders, W/C Stefan Janus, who led I Polish Wing at Northolt, W/C Dickie Milne, who became the second Biggin Hill Wing Leader in captivity, and 124 Wing's W/C Alec Ingle, were all shot down during 1943.

Most RAF aircrew in captivity were held in *Stalag Luft III* at Sagan, a small town some 80 miles south-east of Berlin. This purpose-built camp, unusual in that it was run by *Luftwaffe* personnel, was continually extended throughout the war years. Although Fighter Command aircrew accounted for only a small percentage of its inmates, they were at the forefront of any escape committees, or 'X Organisations', in the camp. In 1943 the leader of a *Stalag Luft III* escape committee was Roger Bushell, the former lawyer shot down over Dunkirk in May 1940. Know as 'Big X', Bushell had a number of fighter pilots in his committee including 610 Sqn's John Ellis as his No 2, and S/Ldr 'Willy' Williams, a New Zealander with 450 Sqn, as his 'head carpenter'.

Following a mass escape through a tunnel on 24 March 1944, which became known as the 'Great Escape', 50 RAF airmen were shot as a reprisal, including 13 from Fighter Command. They included

1942: New boy on the block

'Arriving at Stalag Luft III *was an experience in itself. Here was a large purpose-built, supposedly escape-proof PoW camp administered and run entirely for RAF prisoners by their opposite number, the Luftwaffe.*

Built in a clearing of about 60 to 70 acres in a forest of small pine trees, the camp was planned for expansion and had already been enlarged. There was the original East Compound, the new North Compound and the German Compound, with the Kommandanture *separating them and a* Lazarette *(sick quarters), "cooler", guard rooms and barracks in an adjacent* Vorlager. *To the south and west the site had already been cleared for expansion and the whole area was well clear of the surrounding pine trees.*

Located about 80 miles south-east of Berlin, with a convenient railway station nearby at Sagan township, we could both see and hear the RAF bombing raids on Berlin under certain weather conditions. Indeed, later on, when these raids increased and "block-buster" bombs were used, some claimed to actually feel the detonations.

The North Compound was new and almost a model PoW camp. It was partially occupied by a party of about 250 RAF prisoners, some of whom had initially volunteered to go across to help get the camp ready. These stalwarts of long "X" operations had already made their plans for tunnelling, and when finally transferred from the East Compound soon got at least three going. So when we arrived and were split up between the North and East Compounds, those who went to the North found tunnelling and escape organisation a going concern run by many of their old friends, including the SBO (Senior British Officer).'

Kenneth W. 'Mac' Mackenzie – Fighter

1944: On account

'As the oldest American "Eagle" squadron PoW in Stalag Luft III, *having been down since 2 July 1941, for something to do I started a barber shop and ran it until the camp was evacuated. I was giving guys haircuts, charging them 75 cents a cut. They'd sign a book and leave their address, and I was to bill them after the war.*

I gave haircuts for some time as it was lots of fun, and anyway it was a place for the fellows to sit and talk. The account book kept growing and growing, and on the night of the evacuation, 27 January 1945, it was too heavy to carry. It went into the fire.'

William I. 'Kriegie' Hall – American Volunteer Fighter Command pilot

1945: Chivalry!

'Of the seven men who escaped on the march from Stalag Luft III *at Sagan to Luckenwalde, all were recaptured during the first week in April and were back in camp safe and well, with the exception of Flight Lieutenant Gillet.*

He was captured by two SS Volksturmers, taken to a darkened room and brutally beaten about the face with fists and revolver butts and kicked in the stomach repeatedly – all this despite the fact that his identity as a British officer prisoner of war had been established without question. That was five days ago and he still looks grim. Our chivalrous enemy!'

Roland Prosper 'Bee' Beamont – Fighter Command pilot (ATS)

Roger Bushell and 'Willy' Williams, the two most
senior officers, while the remainder were either RAF
Sergeants or Pilot Officers, none of whom were
British. One of the few who succeeded in carrying
through the escape that day was P/Off van der Stock,
a Dane serving with 41 Sqn, while F/Lt 'Paddy'
Barthropp of 91 Sqn was recaptured.

After the invasion of Normandy in June 1944, the
majority of RAF pilots captured belonged to 2TAF, in
particular the ground support Typhoon units. In the
last six months of the war in Europe several more
high-scoring Wing Leaders were shot down and
captured. On 25 June W/C Bob Braham's Mosquito
was brought down over Denmark on a *Ranger* patrol,
and in October 150 Wing Leader W/C 'Bee' Beamont,
who had destroyed six enemy aircraft and 32 V-1s,
crash-landed his Tempest after being hit by flak over
Germany.

Peterhead Wing Leader, the Polish W/C Jan
Falkowski, was also brought down by flak while
attacking V-2 sites in Holland on 9 March 1945.
Although injured, he managed to escape his captors
while en route to a PoW camp and, with the help of
the Dutch Resistance, managed to meet up with the
advancing Allies and return to his Wing a few days
before VE-Day.

*An RAF Fighter Command
Sergeant Pilot shot down
over France on 5 February
1941 walks into captivity.*

Far left *F/Lt Ken
Mackenzie, who was shot
down by flak while strafing
Lannion airfield in Brittany
in September 1941 and
captured, is seen here
standing second left with
other PoWs of the 'Irish set' in
Stalag Luft III in 1943.*

Left *Free French pilots
P/Off Bernard Scheidhauer
(left) of 131 Sqn with P/Off
Raymond van Wymeesch of
174 Sqn together at Stalag
Luft III at Sagan in June
1943, nine months before
Scheidhauer was shot
following the 'Great Escape'
of 25 March 1944. Van
Wymeesch also escaped but
was sent to Sashsenhausen
concentration camp after
being recaptured.*

Appendices

1. Glossary of fighter terms

Ack-ack	Anti-aircraft gunfire
Angels	Height in thousands of feet
Arse-end/ tail-end Charlie	Pilot protecting the rear of a formation
Balbo	Large formations
Bandit	Enemy aircraft
Blower	Telephone, or supercharger
Bogey	Unidentified aircraft
Buster	Go to full throttle
Cab-rank	Patrol of fighter-bombers over a battle area
Charlies	Aerobatic rolls
Clag	Cloud
Deck	Very low level
Deflection	Deflection angle of bullets fired
Det	Part of a unit detached from the parent unit
Diver	V-1 flying bomb
Drink	Sea
Erk	Groundcrew
Fido	Fog Intensity Dispersal Operation
Flak	German for anti-aircraft gunfire
Flight	Subdivision of a Squadron
Gate	Maximum boost
Glycol	Ethylene glycol, an engine coolant
Gravy state	Fuel state
Green stuff	100 octane aviation fuel
Hack	Operational unit's air taxi
Huff-duff	High-Frequency/Direction-Finding (device)
IFF	Identification Friend of Foe (instrument)
Liner	Cruising speed
Mae West	Inflatable life-jacket
Mayday	Distress call
OTU	Operational Training Unit
Pancake	Land at base
Panic	Air raid alert
Prang	Ground attack or crash
Q-site	Dummy airfield
RDF	Radio Direction-Finding (radar)
Readiness	State of readiness to become airborne
R/T	Radio telephone
Satellite	Auxiliary airfield to a main base
Scramble	Order to take off immediately
Section	Subdivision of a Flight
Sector	Subdivision of a Group
Shagbag	Walrus air-sea rescue amphibian
Snapper	Enemy fighter
Sortie	Individual aircraft's operational flight
Sprog	Junior operational pilot
Spy	Intelligence Officer
Starfish	Decoy airfields
Stood down	Not on call for Operations
Strike	Low-level attack
Sweep	Offensive formation to draw the enemy
TAF	Tactical Air Force
Tally-ho	Enemy aircraft sighted
Top brass	High-ranking officer
Trolley Acc	Engine-starting batteries trolley
Vector	Heading on which to steer
VHF	Very high frequency (radio)
Vic	Aircraft flying in 'V' formation
Wad	Sandwich
Weaver	Aircraft protecting the rear of a formation
Window	Metallic strips dropped to confuse ground radars
X-raid	Unidentified aircraft reports

2. Operation codenames

Fighter Command

Big Ben	Operations against V-2 sites
Channel Stop	Anti-shipping operations over the Straits of Dover
Circus	Fighter escorts for bombers over enemy territory
Flower	Operations against night-fighter bases
Instep	Fighter operations over the Bay of Biscay
Intruder	Offensive patrols over enemy territory
Jim Crow	Operational patrols over the English Channel
Kipper Kites	Fishing fleet protection
Lagoon	Anti-shipping patrols with Coastal Command
Licorice	Aerial smokescreen operations
Mahmoud	Bomber support operations with rear-facing radar
Mandolin	Long-range Night Intruder patrols
Moonshine	Enemy radar-jamming operations
Mutton	Night operations with Long Aerial Mines (LAM)
Nickel	Propaganda leaflet dropping operations
Noball	Operations to attack V-1 facilities
Popular	Photo-reconnaissance missions
Rag	Decoy operations
Ramrod	Operations against enemy ground targets
Ranger	Large-formation freelance intrusions
Rhubarb	Small-formation freelance intrusions
Roadstead	Low-level attacks on enemy shipping
Rodeo	Fighter sweeps over enemy territory
Rover	Armed reconnaissance over enemy territory
Serrate	Device to home in on German night-fighter transmissions

General

Alder Tag (Eagle Day)	*Luftwaffe* mass assault during the Battle of Britain, 15 September 1940
Apostle 1	Allied invasion of Norway, May 1945
Avonmouth	Allied expedition to Narvik, May 1940
Bodenplatte (Ground Plate)	*Luftwaffe* mass attack against Allied airfields in North West Europe, December 1944
Cerberus	German codename for the 'Channel dash' by the warships *Scharnhorst*, *Gneisenau* and *Prinz Eugen*, February 1942
Cobra	Allied breakout from Normandy bridgehead, July 1944
Crossbow	Allied operations against V-1 and V-2 sites, 1944
Dynamo	Evacuation of Anglo-French forces from Dunkirk, May 1940
Fuller	RAF operation against the German warships during the 'Channel dash', February 1942
Gelb (Yellow)	German codename for the invasion of the Low Countries and France, May 1940
Jubilee	Anglo-Canadian raid on Dieppe, August 1942
Market Garden	Allied airborne operation at Arnhem, September 1944
Mars	German codename for the 'Baby Blitz' on England, January 1943
Overlord	Allied invasion of Normandy (D-Day), June 1944
Seelowe (Sealion)	German plan to invade England, 1940
Sickle	Build-up of US 8th Air Force in England, 1942
Steinbock (Ibex)	*Luftwaffe* bombing operations on Britain, 1944
Varsity	Allied airborne crossing of the Rhine, March 1945
Weserubung (Weser Crossing)	German invasion of Denmark and Norway, April 1940

3. Main Fighter Command aircraft types

Type and mark weight	Engine	Crew	Armament	Wingspan	Length	Max
Gladiator I/II	1 x 840hp Mercury IX/VIIIA	1	4 x .303 MG	32.2	27.5	4,750
Hurricane I	1 x 1,030hp Merlin II/III	1	8 x .303 MG	40	31.5	6,600
Hurricane II	1 x 1,280hp Merlin XX	1	4 x 20mm cannon	40	31.5	7,800
Spitfire I	1 x 1,030hp Merlin II/III	1	8 x .303 MG	36.8	29.9	5,748
Spitfire II	1 x 1,150hp Merlin XII	1	8 x .303 MG	36.8	29.9	6,527
Spitfire V	1 x 1,440hp Merlin 45/50	1	8 x .303 MG	36.8	32.1	6,650
			4 x .303 MG + 2 x 20mm cannon			
			4 x 20mm cannon			
Spitfire IX	1 x 1,710hp Merlin 63	1	4 x .303 MG + 2 x 20mm cannon	36.8	31	7,500
Spitfire XIV	1 x 2,050hp Griffon 65	1	4 x .303 MG + 2 x20 cannon	36.8	32.7	8,500
Spitfire XVI	1 x 1,720hp Merlin 266	1	4 x .303 MG + 2 x 20mm cannon	32.6	31.4	7,500
Blenheim IF	2 x 840hp Mercury VIII	2/3	6 x .303 MG	56.3	39.7	11,975
Blenheim IVF	2 x 920hp Mercury XV	2/3	7 x .303 MG	56.3	42.5	13,500
Defiant I	1 x 1,030hp Merlin III	2	4 x .303 MG	39.3	35.3	8,350
Defiant II	1 x 1,260hp Merlin XX	2	4 x .303 MG	39.3	35.3	8,600
Whirlwind I	2 x 885hp Peregrine I	1	4 x 20mm cannon	45	32.7	9,356
Beaufighter IF	2 x 1,425hp Hercules III	2	6 x .303 MG + 4 x 20mm cannon	57.8	41.6	21,600
Beaufighter IIF	2 x 1,280hp Merlin XX	2	6 x .303 MG + 4 x 20mm cannon	57.8	41.6	21,600
Beaufighter IVF	2 x 1,670hp Hercules IV	2	6 x .303 MG + 4 x 20mm cannon	57.8	41.6	21,600
Havoc I/II	2 x 1,200 Twin Wasp S3C4-G	2/3	8 x .303 MG	61.3	47	25,000
Tomahawk I/II	1 x 1,040hp Allison V-1710-33	1	4 x .303 MG + 2 x .50in MG	37.3	31.7	6.400
Typhoon I	1 x 2,200hp Sabre IIB	1	4 x 20mm cannon	41.7	32	13,250
Tempest V	1 x 2,200hp Sabre IIB	1	4 x 20mm cannon	41	33.7	12,820
Mustang I/II	1 x 1,150hp Allison V-1710-39	1	4 x .303 MG	37.1	32.2	8,600
Mustang III/IV	1 x 1,680hp Merlin V-1650-7	1	4 x .50 MG	37.1	32.2	9,200
Mosquito NF.II	2 x 1,111hp Merlin 22	2	4 x .303in MG + 4 x 20mm cannon	54.2	40.5	22,300
Mosquito FB.VI	2 x 1,230hp Merlin 21	2	4 x 20mm cannon	54.2	40.5	22,300
Mosquito NF.XIX	2 x 1,635hp Merlin 25	2	4 x 20mm cannon	54.2	41.7	21,600
Mosquito NF.XXX	2 x 1,690 Merlin 113/114	2	4 x 20mm cannon	54.2	41.7	21,600

4. Aircraft types operated by Fighter Command, ADGB and 2TAF Squadrons

Squadron	Aircraft type(s)	Squadron	Aircraft type(s)
1 (Fighter)	Hurricane, Typhoon, Spitfire	127	Spitfire
2	Defiant, Tomahawk, Mustang, Spitfire	129 (Mysore)	Spitfire, Mustang
		130 (Punjab)	Spitfire
3	Hurricane, Typhoon, Tempest	131 (County of Kent)	Spitfire
4	Spitfire, Mustang	132 (City of Bombay)	Spitfire
16	Gladiator, Mustang, Spitfire	133 (Third Eagle)	Hurricane, Spitfire
17	Hurricane, Spitfire	137	Hurricane, Whirlwind, Typhoon
19	Spitfire, Mustang	140	Spitfire, Mosquito
21	Mosquito	141	Defiant, Beaufighter, Mosquito
23	Blenheim, Havoc, Mosquito	145	Blenheim, Hurricane, Spitfire
25	Blenheim, Beaufighter, Mosquito	151	Hurricane, Defiant, Mosquito
26 (South Africa)	Tomahawk, Mustang, Spitfire	152 (Hyderabad)	Gladiator, Spitfire
29	Blenheim, Beaufighter, Mosquito	153	Defiant, Beaufighter
32	Hurricane, Spitfire	154 (Motor Industries)	Spitfire
33	Spitfire, Typhoon, Tempest	157	Mosquito
41	Spitfire	164 (Argentine-British)	Hurricane, Spitfire, Typhoon
43 (China-British/'Fighting Cocks')	Hurricane, Spitfire	165 (Times of Ceylon)	Spitfire, Mustang
46 (Uganda)	Hurricane, Beaufighter	167 (Gold Coast)	Spitfire
54	Spitfire	168	Mustang, Typhoon
56 (Punjab)	Hurricane, Typhoon, Spitfire, Tempest	169	Mustang, Mosquito
		174 (Mauritius)	Hurricane, Typhoon
63	Spitfire, Mustang	175	Hurricane, Typhoon
64	Blenheim, Spitfire, Mustang	181	Hurricane, Typhoon
65 (East India)	Spitfire, Mustang	182	Hurricane, Typhoon
66	Spitfire, Mustang	183 (Gold Coast)	Hurricane, Typhoon
68	Blenheim, Beaufighter, Mosquito	184	Hurricane, Typhoon
71 (Eagle)	Buffalo, Hurricane, Spitfire	186	Hurricane, Spitfire
72 (Basutoland)	Spitfire	193 (Fellowship of the Bellows)	Typhoon
73	Hurricane	195	Typhoon
74 (Trinidad/'Tiger')	Hurricane, Spitfire	197	Typhoon
79 (Madras Presidency)	Hurricane	198	Typhoon
80	Hurricane, Spitfire, Tempest	212	Spitfire, Hurricane
81	Hurricane, Spitfire	213 (Ceylon)	Hurricane
85	Hurricane, Defiant, Havoc, Mosquito	219	Blenheim, Beaufighter, Mosquito
		222 (Natal)	Blenheim, Spitfire, Tempest
87 (United Provinces)	Hurricane, Spitfire	226 (Rhodesia)	Spitfire
91 (Nigeria/'Jim Crow')	Spitfire	229	Blenheim, Hurricane
92 (East India)	Blenheim, Spitfire	232	Hurricane
93	Harrow, Spitfire, Havoc	234 (Madras Presidency)	Blenheim, Spitfire, Mustang
96	Hurricane, Defiant, Beaufighter, Mosquito	238	Hurricane, Havoc
		239	Mosquito
107	Mosquito	242 (Canadian)	Blenheim, Hurricane
111	Hurricane, Spitfire	245 (Northern Rhodesia)	Blenheim, Hurricane, Typhoon
118	Spitfire, Mustang	247 (China-British)	Gladiator, Hurricane, Typhoon
121 (Second Eagle)	Spitfire	249 (Gold Coast)	Hurricane, Spitfire
122 (Bombay)	Spitfire, Mustang	253 (Hyderabad)	Hurricane
123 (East India)	Spitfire	255	Defiant, Hurricane, Beaufighter
124 (Baroda)	Spitfire	256	Defiant, Hurricane, Beaufighter
125 (Newfoundland)	Defiant, Beaufighter, Mosquito	257 (Burma)	Hurricane, Typhoon
126 (Persian Gulf)	Spitfire, Mustang	260	Hurricane

Squadron	Aircraft type(s)	Squadron	Aircraft type(s)
263 (Fellowship of the Bellows)	Gladiator, Whirlwind, Typhoon	411 (RCAF/'Grizzly Bear')	Spitfire
264 (Madras Presidency)	Defiant, Mosquito	412 (RCAF/'Falcon')	Spitfire
266 (Rhodesia)	Spitfire, Typhoon	414 (RCAF/'Sarnia Imperials')	Tomahawk, Mustang, Spitfire
268	Spitfire, Tomahawk, Mustang	416 (RCAF/'City of Windsor')	Hurricane, Spitfire
274	Hurricane, Spitfire, Typhoon, Tempest	418 (RCAF/'City of Edmonton')	Boston, Mosquito
		421 (RCAF/'Red Indian')	Spitfire
275 (ASR)	Lysander, Walrus, Defiant, Spitfire	430 (RCAF/'City of Sunbury')	Tomahawk, Spitfire, Mustang
276 (ASR)	Lysander, Walrus, Defiant, Spitfire	438 (RCAF/'Wild Cat')	Hurricane, Typhoon
277 (ASR)	Lysander, Walrus, Defiant, Spitfire	439 (RCAF/'Westmount')	Hurricane, Typhoon
278 (ASR)	Lysander, Walrus, Defiant, Spitfire	440 (RCAF/'City of Ottawa')	Hurricane, Typhoon
279	Hurricane	441 (RCAF/'Silver Fox')	Spitfire, Mustang
281	Defiant, Spitfire	442 (RCAF/'Caribou')	Spitfire, Mustang
285	Hurricane, Defiant	443 (RCAF/'Hornet')	Spitfire, Mustang
286	Hurricane, Defiant, Spitfire	451 (RAAF)	Hurricane, Spitfire
287	Hurricane, Spitfire, Beaufighter, Tempest	452 (RAAF)	Spitfire
		453 (RAAF)	Spitfire
288	Hurricane, Spitfire, Defiant	456 (RAAF)	Defiant, Mosquito, Beaufighter
289	Hurricane, Defiant, Spitfire	457 (RAAF)	Spitfire
290	Hurricane, Spitfire	464 (RAAF)	Mosquito
291	Hurricane	485 (RNZAF)	Spitfire, Typhoon, Tempest
302 (Polish/*Poznanski*)	Hurricane, Spitfire	486 (RNZAF)	Hurricane, Typhoon, Tempest
303 (Polish/*Kosciuszko*)	Hurricane, Spitfire, Mustang	487 (RNZAF)	Mosquito
305 (Polish/*Wielkopol*)	Mosquito	488 (RNZAF)	Beaufighter, Mosquito
306 (Polish/*Torunski*)	Hurricane, Spitfire, Mustang	501 (County of Gloucester)	Hurricane, Spitfire, Tempest
307 (Polish/*Lwowski*)	Defiant, Beaufighter, Mosquito	504 (County of Nottingham)	Hurricane, Spitfire, Meteor
308 (Polish/*Krakowski*)	Hurricane, Spitfire	515	Defiant, Beaufighter, Mosquito
309 (Polish/*Czerwienska*)	Hurricane, Mustang	516	Defiant, Beaufighter, Mosquito
310 (Czech)	Hurricane, Spitfire	530	Hurricane, Havoc, Boston
312 (Czech)	Hurricane, Spitfire	531	Hurricane, Havoc, Boston
313 (Czech)	Spitfire	532	Hurricane, Havoc, Boston
315 (Polish/*Deblinski*)	Hurricane, Spitfire, Mustang	533	Hurricane, Havoc, Boston
316 (Polish/*Warsawski*)	Hurricane, Spitfire, Mustang	534	Hurricane, Havoc, Boston
317 (Polish/*Wilenski*)	Hurricane, Spitfire	535	Hurricane, Havoc, Boston
322 (Dutch)	Spitfire	536	Hurricane, Havoc, Boston
326 (French/*Nice*)	Spitfire	537	Hurricane, Havoc, Boston
327 (French/*Corse*)	Spitfire	538	Hurricane, Havoc, Boston
328 (French/*Provence*)	Spitfire	539	Hurricane, Havoc, Boston
329 (French/*Cigognes*)	Spitfire	600 (City of London)	Blenheim, Beaufighter, Mosquito
331 (Norwegian)	Hurricane, Spitfire	601 (County of London)	Blenheim, Hurricane, Airacobra, Spitfire
332 (Norwegian)	Spitfire		
333 (Norwegian)	Mosquito	602 (City of Glasgow)	Spitfire
340 (French/*Ile-de-France*)	Spitfire	603 (City of Edinburgh)	Spitfire
341 (French/*Alsace*)	Spitfire	604 (County of Middlesex)	Blenheim, Beaufighter, Mosquito
342 (French/*Lorraine*)	Boston	605 (County of Warwick)	Gladiator, Hurricane, Boston, Mosquito
345 (French/*Berry*)	Spitfire		
349 (Belgian)	Tomahawk, Spitfire, Tempest	607 (County of Durham)	Gladiator, Hurricane
350 (Belgian)	Spitfire	609 (West Riding)	Spitfire, Typhoon
400 (RCAF/'City of Toronto')	Mustang, Spitfire, Mosquito	610 (County of Chester)	Spitfire
401 (RCAF/'Ram')/1 (Canadian)	Hurricane, Spitfire	611 (West Lancashire)	Spitfire, Mustang
402 (RCAF/'Winnipeg Bear')	Hurricane, Spitfire	613 (City of Manchester)	Tomahawk, Mustang, Mosquito, Spitfire
403 (RCAF/'Wolf')	Tomahawk, Spitfire		
406 (RCAF/'Lynx')	Blenheim, Beaufighter, Mosquito	615 (County of Surrey)	Gladiator, Hurricane, Spitfire
409 (RCAF/'Nighthawk')	Defiant, Beaufighter, Mosquito	616 (South Yorkshire)	Hurricane, Tomahawk, Spitfire, Meteor
410 (RCAF/'Cougar')	Defiant, Beaufighter, Mosquito		

5. Fighter Command Order of Battle

September 1938

No 11 Group
  2 Hawker Fury squadron
  5 Gloster Gauntlet squadrons
  3 Hawker Demon squadrons
  5 Gloster Gladiator squadrons
  1 Bristol Blenheim squadron
  3 Hawker Hurricane squadrons

No 12 Group
  1 Hawker Fury squadron
  4 Gloster Gauntlet squadrons
  4 Hawker Demon squadrons
  1 Gloster Gladiator squadron
  1 Hawker Hurricane squadron

September 1939

No 11 Group
  2 Gloster Gladiator squadrons
  4 Bristol Blenheim squadrons
  11 Hawker Hurricane squadrons
  3 Supermarine Spitfire squadrons

No 12 Group
  1 Gloster Gauntlet squadron
  2 Gloster Gladiator squadrons
  2 Bristol Blenheim squadrons
  5 Hawker Hurricane squadrons
  7 Supermarine Spitfire squadrons

August 1940

No 10 Group
  1 Gloster Gladiator flight
  1 Bristol Blenheim squadron
  3 Hawker Hurricane squadrons
  4 Supermarine Spitfire squadrons

No 11 Group
  2 Bristol Blenheim squadrons
  13 Hawker Hurricane squadrons
  6 Supermarine Spitfire squadrons

No 12 Group
  2 Bristol Blenheim squadrons
  1 Boulton Paul Defiant squadron
  5 Hawker Hurricane squadrons
  6 Supermarine Spitfire squadrons

No 13 Group
  1 Bristol Blenheim squadron
  1 Boulton Paul Defiant squadron
  9 Hawker Hurricane squadrons
  2 Supermarine Spitfire squadrons

June 1941

No 9 Group
  1 Bristol Blenheim squadron
  1 Curtiss Tomahawk squadron
  2 Boulton Paul Defiant squadrons
  4 Hawker Hurricane squadrons
  1 Supermarine Spitfire squadrons

No 10 Group
  1 Boulton Paul Defiant squadron
  1 Douglas Havoc squadron
  2 Bristol Beaufighter squadrons
  1 Westland Whirlwind squadron
  6 Hawker Hurricane squadrons
  5 Supermarine Spitfire squadrons

No 11 Group
  1 Boulton Paul Defiant squadron
  2 Douglas Havoc squadrons
  3 Bristol Beaufighter squadrons
  9 Hawker Hurricane squadrons
  11 Supermarine Spitfire squadrons

No 12 Group
  1 Boulton Paul Defiant squadron
  1 Bristol Beaufighter squadron
  5 Hawker Hurricane squadrons
  6 Supermarine Spitfire squadrons

No 13 Group
  1 Boulton Paul Defiant squadron
  1 Bristol Beaufighter squadron
  2 Hawker Hurricane squadrons
  3 Supermarine Spitfire squadrons

No 14 Group
  5 Hawker Hurricane squadrons

February 1942

No 9 Group
  2 Boulton Paul Defiant squadrons
  1 Douglas Havoc flight
  2 Bristol Beaufighter squadrons
  2 Hawker Hurricane squadrons
  4 Hawker Hurricane squadrons

No 10 Group
  3 Douglas Havoc flights
  1 Westland Whirlwind squadron
  4 Bristol Beaufighter squadrons
  5 Hawker Hurricane squadrons
  10 Supermarine Spitfire squadrons

No 11 Group
  1 Boulton Paul Defiant squadron
  5 Douglas Havoc flights/squadrons
  3 Bristol Beaufighter squadrons
  3 Hawker Hurricane squadrons
  21 Supermarine Spitfire squadrons

No 12 Group
  2 Douglas Boston squadrons
  2 Bristol Beaufighter squadrons
  2 DH Mosquito squadrons
  5 Supermarine Spitfire squadrons
  5 Hawker Typhoon squadrons

No 13 Group
  1 Douglas Boston squadron
  2 Bristol Beaufighter squadrons
  1 DH Mosquito squadron
  4 Supermarine Spitfire squadrons
  2 Hawker Typhoon squadrons

No 14 Group
  4 Supermarine Spitfire squadrons

RAF Northern Ireland
  1 Bristol Beaufighter squadron
  1 Supermarine Spitfire squadron

June 1943

No 9 Group
  2 Bristol Beaufighter squadrons
  1 Hawker Typhoon squadron

No 10 Group
  1 Westland Whirlwind squadron
  1 Hawker Hurricane squadron
  1 Bristol Beaufighter squadron
  4 DH Mosquito squadrons
  9 Supermarine Spitfire squadrons
  4 Hawker Typhoon squadrons
  3 North American Mustang squadrons

No 11 Group
  1 Boulton Paul Defiant squadron
  1 Westland Whirlwind squadron
  1 Douglas Boston squadron
  2 Bristol Beaufighter squadrons
  3 DH Mosquito squadrons
  20 Supermarine Spitfire squadrons
  7 Hawker Typhoon squadrons
  4 North American Mustang squadrons

No 12 Group
  1 Curtiss Tomahawk squadron
  2 Bristol Beaufighter squadrons
  2 DH Mosquito squadrons
  6 Supermarine Spitfire squadrons
  2 Hawker Typhoon squadrons
  5 North American Mustang squadrons

No 13 Group
  3 Bristol Beaufighter squadrons
  4 Supermarine Spitfire squadrons
  1 North American Mustang squadron

No 14 Group
  4 Supermarine Spitfire squadrons

RAF Northern Ireland
  1 Supermarine Spitfire squadron

June 1944

ADGB:
No 10 Group
  2 Bristol Beaufighter squadrons
  1 DH Mosquito squadron
  7 Supermarine Spitfire squadrons
  1 Hawker Typhoon squadron

No 11 Group
  6 DH Mosquito squadrons
  15 Supermarine Spitfire squadrons
  1 Hawker Typhoon squadron

No 12 Group
  1 DH Mosquito squadron
  1 Supermarine Spitfire squadron
  1 North American Mustang squadron

No 13 Group
  3 Supermarine Spitfire squadrons

2TAF:
No 83 Group
  12 Supermarine Spitfire squadrons
  10 Hawker Typhoon squadrons
  3 North American Mustang squadrons

No 84 Group
  15 Supermarine Spitfire squadrons
  5 Hawker Typhoon squadrons
  3 North American Mustang squadrons

No 85 Group
  6 DH Mosquito squadrons
  4 Supermarine Spitfire squadrons
  2 Hawker Tempest squadrons

6. Fighter Command, ADGB and 2TAF airfields, 1939-45

Abbotsinch	Strathclyde	No 13 Group	Eshott	Northumberland	No 9 Group	Montrose	Angus	No 13 Group
Aberporth	Cardiganshire	No 10 Group	Exeter	Devonshire	No 10 Group	Mount Farm	Oxfordshire	No 12 Group
Acklington	Northumberland	No 13 Group	Fairlop	Essex	No 11 Group	Needs Oar		
Aldergrove	Antrim	No 13 Group	Fairwood			Point	Hampshire	No 84 Group
Andreas	Isle of Man	No 9 Group	Common	Glamorgan	No 10 Group	Newchurch	Kent	No 85 Group
Angle	Pembrokeshire	No 10 Group	Filton	Gloucestershire	No 10 Group	Northolt	Middlesex	No 11 Group
Annan	Dumfriesshire	No 9 Group	Finmere	Buckinghamshire	No 9 Group	North Weald	Essex	No 11 Group
Appledram	Sussex	No 84 Group	Ford	Sussex	No 11 Group	Oatlands Hill	Wiltshire	No 10 Group
Baginton	Warwickshire	No 12 Group	Fowlmere	Essex	No 11 Group	Odiham	Hampshire	No 83 Group
Balado Bridge	Kinross	No 9 Group	Friston	Sussex	No 11 Group	Ouston	Northumberland	No 9 Group
Ballyhalbert	Northern Ireland	No 9 Group	Funtington	Sussex	No 83 Group	Pembrey	Carmarthenshire	No 10 Group
Beaulieu	Hampshire	No 11/84 Group	Gatwick	Surrey	No 84 Group	Perranporth	Cornwall	No 10 Group
Bicester	Oxfordshire	No 9 Group	Goxhill	Lincolnshire	No 12 Group	Peterhead	Aberdeenshire	No 14 Group
Biggin Hill	Kent	No 11 Group	Grangemouth	West Lothian	No 13/9 Group	Portreath	Cornwall	No 10 Group
Bircham			Gravesend	Kent	No 11 Group	Predannack	Cornwall	No 10 Group
Newton	Norfolk	No 12 Group	Great Orton	Cumberland	No 9 Group	Prestwick	Ayrshire	No 13 Group
Bognor	Sussex	No 84 Group	Harrowbeer	Devonshire	No 10 Group	Redhill	Surrey	No 83 Group
Bolt Head	Devonshire	No 10 Group	Hartford Bridge	Hampshire	No 85 Group	Ringway	Cheshire	No 12 Group
Boscombe			Hawarden	Flintshire	No 9 Group	Roborough	Devonshire	No 10/70 Group
Down	Wiltshire	No 10 Group	Hawkinge	Kent	No 11 Group	Rochford	Essex	No 11 Group
Boulmer	Northumberland	No 9 Group	Headcorn	Kent	No 11 Group	St Eval	Cornwall	No 10 Group
Bradwell Bay	Essex	No 11 Group	Heathrow	Surrey	No 11 Group	Sawbridgeworth	Hertfordshire	No 12/84 Group
Caistor	Lincolnshire	No 12 Group	Hendon	Middlesex	No 11 Group	Scorton	Yorkshire	No 12 Group
Castle			Hibaldstow	Lincolnshire	No 12/9 Group	Selsey	Sussex	No 11/84 Group
Bromwich	Warwickshire	No 70 Group	High Ercall	Shropshire	No 9 Group	Shoreham	Sussex	No 11 Group
Castle Camps	Cambridgeshire	No 11 Group	Holmsley South	Hampshire	No 11/83 Group	Skeabrae	Orkney Islands	No 14 Group
Castletown	Highlands	No 14 Group	Honiley	Warwickshire	No 12 Group	Snailwell	Cambridgeshire	No 12 Group
Catterick	Yorkshire	No 13 Group	Hornchurch	Essex	No 11 Group	Southend	Essex	No 11 Group
Chailey	Sussex	No 84 Group	Horne	Surrey	No 11 Group	Speke	Lancashire	No 12 Group
Charmy Down	Wiltshire	No 10 Group	Hucknall	Nottinghamshire	No 12 Group	Squires Gate	Lancashire	No 12 Group
Charter Hall	Berwickshire	No 9 Group	Hunsdon	Hertfordshire	No 11/85 Group	Stapleford		
Chilbolton	Hampshire	No 11 Group	Hurn	Dorset	No 11/85 Group	Tawney	Essex	No 11 Group
Church Fenton	Yorkshire	No 12 Group	Hutton			Sumburgh	Shetlands	No 13 Group
Cleave	Cornwall	No 70 Group	Cranswick	Yorkshire	No 12 Group	Sutton Bridge	Lincolnshire	No 12/9 Group
Coleby Grange	Lincolnshire	No 12 Group	Ibsley	Hampshire	No 10 Group	Tangmere	Sussex	No 11/83 Group
Colerne	Wiltshire	No 10 Group	Jurby	Isle of Man	No 9 Group	Tealing	Angus	No 9 Group
Collyweston	Northants	No 12 Group	Kenley	Surrey	No 11 Group	Ternhill	Shropshire	No 12 Group
Coltishall	Norfolk	No 12 Group	Kings Cliffe	Cambridgeshire	No 12 Group	Thorney Island	Sussex	No 84 Group
Coolham	Sussex	No 11/84 Group	Kinnell	Angus	No 9 Group	Turnhouse	Lothian	No 13 Group
Cranage	Cheshire	No 12 Group	Kirton-in-			Twinwood		
Cranfield	Bedfordshire	No 9 Group	Lindsey	Lincolnshire	No 12/9 Group	Farm	Bedfordshire	No 9 Group
Croydon	Surrey	No 11 Group	Lasham	Hampshire	No 11 Group	Usworth	Durham	No 13 Group
Culmhead	Somerset	No 10 Group	Leconfield	Yorkshire	No 12 Group	Valley	Anglesey	No 9 Group
Deanland	Sussex	No 11 Group	Leeming	Yorkshire	No 13 Group	Warmwell	Dorset	No 10 Group
Debden	Essex	No 11 Group	Llanbedr	Merionethshire	No 9 Group	Wellingore	Lincolnshire	No 12 Group
Delquay	Sussex	No 11 Group	Ludham	Norfolk	No 12 Group	Westhampnett	Sussex	No 11/83 Group
Detling	Kent	No 11 Group	Lympne	Kent	No 11 Group	West Malling	Kent	No 11/85 Group
Digby	Lincolnshire	No 12 Group	Manston	Kent	No 11 Group	Wick	Caithness	No 13 Group
Drem	East Lothian	No 13 Group	Martlesham			Winfield	Berwickshire	No 9 Group
Driffield	Yorkshire	No 13 Group	Heath	Suffolk	No 11 Group	Winkleigh	Devonshire	No 10 Group
Duxford	Cambridgeshire	No 12 Group	Matlaske	Norfolk	No 12 Group	Wittering	Northamptonshire	No 12 Group
Dyce	Aberdeenshire	No 13 Group	Merston	Sussex	No 11/84 Group	Woodvale	Lancashire	No 9 Group
Eastchurch	Kent	No 11 Group	Middle Wallop	Hampshire	No 10 Group	Yeadon	Yorkshire	No 12 Group
Eglinton	Northern Ireland	No 9 Group	Milfield	Northumberland	No 13 Group	Zeals	Wiltshire	No 10/85 Group

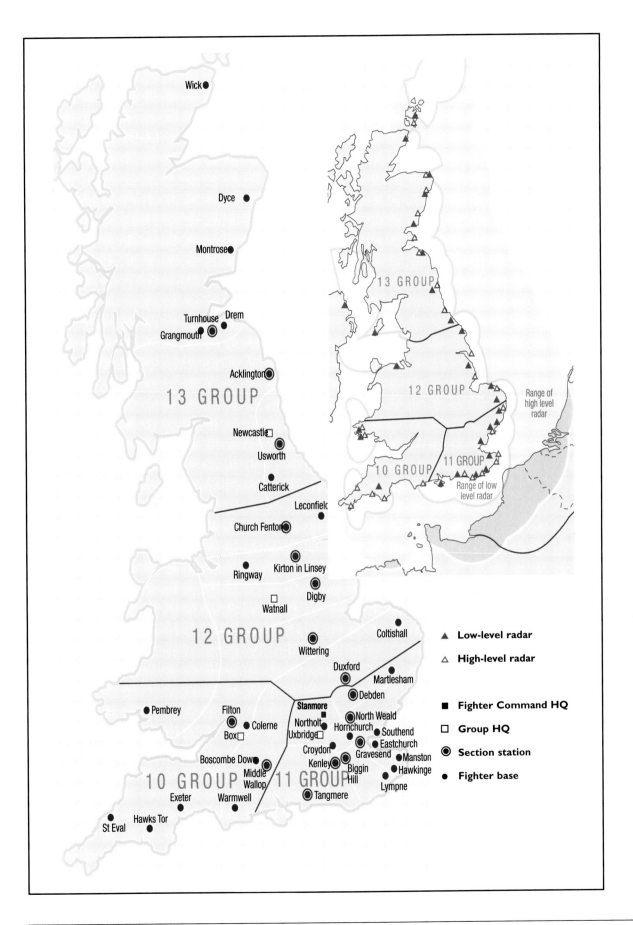

Wick●

Dyce●

Montrose●

13 GROUP

Turnhouse Drem
Grangmouth◉●

Acklington◎

13 GROUP

Newcastle□
Usworth●◎

Catterick●

Leconfield●
Church Fenton◎

Ringway● Kirton in Linsey◎

Digby◎
Watnall□

12 GROUP
Coltishall●
Wittering◎

Duxford◎
Martlesham●
Debden◎

Pembrey● Filton◎ Stanmore■ North Weald◎
Colerne● Northolt◎ Hornchurch◎ Southend●
Box□ Uxbridge□ Eastchurch●
Croydon◎ Gravesend◎ Manston●
Boscombe Down● Kenley◎ Biggin Hawkinge●
Middle Hill
10 GROUP Wallop 11 GROUP Lympne●
Exeter● Warmwell● Hawkinge
St Eval● Hawks Tor● Tangmere◎

13 GROUP

12 GROUP

Range of
high level
radar

10 GROUP 11 GROUP

Range of low
level radar

▲ Low-level radar

△ High-level radar

■ Fighter Command HQ

□ Group HQ

◉ Section station

● Fighter base

Index